LIGHT WEAPONS AND CIVIL CONFLICT

Controlling the Tools of Violence

Edited by
Jeffrey Boutwell
and
Michael T. Klare

CARNEGIE COMMISSION ON PREVENTING DEADLY CONFLICT

CARNEGIE CORPORATION OF NEW YORK

AMERICAN ACADEMY OF ARTS AND SCIENCES

ROWMAN & LITTLEFIELD PUBLISHERS, INC.
Lanham • Boulder • New York • Oxford

ROWMAN & LITTLEFIELD PUBLISHERS, INC.

Published in the United States of America
by Rowman & Littlefield Publishers, Inc.
4720 Boston Way, Lanham, Maryland 20706

12 Hid's Copse Road
Cumnor Hill, Oxford OX2 9JJ, England

British Library Cataloguing in Publication Information Available

Library of Congress Cataloging-in-Publication Data

Light weapons and civil conflict : controlling the tools of violence / edited by Jeffrey Boutwell and Michael T. Klare.
p. cm. — (Carnegie Commission on Preventing Deadly Conflict series)
Includes bibliographical references (p.) and index.
ISBN 0–8476–9484–4 (cloth : alk. paper). — ISBN 0–8476–9485–2 (paper : alk. paper)
1. Firearms. 2. Arms control. 3. Illegal arms transfers. 4. Political violence. I. Boutwell, Jeffrey. II. Klare, Michael T., 1942–. III. Series.
UD380.L54 1999
327.1′743—dc21 98–55389
CIP

Printed in the United States of America

∞ ™The paper used in this publication meets the minimum requirements of American National Standard for Information Sciences—Permanence of Paper for Printed Library Materials, ANSI/NISO Z39.48–1992.

ABOUT THE
Carnegie Commission on Preventing Deadly Conflict Series

Carnegie Corporation of New York established the Carnegie Commission on Preventing Deadly Conflict in May 1994 to address the threats to world peace of intergroup violence and to advance new ideas for the prevention and resolution of deadly conflict. The Commission is examining the principal causes of deadly ethnic, nationalist, and religious conflicts within and between states and the circumstances that foster or deter their outbreak. Taking a long-term, worldwide view of violent conflicts that are likely to emerge, it seeks to determine the functional requirements of an effective system for preventing mass violence and to identify the ways in which such a system could be implemented. The Commission is also looking at the strengths and weaknesses of various internal entities in conflict prevention and considering ways in which international organizations might contribute toward developing an effective international system of nonviolent problem solving. The series grew out of the research that the Commission has sponsored to answer the three fundamental questions that have guided its work: What are the problems posed by deadly conflict, and why is outside help often necessary to deal with these problems? What approaches, tasks, and strategies appear most promising for preventing deadly conflict? What are the responsibilities and capacities of states, international organizations, and private and nongovernmental organizations for undertaking preventive action? The Commission issued its final report in December 1997.

The books are published as a service to scholars, students, practitioners, and the interested public. While they have undergone peer review and have been approved for publication, the views that they express are those of the author or authors, and Commission publication does not imply that those views are shared by the Commission as a whole or by individual Commissioners.

Full text or summaries of Commission publications are available on the Commission's Web site: http://www.ccpdc.org

For more information or to be added to the Commission's mailing list, contact:
Carnegie Commission on Preventing Deadly Conflict
1779 Massachusetts Avenue NW, Suite 715
Washington, DC 20036-2103
Phone: (202) 332-7900 Fax: (202) 332-1919

Members of the Carnegie Commission on Preventing Deadly Conflict

The Carnegie Commission Series

Published in the series:

Bridging the Gap: A Future Security Architecture for the Middle East, by Shai Feldman and Abdullah Toukan

The Price of Peace: Incentives and International Conflict Prevention, edited by David Cortright

Sustainable Peace: The Role of the UN and Regional Organizations in Preventing Conflict, by Connie Peck

Turkey's Kurdish Question, by Henri J. Barkey and Graham E. Fuller

The Costs of Conflict: Prevention and Cure in the Global Arms, edited by Michael E. Brown and Richard N. Rosecrance

Light Weapons and Civil Conflict: Controlling the Tools of Violence, edited by Jeffrey Boutwell and Michael T. Klare

Forthcoming:

The Ambivalence of the Sacred. Religion, Violence, and Reconciliation, by Scott Appleby

Opportunities Missed, Opportunities Seized: Preventive Diplomacy in the Post–Cold War World, edited by Bruce Jentleson

Negotiating to Prevent Escalation and Violence, edited by I. William Zartman

Mediation and Arbitration to Prevent Deadly Conflict, edited by Melanie Greenberg, John Barton, and Margaret McGuinness

For orders and information, please address the publisher: Rowman & Littlefield Publishers, Inc., 4720 Boston Way, Lanham, MD 20706; 1-800-462-6420.

Website: http://www.rowmanlittlefield.com

Selected Reports Available from the Commission

David Hamburg, *Preventing Contemporary Intergroup Violence,* founding essay of the Commission, April 1994.

Preventing Deadly Conflict: Executive Summary of the Final Report, December 1997.

Scott Feil, *Preventing Genocide: How the Early Use of Force Might Have Succeeded in Rwanda,* April 1998.

Edward J. Laurance, *Light Weapons and Intrastate Conflict: Early Warning Factors and Preventive Action,* July 1998.

Donald Kennedy, *Environmental Quality and Regional Conflict,* December 1998.

Essays on Leadership (by Boutros Boutros-Ghali, George Bush, Jimmy Carter, Mikhail Gorbachev, and Desmond Tutu), December 1998.

George A. Joulwan and Christopher C. Shoemaker, *Civilian-Military Cooperation in the Prevention of Deadly Conflict: Implementing Agreements in Bosnia and Beyond,* December 1998.

American Academy of Arts and Sciences

Founded in 1780, the American Academy of Arts and Sciences is an international learned society with headquarters in Cambridge, Massachusetts. The Academy is composed of 3,300 fellows and 600 foreign honorary members representing the academic disciplines as well as the arts, business, and government. Through its multidisciplinary research projects, the Academy addresses major issues of both scholarly and public concern, including international affairs, economic and environmental issues, and the changing nature of higher education, science, and scholarship. The Academy publishes a quarterly journal, *Daedalus;* has regional offices at the University of Chicago and the University of California, Irvine; and oversees U.S. participation in the International Institute for Applied Systems Analysis (IIASA), located in Laxenburg, Austria, outside of Vienna.

The Academy's Committee on International Security Studies (CISS), founded in 1982, oversees a diverse research program focusing on global security issues. Current and previous projects have included Environmental Scarcities, State Capacity, and Civil Violence; Israeli-Palestinian Security in the Final Status Negotiations; and Emerging Norms of Justified Intervention. CISS oversees the activities of the U.S. Pugwash Committee, part of the international Pugwash Conferences on Science and World Affairs, which received the 1995 Nobel Peace Prize.

Among the Academy's CISS publications are:

Lethal Commerce: The Global Trade in Small Arms and Light Weapons, edited by Jeffrey Boutwell, Michael T. Klare, and Laura W. Reed (1995).

Israeli-Palestinian Security: Issues in the Permanent Status Negotiations, by Jeffrey Boutwell and Everett Mendelsohn (1995).

Collective Responses to Regional Problems: The Case of Latin America and the Caribbean, edited by Carl Kaysen, Robert A. Pastor, and Laura W. Reed (1994).

Emerging Norms of Justified Intervention, edited by Laura W. Reed and Carl Kaysen (1993).

Transition to Palestinian Self-Government: Practical Steps toward Israeli-Palestinian Peace, by Ann Mosely Lesch (1992).

Defending Deterrence: Managing the ABM Treaty Regime into the 21st Century, by Antonia H. Chayes and Paul Doty (1989).

To order publications or for more information, please contact CISS at the American Academy of Arts and Sciences, 136 Irving Street, Cambridge, MA 02138. Phone: 617-576-5024; e-mail: ciss@amacad.org; World Wide Web: www.amacad.org.

Contents

Preface and Acknowledgments

The origins of this volume date to February 1994, when the American Academy of Arts and Sciences convened the first major international workshop to explore in depth the increasingly lethal ramifications of the diffusion of small arms and light weapons to areas of conflict around the world. Many of the papers from that workshop were published in 1995 in *Lethal Commerce: The Global Trade in Small Arms and Light Weapons,* itself the first comprehensive volume to examine the dynamics of the trade in light weapons and their use in sectarian, ethnic, and other types of conflict in dozens of countries.

In 1997, the Academy's Committee on International Security Studies joined with the Carnegie Commission on Preventing Deadly Conflict to plan a second international policy workshop that could take account of the many evolving policy initiatives on small arms and light weapons being undertaken by national governments, regional and international organizations, and a large number of nongovernmental organizations (NGOs). More than forty government, military, NGO, and academic specialists met in Washington, D.C., in December 1997 to discuss how best to seek controls on the complex and multifaceted trade in light weapons.

For their support of that conference and of the research and writing of the chapters in this volume, the American Academy and the Commission would like to thank the Ford Foundation, Ploughshares Fund, and an anonymous donor. We also thank the Carnegie Commission itself for providing the necessary funding. In particular, Chris Wing at the Ford Foundation and Sally Lilienthal at the Ploughshares Fund were instrumental in their support and encouragement. Michael Klare also wishes to acknowledge the support he received for research on light weapons from the John D. and Catherine T. MacArthur Foundation. Opinions expressed in the volume are those of the individual authors and do not represent the views of the American Academy, the Carnegie Commission, or the funders.

Carl Kaysen, chair of the American Academy's Committee on International Security Studies, and Thomas J. Leney, senior associate at the Carnegie Commission on Preventing Deadly Conflict, provided much appreciated advice and help during the project. For their continuous administrative and moral support throughout the endeavor, we would like to thank Tracy Sanderson at the American Academy and Esther Brimmer and Robert Lande of the Carnegie Commission. At our Washington conference in December 1997, we were helped greatly by Nancy Ward of the Carnegie Commission and Rachel Stohl and Kate Joseph (both then at the British American Security Information Council).

Looking back from the vantage point of October 1998, great progress has been made in turning small arms and light weapons from the inchoate and little-understood issue that it was in February 1994 to one of the major international policy concerns that it is today. But far more needs to be done—at the local, national, regional, and international levels—for effective policies to be implemented that can constrain the deadly ease with which small arms and light weapons cause untold human and social misery around the world. It is to that aim, however difficult, and the many people and organizations involved in the effort that this volume is dedicated.

Introduction

Jeffrey Boutwell and Michael T. Klare

One of the dominant features of international politics in the 1990s has been the breakdown of civil society in dozens of countries throughout the world. From the former socialist states of the Soviet bloc to dozens of countries in the developing world, the decade since the end of the Cold War has witnessed the outbreak of ethnic, religious, clan, and other forms of violence and the melting away of social norms and government structures that could contain that violence.

Moreover, unlike the traditional warfare between nation-states that characterized the eighteenth and nineteenth centuries and the two major world wars of the twentieth century, the very nature of conflict has shifted from that between states to intrastate ethnic and sectarian conflict. Such conflicts usually involve a wide variety of actors, including not only governments but also rebel movements, armed political militias, ethnic and religious groups, tribal clans, child soldiers, expatriate and diaspora groups, and even criminal gangs and mercenaries.

A common feature of such conflicts is that widespread death and suffering result not from the major conventional weapons (tanks, aircraft, and ships) traditionally associated with warfare but from small arms and light weapons. The widespread global diffusion of assault rifles, machine guns, mortars, rocket-propelled grenades, and other light weapons that can be easily carried by an individual or transported by a light vehicle has greatly intensified the scale of conflict in countries and societies around the world. In the 1990s alone, such weapons have accounted for the vast majority of the four million deaths that have occurred in forty-nine major ethnic and sectarian conflicts. From Bosnia to Zaire, Rwanda to Afghanistan, and Tajikistan to Somalia, the resources of the international community are being overwhelmed as millions of people find themselves caught up in bitter conflicts, deprivation, large-scale refugee movements, and even genocide.

The distinguishing features of small arms and light weapons that make them so suitable to contemporary intrastate and cross-border conflicts include the following:

- *Low cost and wide availability.* Because the production of small arms and light weapons requires little in the way of sophisticated technology, and because these weapons are manufactured for military, police, and civilian use, there are plentiful suppliers around the world. In addition, the existence of many tens of millions of such weapons—whether newly produced, given away by downsizing militaries, or recycled from conflict to conflict—leads to bargain-basement prices in many areas around the world.
- *Lethality.* The increasing sophistication and lethality of rapid-fire assault rifles, automatic pistols, and submachine guns, and their diffusion to nonstate actors, has given such groups a firepower that often matches or exceeds that of national police or constabulary forces. With such weapons capable of firing up to 300 rounds a minute, a single individual can pose a tremendous threat to society. The incorporation of new technology into shoulder-fired rockets, mortars, and light antitank weapons has only increased the firepower that warring factions can bring to bear in civil conflicts.
- *Simplicity and durability.* Small arms are easy to use and maintain, require little maintenance or logistical support, and remain operational for many years. Such weapons require little training to use effectively, which greatly increases their use in conflicts involving untrained combatants and children.
- *Portability and concealability.* Small arms and light weapons can be carried by an individual soldier or light vehicle, are easily transported or smuggled to areas of conflict, and can be concealed in shipments of legitimate cargo.
- *Military/police and civilian uses.* Unlike major conventional weapons, which are most often procured solely by national military forces, small arms and light weapons cross the dividing line separating military and police forces from the civilian population. Depending on the gun control laws of a particular country, citizens are permitted to own anything from pistols and sporting guns to fully automatic rifles. In many countries, moreover, there has been a dramatic increase in the number and size of private militias and security firms—in many cases, equipped with military-type weapons.

It is these characteristics of light weapons that have made them particularly attractive to the sort of paramilitary and irregular forces that have played such a prominent role in recent conflicts. These forces have limited financial and technical means, lack professional military training, and often must operate in remote and inaccessible areas—all conditions that favor the use of small arms and light weapons. At the same time, many states have increased their purchases of small arms and light weapons for use in counterinsurgency campaigns against ethnic and political insurgents and to suppress domestic opposition movements. Thus, through a combination of legal export from the major supplier states, domestic manufacture, and growing sales of black-market weapons, there are literally hundreds of millions of small arms and light weapons circulating in the world today.

In order to meet the challenge posed by this proliferation of weaponry, international organizations, national governments, humanitarian relief organizations, local and international nongovernmental organizations (NGOs), and the policy research community are seeking to understand the dynamics by which the increased availability of low-cost small arms and light weapons contributes to the likelihood, intensity, and duration of armed conflict within states. Equally important are the humanitarian consequences of ever more lethal small arms and light weapons finding their way into the hands of soldiers, civilians, and children engaged in ethnic and sectarian strife. There is also the problem of the rise of criminal and other forms of violence within a society even after "formal" conflict has ended.

In the past several years, a wide range of organizations, from the United Nations (UN) and the Organization of American States (OAS) to national governments and NGOs, have begun to initiate substantive policy controls and public awareness campaigns that could begin to constrain both the availability of small arms and light weapons and their deadly use in conflicts. This constellation of international organizations, national governments, and NGOs is devoting substantial resources to finding ways of curtailing the lethal commerce in small arms and light weapons, in some respects mirroring the experience of the International Campaign to Ban Landmines.

This book, representing the perspectives of the foremost specialists on light weapons from around the world, surveys the wide range of policy options open to the international community. From local initiatives in countries such as South Africa to regional agreements in West Africa to international policies being proposed by the United Nations, the authors take a critical look at the feasibility of various types of instruments for controlling the trade in small arms and light weapons. These include various export and import controls, law enforcement strategies to break up light weapons black markets, collection and destruction of weapons following the end of conflict, and greater transparency efforts to illuminate just how small arms and light weapons make their way to the killing grounds of the 1990s. Several of the chapters focus on

Africa because the ongoing conflicts have been particularly virulent there. The lessons learned about the ready availability of light weapons and escalating cycles of violence are applicable to continuing conflicts in other regions, such as those in Afghanistan, Colombia, and Kosovo.

In part 1, Michael Klare reviews how much the policy and research communities have learned, in a relatively few years, about the dynamics of light weapons diffusion to and within areas of conflict. In their chapters, Kathi Austin and Tara Kartha focus especially on the illicit trade in small arms and light weapons and the effect of this trafficking in both facilitating and prolonging conflict in East Africa and South Asia, respectively.

Part 2 highlights the critical role played by the world's major manufacturers and suppliers of light weapons. Lora Lumpe notes that, despite several new and promising U.S. government policies aimed at better regulating the light weapons trade, there remains a need for still tighter controls on the legal transfer of weapons. Paul Eavis and William Benson review both the progress to date and the need for still greater efforts on the part of the European Union and the major European weapons suppliers. Natalie Goldring demonstrates how a country's domestic laws and attitudes on gun control directly affect both the legal and the black-market trade in light weapons.

The chapters in part 3 analyze emerging regional efforts to control both the external supply and the internal diffusion of small arms and light weapons in areas with a high incidence of conflict. Joseph Smaldone reviews one of the most promising of these, the Mali initiative, and its effect on curbing light weapons availability in West Africa. By contrast, Hussein Solomon notes the much more difficult task of curbing the circulation of vast quantities of weapons in southern Africa, despite recent initiatives toward greater regional coordination undertaken by the governments of South Africa, Mozambique, Zimbabwe, Namibia, and others.

The wide range of initiatives being proposed at the international level is the subject of part 4. Graciela Uribe de Lozano reviews the central role being played by the United Nations in highlighting the issue and proposing solutions, particularly through its Group of Governmental Experts on Small Arms and the UN Crime Prevention Panel and through support for regional initiatives. One such regional mechanism, the 1997 OAS Convention, focuses on the importance of greater cooperation among law enforcement officials in tracking and interdicting the flow of illegal arms, as is covered in the chapter by James McShane.

Increasingly, as part 5 demonstrates, the destructive impact of light weapons on civil society, human rights, and social reconstruction is being emphasized by international aid donors and NGOs. Edward Laurance analyzes how a profusion of light weapons in areas of conflict can have devastating effects for human development but also how greater transparency and early warning measures can help break the cycle of violence such weapons engender. Peter Herby notes the importance of strengthening international humanitarian law and other norms relating to armed conflict as a way of reducing the flow of light weapons to those governments and armed groups who violate such norms. The increased need for combining development aid with disarmament, demobilization, and other social reconstruction policies on the part of international donor agencies, such as the World Bank, is the subject of the chapter by Nat Colletta.

In the concluding chapter, Jeffrey Boutwell and Michael Klare review the wide range of policy initiatives being proposed and implemented at many different levels and in diverse regions around the world. They note the widespread recognition in the international community that efforts to mitigate the murderous effects of small arms and light weapons will be difficult, far more so than the international campaign to ban just one type of weapon—antipersonnel land mines. Nonetheless, the past several years have seen the building of an incredible momentum for far stronger controls on small arms and light weapons. There is greater media exposure than ever before on the devastation, to both individuals and societies, caused by such weapons. Local communities, national governments, regional and international organizations, and a wide array of NGOs are devoting themselves to ending the violence caused by this scourge of small arms and light weapons. Because of the complexity of the issue, it will indeed take a wide range of initiatives on many different levels to minimize the murderous effects of small arms and light weapons. To that end, however, we hope this volume will contribute to the ongoing debate and search for the most promising and feasible mix of policies and strategies for controlling small arms and light weapons and the deadly legacy they leave in their wake.

Part One

Light Weapons and International Conflict

1

The International Trade in Light Weapons: What Have We Learned?

Michael T. Klare

THROUGHOUT THE COLD WAR ERA, interest in arms transfers and the proliferation of military technology was focused almost entirely on major weapons systems—tanks, jet aircraft, naval vessels, artillery pieces, and so on. Policymakers and arms control advocates were understandably concerned with the impact of major weapons transfers on the military balance in areas of strategic importance and on the relative strength and durability of military alliances. Although a great many small arms and light weapons were sold or given away during this period, scant attention was paid to the policy implications of such transfers. As a result, very little research was conducted on the production and trade in light weapons, and no effort was made to track these transfers on a systematic basis.

Since the end of the Cold War, however, there has been a surge of interest in the light weapons trade. This is due, in large measure, to the changing nature of international conflict: whereas most major conflicts of the Cold War era entailed a clash between the regular armed forces of established states, conflict in the current era has consisted largely of ethnic and sectarian warfare within states. Typically, the fighting in such conflict is conducted by irregular forces—guerrillas, ethnic separatists, private militias, criminal bands, and so on. These forces are rarely in a position to obtain and operate major weapons systems and so rely, for the most part, on small arms and light weapons.

As the death toll from ethnic and internal conflicts has risen, the international community has devoted greater effort and resources to the control, prevention, and mitigation of such conflict. Numerous peacekeeping operations have been initiated by the United Nations and associated bodies, and vast sums have been spent on the reconstruction of war-torn nations. These efforts have been hampered, however, by the persistence of armed violence in divided and dysfunctional societies. Because firearms have been so widely disseminated in these societies, and the warring parties are so fragmented, it is often impossible for international peacekeepers to restore order and ensure the delivery of humanitarian assistance.

The difficulties encountered by international peacekeepers and humanitarian aid organizations in the performance of their respective functions has led, in turn, to an interest in the proliferation of small arms and light weapons. Believing that international efforts to reduce the intensity and duration of internal warfare have been undermined by the flow of firearms into areas of conflict, many policymakers have called for tightened controls on the trade in such weapons. In one of the earliest of these statements, then Secretary-General Boutros Boutros-Ghali told the UN Security Council in 1995, "I wish to concentrate on what might be called 'micro-disarmament.' " By this, he explained, "I mean practical disarmament in the context of the conflicts the United Nations is actually dealing with, and of the weapons, most of them light weapons, that are actually killing people in the hundreds of thousands."[1]

This interest in light weapons and their role in contemporary conflict has generated a growing demand for information and analysis on the trade in such munitions. However, the neglect of this subject during the Cold War era has proved a significant obstacle to research in the field. While much data have been accumulated on the trade in major weapons, very little has been accumulated on light weapons trafficking. As a result, those with an interest in this topic have had to create a new field of research, requiring the assembly of data not previously available to scholars.

In February 1994, the American Academy of Arts and Sciences held a two-day workshop on the international trade in light weapons to survey the state of the field and to stimulate further interest in the topic. That meeting, the first of its kind on light weapons, illuminated many aspects of the problem and pointed to the need for new international initiatives to control the trade. But the workshop also revealed huge gaps in our knowledge, leading many participants to conclude that additional research would be required before effective control measures could be devised. This view was given expression in the preface to *Lethal Commerce*, the publication derived from the 1994 workshop:

> The [1994 Academy] meeting highlighted the enormous gaps in our current understanding of the nature and scope of the trade and underscored the need for further analysis and debate. . . . What is needed, then, is a systematic survey of

the available information to provide a more reliable assessment of the nature and scope of the trade in small arms and light weapons, and the initiation of additional studies to develop concrete steps for monitoring and ultimately controlling these weapons.[2]

Now, four years after the 1994 Academy meeting, it can be said that much of the necessary research has been completed. While not every gap in our knowledge has been closed, much more has been learned about the nature, scope, and consequences of the light weapons trade. Extensive studies of particular aspects of the trade have been produced by such organizations as the Arms Division of Human Rights Watch (HRW), the British American Security Information Council (BASIC), the Bonn International Center for Conversion (BICC), the Federation of American Scientists (FAS), the Institute for Security Studies of South Africa (ISS), and the UN Institute for Disarmament Research (UNIDIR). It is appropriate, therefore, that we take stock of what has been learned and consider how it can guide us in the development of effective control systems.

On Methodology

When the earliest studies of the light weapons trade were first getting under way, considerable effort was expended in the search for a uniform database of information on this topic. We assumed that a database of this sort—modeled on the annual "register" of major weapons transfers published by the Stockholm International Peace Research Institute (SIPRI)—would be located or could be easily constructed. As it turned out, no such "holy grail" was found to exist. While much data have been collected on the topic, no uniform set of statistics has yet been discovered. What information has been acquired, moreover, does not fit neatly into the sort of tables and charts provided by SIPRI (and other arms control organizations) on the trade in major weapons systems.

This has not, however, proved to be an insurmountable obstacle to our work. Rather, it has been in some ways a positive development, in that it has forced us to develop new sources and methodologies—and thus to acquire a more intimate and detailed understanding of our subject. Indeed, we have seen the emergence of several fruitful approaches to research on the topic.

(1) *The acquisition of national government data.* Several channels have been employed to obtain data on various aspects of the light weapons trade from government agencies. Considerable information on U.S. arms exports, for instance, has been obtained from the U.S. government by FAS using the Freedom of Information Act, much of which has since been published in FAS publications.[3] In addition, some researchers have obtained valuable information on arms smuggling from national police and military records in other coun-

tries. For example, data on arms intercepts by South African authorities are summarized in an essay by Chris Smith in *Small Arms Management and Peacekeeping in Southern Africa,* published by UNIDIR in 1996.[4] Many governments have also supplied detailed information on domestic firearms ownership to the UN Commission on Crime Prevention and Criminal Justice.[5]

(2) *Field research.* Some of the most valuable data on light weapons trafficking have been collected "on the ground" in areas of conflict by researchers who have traveled to the region, collecting documents and interviewing key actors. Especially noteworthy in this regard are the studies of arms trafficking in Angola, Burundi, Rwanda, Sudan, and Zaire by the Arms Project (now Arms Division) of HRW.[6] Equally valuable are the studies of South Asia and southern Africa by Chris Smith of King's College, London,[7] and the work of the ISS in South Africa.[8]

(3) *"Incident reports."* The closest we can probably come to a full-blown database on the light weapons trade is through the collection and tabulation of "incident reports" on individual instances of weapons sales, deliveries, thefts, and interceptions. Such compilations rely, for the most part, on newspaper, radio, and television reports from around the world as collected and translated by the Foreign Broadcast Information Service (FBIS). Efforts of this sort, as undertaken by the Institute on Small Arms in International Security (IRSAIS) and the Monterey Institute of International Studies (MIIS), have proved especially useful in studying the illicit trade in small arms and light weapons.[9]

(4) *Information collected in the course of peacekeeping operations.* One of the tasks of UN peacekeepers in many recent missions has been to collect, store, and (in some cases) destroy the weapons turned in by the warring parties in areas of conflict. Such activities can be an extremely useful source of information on the types and numbers of weapons employed by the belligerents in ethnic and internal conflicts. Much of this information has been summarized and analyzed in the series "Managing Arms in the Peace Process" by UNIDIR.[10]

The information collected through these various endeavors has been used over the past few years to produce a number of important monographs, studies, and papers on various aspects of the light weapons trade. These include *Light Weapons and International Security,* edited by Jasjit Singh (1995); *A Scourge of Guns,* by Michael Klare and David Andersen (1996); *The New Field of Micro-Disarmament,* by Edward Laurance (1996); *Small Arms, Big Impact,* by Michael Renner (1997); *Society under Siege,* edited by Virginia Gamba (1997); and *Light Weapons and Intrastate Conflict,* by Edward Laurance (1998).[11] This information was also utilized by the Panel of Governmental Experts on Small Arms in preparing its 1997 report to the UN General Assembly.[12]

Each of these authors has derived a variety of conclusions about the nature and scope of the international trade in light weapons. For the most part, there is considerable agreement among these authors concerning the basic dynamics of the trade and its impact on international peace and security. While it is impossible to capture the results of this research in a single chapter, I will try to summarize what I see as the major findings and conclusions of these studies.

Major Findings

There is a close and symbiotic relationship between light weapons trafficking and contemporary forms of violent conflict.

Although no two conflicts are ever exactly alike, it can be said that the wars of the post–Cold War have generally taken a particular form: one in which the forces involved are predominantly of a paramilitary or irregular nature and the fighting is confined largely to the national territory of the state in question (and to the border zones of neighboring countries). The conflicts that fit this pattern have, for the most part, entailed a struggle over the ethnic composition of a disputed area or the possession of valuable resources (including, in some cases, control of the state itself). In such circumstances, the parties in question are not so much interested in defeating an enemy's regular military forces as in controlling territory or resources, punishing or driving off hostile groups, and terrorizing or killing those who resist.[13]

Such conflicts, by their very nature, tend to be conducted primarily with small arms and light weapons. This is so because the belligerents involved—state security forces, insurgent organizations, ethnic militias, warlords, death squads, and so on—are normally barred from access to major weapons systems and/or lack the training and logistical capacity to operate such systems. On the other hand, these forces are usually able to acquire small arms and light weapons—whether through gifts from the government, theft, or purchases from black-market dealers—and normally encounter little difficulty in using them. The ease with which light weapons can be operated is of particular salience to child and teenaged soldiers, who often make up a significant proportion of the combatants in many ethnic militias and irregular armies.[14]

The prevalence of light weapons in conflicts of this sort is also a product of the relative poverty of the belligerents involved—whether they be state or nonstate actors—and, in many cases, of the need for secrecy in their arms procurement activities. All too often, ethnic and internal warfare has broken out in states that are poor or are suffering from economic hardship of one sort or another. The end of the Cold War has also produced a sharp reduction in the military aid programs of the wealthier countries. As a result, governments engaged in internal conflicts often have had to confine their arms procurement to small arms and light weapons. Most substate actors are even less well endowed with funds, and so they, too, have had to limit their purchases to smaller and less costly items.

The need for concealment also favors the acquisition of small arms and light weapons. In many of these conflicts, the belligerents involved have been subjected to arms embargoes by the United Nations, the European Union, or other bodies and so have had to conceal their procurement activities from outside observers. This applies as well to their suppliers, who risk censure or prosecution if found to be in violation of international embargoes. On both accounts, this produces a natural preference for deliveries of small arms and light weapons, as these systems are far easier to disguise or conceal than are large and heavy weapons.[15]

There is, then, a close relationship between the particular nature of contemporary conflict and the unique characteristics of small arms and light weapons. While the worldwide diffusion of such weapons is not a cause of these conflicts—most of which have deep and complex roots, often stretching back many generations—the widespread abundance of such munitions has made it much easier for potential belligerents to initiate and sustain armed combat. At the same time, the outbreak of such conflict has produced a substantial demand for weapons of this type.

It is in this sense that the relationship between the two is symbiotic: the proliferation of ethnic and internal conflict has produced a rising demand for light weapons, which, in turn, has induced arms suppliers to increase the available supply of such weaponry; as the supply increases, it becomes easier for those already at war to expand or prolong their operations and for potential belligerents to commence fighting.[16] This pattern, more than anything, explains the persistence and intensity of armed conflict in such locations as Angola, Bosnia, Burundi, Kashmir, Liberia, Sierra Leone, Somalia, Sri Lanka, Sudan, Uganda, Tajikistan, and the Great Lakes region of Africa.[17]

The symbiosis between light arms trafficking and contemporary forms of conflict is underscored in all of the recent studies of the issue. In *Small Arms, Big Impact,* Renner notes, "Small arms are the weapons of choice in today's typical conflict—fighting that rages within, rather than between, countries. The wide availability of these weapons is contributing both to the intensity and duration of conflicts."[18] Likewise, in his 1996 report to the BICC, Laurance notes that "the dominant type of warfare in the post–Cold War era is defined by insurgency, terrorism, and a heavy emphasis on the psychological aspects of warfare. This leads to a preference for light weapons so that combatants can rely on being aggressive and mobile."[19]

The outbreak of ethnic and internal conflict in weak and divided societies often produces an "internal arms race" that further drives the acquisition of small arms and light weapons.

For the reasons given above, insurgents and other nonstate actors are naturally drawn to small arms and light weapons when seeking the wherewithal to initiate and sustain internal conflicts. By the same token, the growing prevalence of ethnic and sectarian conflict has also generated an increased demand for light weapons on the part of established governments. Although state actors will sometimes employ the regular military (with heavy equipment in tow) to root out and destroy insurgent movements, they tend to rely, for the most part, on police and paramilitary forces (which are normally equipped with light and medium weapons only) for these purposes. This is so because much of the fighting tends to occur in populated areas—urban slums, suburban shantytowns, and rural villages—where the use of regular forces and heavy weapons would produce high collateral damage, thereby turning the population against the government. Thus, while there has been a worldwide decline in the demand for heavy weapons since 1990, many states have increased their purchases of light arms and counterinsurgency equipment.[20]

The accelerated procurement of light weapons by both state and nonstate actors often produces an "internal arms race" in which each warring party seeks to outmatch the capabilities of the other (or others).[21] This is evident, for example, in Angola, where the collapse of the Bicesse peace accords following the elections of 1992 led to a mad scramble by both the government and National Union for the Total Independence of Angola (UNITA) to acquire vast quantities of arms from foreign sources.[22] A similar pattern is evident in Sri Lanka, where both the government and the Tamil insurgents have engaged in a substantial and costly arms procurement effort—the government through established trade channels, the Tamil Tigers through an elaborate black-market network stretching across Asia.[23]

An internal arms race of this sort often develops in weak or failed states when representatives of various ethnic and religious groups clash with one another over control of the state apparatus and/or the national territory. In such a setting, it is not uncommon for the government in power—itself a faction in a multiparty conflict—to provide arms to its political or ethnic allies and for the military establishment to split up into rival groups, each with a share of the state's war-making capability.[24] This was the case in Somalia in the early 1990s, when the flight of longtime dictator Mohammed Siad Barre ignited a bitter rivalry between the various clan-based militias that had cooperated in forcing his ouster. A similar pattern occurred in Liberia following the arrival of Charles Taylor's insurgent force in late 1989 and the subsequent capture and execution of President Samuel Doe.[25]

That the outbreak of internal arms races in many countries around the world has stimulated the expansion of global arms-trafficking networks is apparent from the data collected by HRW, UNIDIR, and other organizations. In a 1996 report on Rwanda and Zaire, for instance, Austin of HRW showed how the former Rwandan army forces in Zaire established an elaborate arms-procurement system from their temporary bases inside UN-managed refugee camps.[26] Similarly, in a 1996 report for UNIDIR, Smith described the profusion of covert arms networks that have been established to smuggle weapons from Angola, Mozambique, and Namibia to criminal and extremist organizations in South Africa.[27]

At the same time, the proliferation of channels for the dissemination of light weapons in areas of conflict has clearly made it easier for the protagonists involved to sustain conflicts of great violence and destructiveness. As noted by the UN Panel of Governmental Experts on Small Arms in its 1997 report to the General Assembly,

> Accumulations of small arms and light weapons by themselves do not cause the conflicts in which they are used. The availability of these weapons, however, contributes towards exacerbating conflicts by increasing the lethality and duration of violence, by encouraging a violent rather than a peaceful resolution of differences, and by generating a vicious circle of a greater sense of insecurity, which in turn leads to a greater demand for, and use of, such weapons.[28]

The widespread outbreak of ethnic and internal conflict has also produced a growing demand for small arms and light weapons on the part of individuals and private entities. Even when not aligned with any of the major factions in such conflicts, individuals are often put at risk because they are members of a targeted ethnic or religious group or simply because they live in villages or neighborhoods that are being fought over. And, when the established government is unable to provide adequate protection, such individuals (or firms) are likely to arm themselves or to hire private security companies in order to obtain some measure of safety. As shown by Renner, this accounts for the proliferation of private security firms and neighborhood protection organizations in areas of conflict—a process that is naturally accompanied by the growing diffusion within civil society of guns and other light weapons.[29]

The emergence of internal arms races and the outbreak of conflict in weak and divided societies is fostered by an immense worldwide abundance of small arms and light weapons.

Greatly contributing to the widespread instability described in the 1997 UN report on small arms is the presence in the world today of vast quantities of firearms—many of them left over from superpower competition of the Cold War era and the proxy wars of the 1980s. It is impossible to produce an exact tally of all small arms and light weapons in worldwide circulation today, but the numbers are surely substantial. An estimate of 500 million firearms in current use has been provided by Air Commander Jasjit Singh of the Institute of Defense Studies and Analyses in New Delhi, and this is probably as close as we can come to the actual number.[30] It has been further estimated that this figure incorporates at least 100 million modern rifles, including large numbers of Kalashnikov AK-47s (of which some 50 million had been produced by 1990), U.S. M16s (8 million produced), and Fabrique Nationale FALs (7 million produced).[31]

The fact that so many weapons are in existence today is due, to a considerable extent, to the military competition of the Cold War era. Both of the superpowers produced vast quantities of small arms and light weapons for their own forces and for transfer to their allies. To give just one example of such largess, between 1950 and 1975, the United States donated a total of 312,000 M1 rifles to Turkey, 296,000 to South Korea, 232,000 to France, 220,000 to South Vietnam, 186,000 to Greece, 165,000 to Iran, 150,000 to Pakistan, 73,000 to Norway, 70,000 to Denmark, 60,000 to Israel, 56,000 to Venezuela, 55,000 to Indonesia, and comparable numbers to several other states, for a grand total of 2,174,000.[32] Many of these weapons, and the millions of other firearms produced by the two superpowers (and their allies) during the Cold War era, remain in use or are piled up in warehouses and arsenals, awaiting delivery to future customers.

The vast quantities of light weapons left over from the Cold War period are likely to be recycled into the global arms traffic through a variety of channels. In some cases, the former owners of these weapons have agreed to transfer them to the military forces of friendly states. After taking possession of the arsenals of the former East German military establishment in 1990, for instance, the reunified German government donated some 304,000 Kalashnikov rifles (along with 83 million rounds of ammunition) and 5,000 RPG-7 grenade launchers to the Turkish military.[33] The United States has also transferred large quantities of surplus weapons to friendly states in the developing world through its Excess Defense Articles (EDA) program, which was significantly expanded in 1989–90.[34] Similarly, Russia is believed to have transferred large quantities of ex-Soviet arms to Armenia, Georgia, and other friendly states in the space of the former Soviet Union.[35] In addition, many weapons left over from the Cold War have fallen into the hands of black-market dealers. Large numbers of ex-Soviet weapons, for instance, have been acquired by criminal gangs in Russia and the former Soviet Union and sold to the belligerents in the former Yugoslavia.[36]

Adding to the global circulation of surplus weapons are the many weapons left over from the proxy wars of the 1980s—wars in which the United States and the Soviet Union sought regional advantage by providing arms to insurgent forces seeking the overthrow of governments allied with the opposite superpower. When the Soviets occupied Afghanistan, for instance, the United States provided the rebel *mujahideen* with several million AK-47 rifles and other light weapons, many of which remained in rebel supply depots in northern Pakistan at the time of the Soviet pullout. As shown by Smith in his studies of arms trafficking in South Asia, many of these weapons have since been used to sustain the fighting in Afghanistan as well as ethnic violence in Pakistan, Kashmir, and Punjab.[37] Likewise, many of the weapons provided by the United States and the Soviet Union to the belligerents in Central America in the 1980s have since been used to fuel insurgent and criminal violence in the Western Hemisphere.[38]

Although many of the weapons used in future conflicts are likely to be derived from surplus stocks of one sort or another, the world continues to produce small arms and light weapons of various types. Many of the traditional producers of firearms—the United States, Russia, China, Belgium, Germany, Italy, and the Czech Republic, among others—continue to manufacture and sell weapons of the types they produced during the Cold War era. According to the U.S. Arms Control and Disarmament Agency (ACDA), small arms and ammunition represent about 13 percent of the total worldwide trade in conventional weapons; if applied to the ACDA's estimate of $172 billion for total world arms exports in 1990–95, this would yield a figure of $22.3 billion.[39]

Unfortunately, it is impossible to translate these numbers into specific numbers of particular items. It is, however, sometimes possible to learn of major transactions from trade or government publications. In 1997, for instance, the U.S. Department of Defense announced the sale of 37,500 M16 rifles, 4,700 M4 carbines, and 2,600 M203 grenade launchers to Thailand in a deal worth some $40 million.[40] More recently, Washington promised to supply Estonia with 40,500 surplus M14 rifles (along with 1.3 million rounds of ammunition) and Lithuania with 40,000 M14s (plus 1.5 million rounds).[41] Many similar transactions (although usually on a smaller scale) occur around the world on a daily basis.

Nor are the traditional arms producers the only suppliers of such munitions: over the past few decades, the technology to manufacture small arms and light weapons has spread to a significant number of developing countries. According to *Jane's Infantry Weapons* and other sources, twenty-two developing nations now manufacture light weapons of one sort or another. In most cases, this entails the licensed production of arms developed by the industrialized countries; in some countries, however, it also involves the manufacture of indigenously designed systems. Brazil, for instance, produces the Belgian-designed FAL assault rifle along with the indigenous Uru submachine gun; Singapore makes the U.S. M16 rifle as well as the locally designed Ultimax light machine gun.[42]

While it is likely that the rate of firearms production has dropped in some countries since the end of the Cold War, most of these nations continue to produce and export a variety of light weapons, further adding to global supplies. The multiplicity of suppliers also facilitates the acquisition of arms by potential belligerents, particularly those that might be shunned by the traditional suppliers for political or human rights reasons. Prior to the massacres of 1994, for instance, the government of Rwanda was able to purchase large quantities of small arms from producers in Egypt and South Africa.[43] The two sides in the Angolan civil war have also benefited from the proliferation of potential sources of supply.[44]

Even relatively small quantities of light weapons can prove highly destabilizing in vulnerable and fractured societies.

When societies are deeply divided along ethnic, religious, or sectarian lines and the existing government is unwilling or unable to protect minorities and maintain domestic order, the introduction and use of even small quantities of small arms and light weapons can have profoundly destabilizing effects. This was made painfully evident at the 1994 American Academy meeting when, on the second day of the workshop, it was learned that an Israeli settler had walked into an Islamic mosque in Hebron and opened fire on the assembled worshipers with a Galil assault rifle—killing or wounding dozens of Palestinians and producing a serious breach in the Israeli-Palestinian peace process. Since then, the world has witnessed many similar incidents, including periodic massacres in Algeria, the November 1997 attack on foreign tourists in Luxor, and the December 1997 slayings in Chiapas.

The great impact of such events is a consequence of the troubled world in which we live. While the risk of major interstate conflict has declined in recent years, we find that many societies are deeply stressed through some combination of economic hardship, population growth, environmental decline, and political polarization. One consequence of these pressures is the phenomenon of failed states, which occurs when an established government falls apart in the face of unrelenting internal pressures; another consequence is the rise of hate groups and militant ethnic/religious organizations. In such an environment, it takes only a single incident—the assassination of an important leader, the slaughter of worshipers in a crowded church or mosque, or a racial brawl—to ignite a national crisis or upheaval. It is against this backdrop that the widespread availability of assault rifles and other light weapons must be examined.[45]

The potentially catastrophic impact of even small quantities of light weapons on vulnerable societies is evident in many recent conflicts. Liberia is perhaps the most depressing example: according to *The Economist,* at least 200,000 people have been killed in the fighting there—most of them by small arms and light weapons.[46] In addition, one million people have been rendered homeless, the economy has been shattered, famine is rampant, health facilities are nonexistent, and large areas of the countryside have been abandoned. All of this is the product of a civil war that began on Christmas Eve 1989, when Charles Taylor invaded Liberia with 100 lightly armed insurgents. By gradually selling off Liberia's mineral and timber wealth to finance the procurement of additional weapons, Taylor was able to build an army big enough to seize control of large parts of the country.[47] At the same time, other factions arose in other parts of the country to contest Taylor's rule, producing a bloody internecine conflict that lasted for seven grueling years.[48]

The destabilizing impact of small arms on vulnerable societies is also evident in the Great Lakes region of Central Africa, where first Rwanda and then Zaire imploded in a maelstrom of ethnic and political violence. Here, too, a catastrophic chain reaction of events began with the arrival of a small, lightly equipped insurgent force. When the Tutsi-led Rwandan Patriotic Front

(RPF) entered Rwanda in 1990 (with arms supplied by Uganda), the existing, Hutu-controlled government of Rwanda created militant ethnic militias known as *Interahamwe* and provided them with an array of light weapons (including machetes imported for this purpose). These forces were deeply implicated in the 1994 massacre of some 800,000 Tutsi and moderate Hutu.[49]

Subsequently, when the RPF seized control of Rwanda, the former government (along with what remained of the Rwandan army and the *Interahamwe* militias) fled to Zaire, where—with the aid of the Mobutu regime—they began to prepare for the reconquest of Rwanda.[50] This, in turn, led the new government of Rwanda to arm antigovernment forces in Zaire and eventually to orchestrate the rebellion that resulted in the collapse of the Mobutu dictatorship. While it is true, of course, that many factors contributed to these outcomes, it is also evident that, at each stage in this process, the acquisition of relatively small quantities of light weapons—never exceeding a few million dollars' worth at any given time—played a decisive role in sustaining and escalating the violence.

The acquisition of relatively small quantities of light weapons by extremist organizations, ethnic militias, and criminal groups can also contribute to social instability in troubled nations, undermining economic development and the democratic process. This is especially evident in South Africa, where efforts to establish a stable, multiethnic society have been severely hampered by the acquisition and use of military-type firearms by political extremists and criminal gangs.[51] In 1995, Jacklyn Cock of the University of the Witwatersrand observed, "The level of violent crime linked to [light weapons] proliferation threatens the consolidation of democracy."[52] A similar picture is described by Laurance regarding the situation in El Salvador, where many former combatants—unable to find employment in the civil sector—"have taken up arms and formed criminal gangs responsible for the violence threatening to overwhelm [the country]."[53]

Light weapons flow to existing and potential belligerents through a wide variety of channels, both public and private, licit and illicit.

The many studies conducted on the light weapons traffic over the past few years have revealed a vast and complex system, involving multiple channels of trade and a wide variety of actors. Although this trade employs some of the same channels used in the transfer of major weapons systems—particularly with respect to government-to-government sales—it also embraces a variety of other, less familiar channels (many of them of an illicit or clandestine nature). Some of these channels involve government entities at one stage or another in the arms transfer process, while others rely entirely on nonstate actors. Research suggests that all of these channels play an important role in supplying weapons to the various belligerents in the multiple conflicts of the post–Cold War era.[54]

To capture the distinctive character of the light weapons trade, and to distinguish it from the more familiar pattern of arms *proliferation* (meaning the spread of a particular weapons type from one or two states to many), I prefer to speak of the *diffusion* of arms, meaning the transfer of arms across and within national boundaries, at both the state and the substate level.[55] Laurance also speaks of the *circulation* of arms, suggesting the recycling of weapons from one belligerent to another, whether through sale, gift, or barter.[56] In some settings, such as Colombia, El Salvador, and Somalia, we can even speak of the *saturation* of society with such weapons. Whichever term is used, it is important to accurately portray the complexity of the distribution system for small arms and light weapons.

In approaching this task, it is useful to distinguish between four basic types of light weapons transfers: (1) government-to-government sales or deliveries, (2) government-sanctioned commercial sales, (3) covert deliveries by government agencies or government-backed private firms (also known as "gray-market" sales), and (4) black-market (or illicit) transactions. Each is described briefly below.

(1) *Government-to-government transfers.* Such transfers entail the sale or gift of arms from one government to another through overt, legal channels. Very large quantities of light weapons were given to Third World governments in this fashion during the Cold War period by the two superpowers and their allies. Some governments continue to sell or give away arms through such channels—the U.S. government, for instance, continues to provide arms to certain governments for use in antinarcotics operations—but government-to-government transfers of this sort have become less common in the post–Cold War period.

(2) *Government-sanctioned commercial sales.* Such transfers entail the sale of arms on a commercial basis by private firms in accordance with government-approved and -supervised export/import procedures. Such sales usually require a license or "end-user certificate" demonstrating that the intended recipient is a government agency or a government-approved commercial entity in an allowable destination. Most transfers of small arms and light weapons are conducted in this fashion.

(3) *Covert or "gray-market" operations.* Such transfers entail the covert sale or delivery of arms to illicit recipients in another country by government agencies or government-backed private firms in pursuit of political or strategic advantage. During the Cold War period, the United States and the Soviet Union provided large quantities of arms in this fashion to insurgent groups seeking the overthrow of regimes considered friendly to the other superpower. Today, the Cold War no longer provides the impetus for such transactions, but some governments continue to aid insurgent forces in this fashion (usually on the basis of ethnic or religious ties). Such transactions can also entail the delivery of arms to ethnic militias, death squads, and local warlords operating within the country in question.

(4) *Black-market transactions and theft.* Such transfers entail the covert sale of illicitly procured arms by private entities in knowing violation of established government laws and policies. Those engaged in such sales normally do so for the high profits to be made and risk large fines and incarceration if caught. Transactions of this sort are the main source of supply for insurgents, ethnic militias, warlords, and other groups barred from obtaining arms through normal, licit trade channels. Such groups may also acquire arms through theft from government arsenals or through the collusion of friendly (or corrupt) military officials.[57]

When examining these channels, moreover, it is also useful to distinguish between various types of recipients: domestic consumers, foreign governments, and foreign nonstate actors. The resulting labyrinth of supply channels can be represented by the twelve-part matrix shown in table 1.1.

Although every one of the transaction types identified above contributes to the worldwide diffusion of light weapons, recent events suggest that arms transferred through black-market and covert government channels play a disproportionate role in fueling ethnic and internal conflicts. This is so because

TABLE 1.1
Channels Used in the Transfer of Small Arms and Light Weapons

	Recipient		
Supplier	Foreign governments	Nonstate actors (domestic)	Nonstate actors (foreign)
State (via legal channels)	State-to-state military aid and sales programs	Sales to private firms and individuals, gun clubs, etc.	Sales to private entities backed by recipient government
State (via covert channels)	Covert sales or deliveries to pariah or embargoed states	Transfers to friendly militias, warlords, and political groups	Covert transfers to friendly insurgent and separatist forces
Private firms (via legal channels)	Government-sanctioned commercial sales	Government-sanctioned sales to private firms and individuals	Government-sanctioned sales to private dealers for domestic resale
Black-market dealers	Sales to pariah and embargoed governments	Sales to insurgents, warlords, brigands, etc.	Sales to insurgents, warlords, brigands, etc.

such channels often constitute the only source of arms for insurgents, separatists, warlords, brigands, and other nonstate actors. And because black-market and covert government transfers have enabled such actors to sustain relatively high levels of combat for extended periods of time, they clearly represent a significant factor in the global conflict equation.[58]

The role of black-market transfers is evident in many of the cases cited above. Taylor could not have terrorized Liberia for as long as he did had he not been able to resupply his forces on a regular basis through such channels. Likewise, the former Rwandan army forces in Zaire were able to retain a military capability of sorts through their access to black-market arms. Illicit arms trafficking has also contributed to the lawlessness and banditry that currently afflicts many societies—especially when such trafficking is linked to the trade in illegal narcotics, as is the case in many areas.[59]

Of equal concern is the transfer of arms by government agencies to insurgent groups in other countries. During the Cold War period, the two superpowers funneled large quantities of weapons in this fashion to opponents of governments linked to their respective adversary. Covert operations of this type largely ceased with the end of the Cold War, but other governments continue to supply arms through clandestine channels to insurgent and separatist groups in neighboring countries. Pakistan, for instance, has been accused of supplying arms to Muslim separatists in Kashmir, Iran of supplying Kurdish separatists in Turkey, Rwanda of supplying anti-Mobutu forces in Zaire, Zaire of supplying antigovernment forces in Angola, Sudan of supplying antigovernment forces in Uganda, and so on.[60] Such transactions, although rarely acknowledged by the governments involved, play a significant role in supplying insurgent forces around the world.

Conclusion

These findings represent some of the most important results of the extensive research conducted by scholars in the field between 1994 and 1998. It is hardly a complete picture of the trade in light weapons, but it serves to highlight aspects of this trade that deserve close attention from policymakers. In particular, it highlights the complexity of the trade, its multiple dimensions, and its great impact on the international security environment of the post–Cold War era.

No doubt we would be well served by additional research on the trade in small arms and light weapons. Much more needs to be learned, for instance, about the black-market trade in these munitions. But we surely possess a much clearer and more substantial picture of the trade than we did in 1994 at the first American Academy workshop on this topic. Many of the gaps revealed at that earlier meeting have now been closed. We have also begun to establish significant archives on the subject. But most of all, we now possess a sufficiently thorough assessment of the trade to begin the vital task of devising effective control measures.

Notes

1. Boutros Boutros-Ghali, *Supplement to an Agenda for Peace: Position Paper of the Secretary-General on the Occasion of the Fiftieth Anniversary of the United Nations,* UN document A/50/60, January 3, 1995, p. 14.

2. Jeffrey Boutwell, Michael T. Klare, and Laura W. Reed, *Lethal Commerce: The Global Trade in Small Arms and Light Weapons* (Cambridge, Mass.: American Academy of Arts and Sciences, 1995), p. 5.

3. See, in particular, Michael Klare and David Andersen, *A Scourge of Guns: The Diffusion of Small Arms and Light Weapons in Latin America* (Washington, D.C.: Federation of American Scientists, 1996), and the *Arms Sales Monitor,* a periodic publication of the Federation's Arms Sales Monitoring Project.

4. Chris Smith, "Light Weapons and the International Arms Trade," in United Nations Institute for Disarmament Research (UNIDIR), Disarmament and Conflict Resolution Project, *Small Arms Management and Peacekeeping in Southern Africa* (New York and Geneva: UNIDIR, 1996), pp. 41–48.

5. See UN Commission on Crime Prevention and Criminal Justice, *United Nations International Study on Firearms Regulation*, E.89.IV.2(New York:United Nations, 1998).

6. Human Rights Watch Arms Project (HRWAP), *Angola: Arms Trade and Violations of the Laws of War since the 1992 Elections* (New York and Washington, D.C.: HRWAP, 1994); *Arming Rwanda* (New York and Washington, D.C.: Human Rights Watch [HRW], January 1994); *Rwanda/Zaire: Rearming with Impunity* (New York and Washington, D.C.: HRW, May 1995); *Stoking the Fires: Military Assistance and Arms Trafficking in Burundi* (New York and Washington, D.C.: HRWAP, 1997); Human Rights Watch, *Sudan: Global Trade, Local Impact* (New York and Washington, D.C.: HRW, August 1998).

7. Chris Smith, "Light Weapons and Ethnic Conflict," in Boutwell et al., eds., *Lethal Commerce,* pp. 61–80, and "Light Weapons and International Conflict."

8. See, for example, Virginia Gamba, ed., *Society under Siege: Crime, Violence and Illegal Weapons* (Halfway House, South Africa: Institute for Strategic Studies, 1997).

9. Data of this sort are available online from the Monterey Institute's Program for Arms Control, Disarmament and Diversion at http://cns.miis.edu/pacdc/salw proj.html.

10. Case studies in this series include Somalia, Rhodesia/Zimbabwe, Croatia and Bosnia-Herzogovina, Cambodia, Mozambique, Liberia, and Southern Africa.

11. See Gamba, ed., *Society under Siege;* Klare and Andersen, *A Scourge of Guns;* Edward Laurance, *The New Field of Micro-Disarmament,* Brief 7 (Bonn: Bonn International Center for Conversion, September 1996), and *Light Weapons and Intrastate Conflict: Early Warning Factors and Preventive Action* (Washington, D.C.: Carnegie Commission on Preventing Deadly Conflict, 1998); Michael Renner, *Small Arms, Big*

Impact: The Next Challenge for Disarmament, Worldwatch Paper 137 (Washington, D.C.: Worldwatch Institute, October 1997); and Jasjit Singh, ed., *Light Weapons and International Security* (New Delhi: Indian Pugwash Society and British American Security Information Council, December 1995).

12. United Nations General Assembly, *General and Complete Disarmament: Small Arms,* UN document A/52/298, August 27, 1997.

13. For discussion, see Mary Kaldor and Basker Vashee, eds., *New Wars,* Restructuring the Global Military Structure, vol. 1 (London: Pinter, 1997). See also Human Rights Watch, *Slaughter among Neighbors* (New Haven: Yale University Press, 1995).

14. For a poignant discussion of the use of child soldiers by the Lord's Resistance Army (LRA) in Uganda, see Elizabeth Rubin, "Our Children Are Killing Us," *The New Yorker,* March 23, 1998, pp. 56–65.

15. On the need for concealment as a factor in the international arms trade, see Human Rights Watch Arms Project, *Stoking the Fires,* esp. pp. 30–34.

16. The author first argued this point in Klare, "Light Weapons Diffusion and Global Violence in the Post–Cold War Era," in Singh, ed., *Light Weapons and International Security,* pp. 1–40.

17. This is most evident, perhaps, in the Human Rights Watch reports on Burundi, Rwanda, and Zaire. See Human Rights Watch Arms Project, *Arming Rwanda, Rearming with Impunity,* and *Stoking the Fires.*

18. Renner, *Small Arms, Big Impact,* p. 10.

19. Laurance, *The New Field of Micro-Disarmament,* p. 16.

20. This is evident largely from anecdotal evidence, involving purchases by particular states. Mexico, for instance, reportedly sought additional antiriot systems following the uprising in Chiapas. See John MacCormack and Carmina Danini, "Mexico Importing Riot-Control Vehicles," *San Antonio Express News,* April 27, 1994. Likewise, Colombia has built up its internal security forces for combat against guerrillas and narcotraffickers, with U.S. assistance. See Human Rights Watch/Americas, *State of War: Political Violence and Counterinsurgency in Colombia* (New York and Washington, D.C.: Human Rights Watch, 1993). The same pattern is visible in Burma, where government forces are battling ethnic separatists. See Barbara Crossette, "Burmese Warning on Arms Build up," *New York Times,* November 19, 1991. Many other such cases have been documented by Human Rights Watch and Amnesty International.

21. For discussion of this process, see Barry R. Posen, "The Security Dilemma and Ethnic Conflict," *Survival,* vol. 35, no. 1 (Spring 1993), pp. 27–47.

22. For an excellent account of this episode, see Human Rights Watch Arms Project and Human Rights Watch/Africa, *Angola: Arms Trade and Violations of the Laws of War since the 1992 Elections* (New York and Washington, D.C.: Human Rights Watch, 1994).

23. See Raymond Bonner, "Tamil Guerrillas in Sri Lanka: Deadly and Armed to the Teeth," *New York Times,* March 7, 1998; Barbara Crossette, "Sri Lanka Buys Arms to Fight Rebels," *New York Times,* May 20, 1985; and Anthony Davis, "Tamil Tiger International," *Jane's Intelligence Review,* October 1996, pp. 469–73.

24. On the ties between the Hutu-controlled government of Rwanda (prior to 1994) and extremist Hutu militias, see Africa Rights, *Rwanda: Death, Despair and Defiance* (London: Africa Rights, 1995).

25. See discussion in Klare, "Light Weapons Diffusion and Global Violence in the

Post–Cold War Era," pp. 17–22. See also William Reno, *Warlord Politics and African* States (Boulder, Colo.: Lynne Rienner, 1998).

26. Human Rights Watch Arms Project, *Rwanda/Zaire.*

27. Smith, "Light Weapons and the International Arms Trade," pp. 41–57.

28. UN General Assembly, *Small Arms,* p. 10.

29. Renner, *Small Arms, Big Impact,* pp. 14–18.

30. Singh, "Introduction," *Light Weapons,* p. ix.

31. The 100 million estimate is from Renner, *Small Arms, Big Impact,* p. 20. The figures on assault rifle production are from Virginia Hart Ezell, "Small Arms Proliferation Remains Global Dilemma," *National Defense,* January 1995, pp. 26–27.

32. John Walter, *Rifles of the World* (Northbrook, Ill.: DBI Books, 1993), p. 73.

33. Otfried Nassauer, "An Army's Surplus—the NVA's Heritage," in Edward J. Laurance and Herbert Wulf, eds., *Coping with Surplus Weapons,* Brief 3 (Bonn: Bonn International Center for Conversion, 1995), pp. 45–46, 58–59.

34. For background on this program, see Paul F. Pineo and Lora Lumpe, *Recycled Weapons: American Exports of Surplus Arms 1990–1995* (Washington, D.C.: Federation of American Scientists, 1996).

35. For discussion, see Pavel Baev, *Russia's Policies in the Caucasus* (London: Royal Institute of International Affairs, 1997).

36. See Roger Cohen, "Arms Trafficking to Bosnia Goes On despite Embargo," *New York Times,* November 5, 1994; Daniel N. Nelson, "Ancient Enmities, Modern Guns," *Bulletin of the Atomic Scientists,* December 1993, pp. 21–27; and Smith, "Light Weapons and the International Arms Trade," pp. 11–13.

37. See Smith, "Light Weapons and Ethnic Conflict in South Asia," in Boutwell et al., eds., *Lethal Commerce,* pp. 61–80.

38. See Klare and Andersen, *A Scourge of Guns,* pp. 58–62.

39. The 13 percent figure comes from U.S. Congress, Senate Committee on Governmental Affairs, *A Review of Arms Export Licensing,* Hearing, 103rd Cong., 2d Sess., June 15, 1994, p. 37. The ACDA figures (in constant 1994 dollars) are from the U.S. Arms Control and Disarmament Agency (ACDA), *World Military Expenditures and Arms Transfers 1995* (Washington, D.C.: ACDA, 1996), p. 103.

40. U.S. Department of Defense, "Memorandum for Correspondents," no. 112-M, July 9, 1997; electronic communication accessed at www.dtic.mil/defenselink/news.

41. From U.S. government sources as reported in Federation of American Scientists, *Arms Sales Monitor,* April 10, 1998, pp. 7–8.

42. The twenty-two developing-world producers are Argentina, Brazil, Chile, the Dominican Republic, Egypt, India, Indonesia, Iran, Iraq, Israel, Mexico, North Korea, Pakistan, Peru, the Philippines, Saudi Arabia, Singapore, South Africa, South Korea, Taiwan, Turkey, and Venezuela. Extensive data on the arms production activities of these countries are available in various editions of *Jane's Infantry Weapons.* See also Klare, "Light Weapons Production in Developing Countries," in Singh, ed., *Light Weapons and International Security,* pp. 26–36.

43. Human Rights Watch Arms Project, *Arming Rwanda.*

44. See Human Rights Watch Arms Project, *Angola,* pp. 35–57.

45. For discussion of this point, see Smith, "Light Weapons and the International Arms Trade," pp. 4–8. See also Human Rights Watch, *Slaughter among Neighbors.*

46. "Liberia: Farewell, Guns?" *The Economist,* July 26, 1997, p. 39.

47. On Taylor's arms-buying activities, see William Reno, "The Business of War in Liberia," *Current History,* May 1996, pp. 211–15.

48. For background and discussion, see Howard W. French, "As War Factions Shatter, Liberia Falls into Chaos," *New York Times,* October 22, 1994, and Jeffrey Goldberg, "A War without Purpose in a Country without Identity," *New York Times Magazine,* January 22, 1995, pp. 36–39.

49. For background, see Africa Rights, *Rwanda: Death, Despair and Defiance* (London: Africa Rights, 1995).

50. See Human Rights Watch Arms Project, *Rwanda/Zaire.*

51. For further discussion, see the essays by Peter Batchelor and Jakkie Potgieter in *Society under Siege.*

52. Jacklyn Cock, "A Sociological Account of Light Weapons Proliferation in Southern Africa," in Singh, ed., *Light Weapons and International Security,* p. 87.

53. Laurance, *The New Field of Micro-Disarmament,* p. 60.

54. The author first emphasized this point in Klare, "Light Weapons Diffusion and Global Violence in the Post–Cold War Era."

55. I first employed this term in Klare, "Light Weapons Diffusion and Global Violence in the Post–Cold War Era," p. 3.

56. Laurance, *The New Field of Micro-Disarmament,* p. 15.

57. For background on the illicit arms trade, see "The Covert Arms Trade," *The Economist,* February 12, 1994, pp. 21–23; Aaron Karp, "The Rise of Black and Gray Markets," *Annals of the American Academy of Political and Social Science,* vol. 535 (September 1994), pp. 175–89; Michael Klare, "The Thriving Black Market for Weapons," *Bulletin of the Atomic Scientists,* April 1988, pp. 16–24, and "The Subterranean Arms Trade," in Andrew J. Pierre, ed., *Cascade of Arms* (Washington, D.C.: Brookings Institution Press, 1997), pp. 43–71; and Edward J. Laurance, "Political Implications of Illegal Arms Exports from the United States," *Political Science Quarterly,* vol. 107, no. 3 (Fall 1992), pp. 109–40.

58. On the growing role of black-market dealers in supplying the warring parties in Burundi, see Human Rights Watch Arms Project, *Stoking the Fires.*

59. For discussion of the links between illicit arms trafficking and illicit drug trafficking in South and Southeast Asia, see Tara Kartha, "Southern Asia: The Narcotics and Weapons Linkage," in Singh, ed., *Light Weapons and International Security,* pp. 63–86.

60. See John Anderson, "Pakistan Aiding Rebels in Kashmir," *Washington Post,* May 16, 1994, and "Iran Is Reported to Aid Turkish Kurds in Iraq," *New York Times,* October 25, 1992; Howard W. French, "Zairian Crisis Part of Broad Web of African Subversion and Revolt," *New York Times,* November 23, 1996; James Rupert, "Zaire Reportedly Selling Arms to Angolan Ex-Rebels," *Washington Post,* March 21, 1997; Donatella Lorch, "Rebels without a Cause Terrorize Uganda," *New York Times,* June 21, 1995; and Human Rights Watch, *Sudan,* pp. 39–43.

2

Light Weapons and Conflict in the Great Lakes Region of Africa

Kathi Austin

SINCE THE END OF THE COLD WAR, the Great Lakes region of Africa—an area that includes Rwanda and Burundi as well as parts of Uganda, Tanzania, and the Democratic Republic of Congo (formerly Zaire, now commonly referred to as the DRC)—has experienced a rising tide of militarization and conflict with a corresponding decrease in human security. Contributing to this tragic state of affairs is the seemingly unstoppable flow of small arms and light weapons into the region. The proliferation of weapons in this conflict-ridden zone underscores the failure of regional and international actors to curb arms flows to governments, insurgents, armed political factions, militias, and others who use these weapons to undermine responsible governance and democracy, commit serious violations of human rights and international law, and target civilian populations in their pursuit of political and financial gain.

Over the past few years, civil war, genocide, ethnic cleansing, military operations, and political strife have taken the lives of more than one and a half million people in this region and produced more than six million refugees and internally displaced. But these high figures cannot do justice to the traumas and scars produced by the region's recent conflicts: the 1990–94 civil war in Rwanda; the ethnic slaughter of roughly 50,000 Burundians in a single week following Burundi's abortive 1993 military coup; the 1994 Rwandan genocide, which claimed upwards of one million lives within a three-month period;

the ethnic killing of tens of thousands in eastern Zaire/Congo[1] by both Hutu and Tutsi forces; the ousting of the Mobutu regime by an insurgent drive in early 1997; and the outbreak of army mutinies and militia violence in the Central Africa Republic and Congo-Brazzaville in 1996 and 1997, respectively.

Currently, the killing continues in both Rwanda and Burundi. In the neighboring DRC, Laurent Kabila came to power amid allegations that his forces massacred thousands of Hutu refugees during the civil war in Zaire, and local and international human rights organizations have reported serious and widespread infringements on fundamental human rights in the DRC.[2] Political and military violence had become the norm under Kabila's presidency and led to the outbreak of a rebellion sponsored by Rwanda and Uganda. Presently, Rwanda, Uganda, and, to a lesser extent, Burundi are fighting in the new civil war against Kabila, who in turn is relying on troops or military assistance mainly from Angola, Zimbabwe, Namibia, Chad, and Sudan as well as former Hutu genocidaires and Burundian insurgents.[3] Within Uganda, low-intensity conflicts are being fought between the government and the Allied Democratic Forces (ADF) in the west and the Lord's Resistance Army (LRA) and West Nile Bank Front (WNBF) in the north. Military assistance continues to be funneled through Uganda to the Sudanese rebels fighting against the Islamic government in Khartoum. Tanzania, alone, has remained relatively peaceful throughout the Great Lakes crises; however, it is increasingly experiencing an upsurge in criminal violence on its western frontier, where refugee camps for Rwandans, Burundians, and Congolese have been situated and are known to harbor rebels active against their countries' governments. What is especially troubling to both residents and outside observers is the chronic nature of the Great Lakes conflicts, which tend to spill over into one another with an enormous humanitarian toll. The constant flow of new weaponry into the region extends and intensifies these conflicts. Clearly, any effort to reduce the violence in the Great Lakes region must tackle the high degree of internal militarization resulting from unimpeded flows of weapons and foreign military assistance. Of particular concern is the growing reliance by belligerents on private arms networks—most of them criminal—which operate with little public accountability and a high degree of secrecy.

Background

The current period of turbulence in the Great Lakes region began with the civil war in Rwanda, fought largely between the Habyarimana regime and the rebel Rwandan Patriotic Front (RPF). During the fighting of 1990–94, France was the key supplier of arms, training, and military assistance to the Habyarimana government and the Hutu-controlled Armed Forces of Rwanda (FAR, by its initials in French). President Juvenal Habyarimana also acquired rifles, machine guns, and ammunition from South Africa in contravention of an international ban on South African arms exports.[4] In addition, the Egyptian government provided Habyarimana with long-range artillery pieces, artillery shells, explosives, grenades, land mines and Egyptian-made Kalashnikov rifles in exchange for cash and tea; this $6 million transaction was financed with a loan provided by the French government bank, the Credit Lyonnais.[5] The RPF, meanwhile, was supplied largely by Uganda, which permitted its territory to be used as a base for recruitment, training, and the launching of armed attacks into Rwanda.

The civil war in Rwanda corresponded with serious political turmoil in Burundi. The Tutsi-dominated military had intervened in state affairs repeatedly since the country's independence from Belgium in 1962, largely in order to suppress challenges by the Hutu majority to Tutsi domination. After a number of successive military coups, the first national democratic elections were held in 1993. Tragically, an aborted military coup by Tutsi army officers resulted in the death of the first elected Hutu president along with the outbreak of ethnic violence that claimed the lives of over 50,000 people in a single week. After international condemnation, the coup was aborted and a power-sharing arrangement negotiated. During most of this period, the Tutsi-dominated Burundian military received training and munitions from France, Egypt, Russia, China, North Korea, and the United States, through either direct purchases or military cooperation agreements.[6] At the same time, sporadic attacks were being waged against the country by small Hutu guerrilla groups based in neighboring Tanzania and Zaire. These groups had various business and political patrons in the region from whom they received political support and small quantities of light weapons.[7]

The Burundian bloodbath of 1993 should have served as a warning to the international community of the volatility of ethnic tensions in the region. However, in Rwanda, the UN-brokered 1993 Arusha peace agreement between the government and the RPF, along with the arrival of UN peacekeepers in the country, lulled policymakers into believing that everything was under control. Under the Arusha accords, weapons flows were expected to cease and the peacekeeping forces were to monitor security. But while UN intelligence and reports by human rights organizations warned of impending violence, nothing was done to impede the planning and execution of the 1994 genocide by Hutu extremists of Tutsi and moderate Hutu. The mass slaughter was initiated, organized, and often supervised by members of the Rwandan security forces, some of whom were armed and trained by the French. Much of the killing was carried out with traditional weapons and farming implements, including machetes, knives, and hoes; however, the security forces often finished off the survivors seeking refuge in churches, stadiums, or school buildings with automatic rifles and grenades. Sadly, a UN arms embargo was not imposed on Rwanda until a month and a half after the genocide had commenced.

Following their defeat by the RPF in the fall of 1994, the perpetrators of the Rwandan genocide led a mass exodus of Hutu refugees out of the country into neighboring Zaire, Burundi, and Tanzania. The immediate impact of the refugee crisis was to extend Rwanda's political strife throughout the region and lay the groundwork for continued regional warfare. Although some weapons were confiscated from the defeated Rwandan army (the ex-FAR) and its allied militias as they crossed international borders, the refugee camps were quickly militarized and served as significant bases for the further destabilization of Rwanda, Burundi, and eastern Zaire. In contravention of the UN arms embargo, weapons poured into eastern Zaire for the ex-FAR from governments or traffickers based in Belgium, China, France, South Africa, and the Seychelles.[8]

A successfully rejuvenated ex-FAR and its allied militias forged alliances with local Zairean military and political authorities as well as Burundian insurgents, with whom they shared recruitment, training, and arms procurement from bases within certain refugee camps.[9] This constellation of forces undertook attacks, with limited success, against Rwandan, Burundian, and Tutsi ethnic groups within eastern Zaire, particularly the Banyarwanda of the Masisi region and the Banyamulengue of South Kivu.

Growing conflict within Rwanda and eastern Zaire coincided with all-out civil war in Burundi and the collapse of the power-sharing arrangement by a Tutsi-led coup in July 1996. The rapid growth of armed factions dedicated to the advance of their ethnic and political causes, as well as the ethnic partisanship of the Tutsi-dominated Burundian army, completely overwhelmed the political process in the country. Despite a regional trade embargo imposed against the new Buyoya regime, the army continued to receive light weapons and assistance from former military sources such as China and Russia; however, it began to rely heavily on private networks that were willing to break the embargo and evade scrutiny.[10] Insurgents continued to receive arms, financing, and military support from private networks operating out of numerous countries abroad.[11]

The war in Zaire in 1996–97 was an outgrowth of the regional destabilization carried out by allied Hutu insurgent forces. Both the Rwandan and the Burundian governments became actively involved in invasive military operations to stymie the constant insurgent attacks on their territories. A significant number of soldiers—artificially identified as Banyamalengue[12] but inclusive of nebulous elements of the Alliance of Democratic Forces for the Liberation of Congo-Zaire (ADFL)—received arms, training, and military assistance from Rwanda and Burundi. These soldiers, along with the Rwandan army and elements of the Burundian military, were deployed in Zaire with the primary objective of disbanding the vast Hutu refugee camps situated in the border area. The war widened as arms and other forms of military support were provided to the ADFL from Angola, Eritrea, Uganda, and Zambia. Kabila, the leader of the ADFL, previously had been under investigation by the author as an arms smuggler with links to Burundi, Tanzania, and Zaire.[13] During the war, Kabila also received direct support for his war effort from U.S., British, and Canadian corporations that sought new investment opportunities in Zaire's rich mining regions.

To counter the ADFL, Mobutu and his cronies quickly elicited the support of Serbian, French, and Belgium mercenaries.[14] Arms were acquired from China, North Korea, and France. In an attempt to shore up his own fighting forces, Mobutu made sure that the ex-FAR and allied Hutu militias were provided with weaponry.[15] Despite Mobutu's desperate attempts at using force to retain power, the ADFL, led by Kabila, captured the capital of Kinshasa in a spray of "wild gunfire."[16] Many of Mobutu's forces fled to Congo-Brazzaville, where some of their weapons reportedly wound up in the hands of armed gangs.

In less than fifteen months after Mobutu was toppled, a Tutsi-propelled armed movement, now known as the Rassemblement Congolais pour la démocratie (RCD), dissatisfied with President Kabila's policies of exclusion and harboring political and economic ambitions of its own, began a second "war of liberation" within two years. In what amounts almost to an instant replay, the rebellion, backed with troops and military assistance from Rwanda and Uganda, launched an offensive on August 2, 1998, from the eastern region of Kivu and quickly overtook a number of key towns. Angola, Zimbabwe, Namibia, Chad, and Sudan, among others, have all come to the aid of Kabila's debilitated Congolese armed forces by sending troops and arms to counter the insurrection in the DRC. Adding further fuel to the fire, Kabila has armed a number of guerrilla groups, including the indigenous Mai-Mai, the Rwandan ex-FAR and its militias, the Burundian Hutu insurgents, and the Ugandan ADF, in an effort to help him restore the military balance in the east. The pursuit of the military option to resolve conflict in this heart of Africa, which so far includes aerial bombardments of cities and the shooting down of a commercial airplane, portends a protracted, bloody crisis consuming nearly a third of the sub-Saharan continent.

The Demand for Arms

The conflicts described above have generated an insatiable demand for weapons throughout the Great Lakes region on the part both of governments and of various substate actors. Historically, weaponry and military training have been obtained by governments in the Great Lakes region through military assistance agreements with the major powers, as in the case of the French aid to the Habyarimana regime in Rwanda. Insurgent groups, meanwhile, have often received weapons through covert channels from regional allies that supported their military campaigns as part of a common struggle against a shared enemy, as in the case of Uganda's arms transfers to the RPF for use against the Habyarimana regime and President Mobutu's military assistance to the remnants of the Rwandan army and allied militia groups following the 1994 genocide.[17] Other nonstate actors, such as militia groups and youth gangs, have bought weapons on the black market or acquired them from allies within the local armies or political structures.

The continuing flow of arms to the Great Lakes region through both licit and illicit channels has stood in sharp contrast to a global picture of declining arms transfers. While the end of the Cold War saw a decline in arms transfers within the industrialized north and much of the developing world, small arms imports by sub-Saharan Africa have been on the rise. Between 1992 and 1994, Rwanda was the region's third-largest importer of weapons (behind Angola and Nigeria), with cumulative military imports totaling $100 million.[18] It must be recognized, moreover, that the standard arms-trade statistics do not begin to capture the illicit arms trade or weapons flows that are diverted from legitimate recipients to illicit end users.[19] As disclosed by primary field research in the Great Lakes region over the past several years, both illicit and diverted arms transfers are prolific and are fast becoming the mainstay of most of the warring parties.[20]

The Increasing Reliance on Light Weapons

The surge in intrastate tensions throughout the 1990s has led to a persistent and rising demand for weapons in central Africa. At the same time, governments in the region have received fewer heavy weapons and lucrative military assistance packages from their traditional patrons in the north. As a result, small arms and light munitions are the weapons of choice for government armies, ethnic militias, rebel groups, and civilian defense forces. Such weapons are less expensive to procure and maintain, giving them a distinct advantage in this profoundly poverty-stricken region.

Light weapons also can be more readily concealed than heavy weapons from the scrutiny of international observers, whether they are disguised as nonlethal cargo or as humanitarian supplies. These transfers are often discovered only after a trafficker is detained for refusing to pay bribes to local police and customs officers or when a plane crash reveals the hidden nature of its cargo. The ability to conceal weapons flows is significant, given the regional and international embargoes that have been imposed on belligerents in the region, the pariah status of various governments and rebel groups, and the campaigns being mounted by human rights and humanitarian organizations to curb the flow of arms into the region.[21]

Tragically, it is small arms and light weapons that account for most of the casualties and displaced populations that have resulted from the conflicts in the Great Lakes region. These weapons are more readily obtainable than heavy weapons and easier to use against civilians in communal conflict situations, where populations are characteristically targeted for being of the wrong ethnicity, political party, or military faction. As the governments of the Great Lakes states weaken and favor one group within society over others, armed groups acting as self-defense forces for their various communities are appearing everywhere. Under these circumstances, armed factions or even neighbors within a communal conflict area can more readily initiate slaughter against those accused of harboring or providing support to a suspected "enemy." This, in turn, has generated the widespread need felt by individual citizens to arm themselves as a prerequisite for survival.[22]

Impediments to Demand-Side Controls

As elsewhere in the world, arms acquisitions have been justified by governments in the Great Lakes region as integral to their ability to defend vital interests and to address domestic concerns.[23] However, what is of particular concern in this region is the emergence of *regional* alliances of warring parties, linking governments, rebel groups, and ethnic or political militias that share a common political agenda. Witness the initial backing of Kabila's ADFL of Congo-Zaire by the governments of Rwanda, Burundi, Uganda, Angola, Zambia, and Eritrea. Increasingly, though alignments may change, these regional allies are banning together to procure arms, train, fight, and provide both economic and political support for one another.[24]

Moreover, a sophisticated understanding of the politics of the Great Lakes region is required for successful arms control attempts at the recipient end. For example, disarmament campaigns launched by the Tutsi-dominated governments of both Rwanda and Burundi have been used as a guise to intimidate, harass, and facilitate counterinsurgency operations against opposing ethnic groups, resulting in numerous civilian deaths.[25] Arms control efforts also require complex interactions between donor and international organizations as well as the warring parties and other local elements in a region where there is considerable distrust on all sides. Consider, for example, how difficult it has been for the UN High Commissioner for Refugees (UNHCR) to obtain access and consent for humanitarian operations in the region.[26]

It may be true that, without consent, even well-managed local arms control efforts would be rendered deficient and incomplete. Enforced consent may not yield adequate results either. Even when there is seeming political will for regional cooperation, effective implementation may be lacking. (A notable example was the porousness of the regional trade embargo against the Burundian government.[27]) While an international arms embargo against the entire region would hold the most promise for curbing arms proliferation, such a measure is opposed by France and the United States—both of which continue to vie for strategic advantage in the region. Given the region's high degree of conflict and lack of respect for the rule of law, it would appear timely and useful to institute better controls on the supply side of the arms equation.

The Supply Side

Throughout this period, foreign governments supplied a wide variety of arms to selected governments and substate forces in the Great Lakes area or allowed their territory to be used for the transshipment of arms to belligerents in other countries or to rebel groups operating from bases within their own territory. Initially, much of the military equipment flowing into the Great Lakes area was supplied by foreign governments as part of official military cooperation agreements with states in the region. Since 1994, however, direct supply activities of this sort have become less common, as suppliers and recipients alike have come to rely more on private arms networks, often operating illegally.

In many cases, the switch from overt government aid to covert arms transfers was driven by a desire on the part of both suppliers and recipients to disguise their mutual ties. During the Rwandan civil war of 1990–94, for example, both sides wanted to conceal their various military backers, particularly as international calls for peace negotiations grew louder. Later, when a UN arms embargo was imposed on Rwanda following the outbreak of the genocide, suppliers to both sides sought to conceal their role for fear of being censured. Similarly, Kabila's ADFL wanted to conceal its foreign military support in order to maintain its image as an indigenous movement; by the same token, foreign backers of the ostracized Mobutu regime required a means of circumventing both European Union (EU) and U.S. prohibitions.

In turning to covert operations of this sort, foreign governments have found creative channels for aiding their regional allies. For example, France used private contractors to provide light weapons to ex-FAR units based in refugee camps in eastern Zaire and provided financial assistance to the Mobutu regime in 1996 for third-party arms transfers.[28] China has hidden behind nominally autonomous companies that disguised light weapons transfers under the cover of humanitarian deliveries.[29] At the height of the war in Zaire, the U.S. government transferred large stocks of military equipment to Uganda, Ethiopia, and Eritrea—at least some of which wound up in the hands of the ADFL combatants.[30]

Foreign governments have also aided their regional allies in a passive manner by failing to prevent their nationals from engaging in private arms trafficking or mercenary activities or by failing to interdict arms transfers that are transshipped through their ports and airfields or ferried by train or truck across their territory. These governments may also take steps to shield private arms networks from exposure or prosecution when this might interfere with other covert operations in the Great Lakes region or elsewhere in Africa. For example, diplomats in the region have cited U.S. pressure to refrain from exposing the arms networks catering to both Rwandan and Burundian Hutu rebels in Kenya, as these same networks also serve U.S.-supported Sudanese rebels, such as the Sudanese People's Liberation Army. Moreover, governments are generally reluctant to provide information to foreign or international investigating bodies on the criminal activities of their nationals, often citing domestic laws.[31]

Motives: Politics and Profit

Arms traffickers have themselves acknowledged that their networks often serve several agendas simultaneously. In some cases, foreign governments may employ such networks in the furtherance of their regional political objectives. This has been true, for example, in the case of French operations in Rwanda and U.S. operations in Uganda and southern Sudan. In other cases, the networks serve the interests of a regional political alliance, such as linking Yoweri Museveni's Uganda with Paul Kagame's Rwanda. Finally, and most commonly, private networks operate for profit, as in the case of the Belgian traffickers who have been supplying weapons to the Hutu rebel forces based in Tanzania as well as the current Burundian government military.[32]

The covert networks that supply the weapons to the various armed parties in the Great Lakes region overlap with wider networks that cater to the demand for weapons throughout Africa (as well as other continents) and whose clients can often be found on both sides of a conflict. The South African company GMR Group, for example, offered weapons to the Burundian military before selling the same stocks to Burundian rebels based in Tanzania. Networks operating out of Belgium have transferred weapons from the Soviet Union and eastern Europe to the Burundian government, the Zairean military (before the establishment of the DRC), and Hutu rebel forces based in eastern Zaire (at least until the end of 1996). These networks also supply other clients in southern Africa, such as the rebels of the National Union for the Total Independence of Angola (UNITA) in Angola.[33]

In the Great Lakes region, it is still difficult to discern the line between illegal (black) arms transfers and government-sponsored (gray) covert activities. Many of the existing arms pipelines are holdovers from the Cold War or the former South African government's regional destabilization effort. While many of these former government-backed covert operations were officially shut down in the early 1990s, the aircraft, airstrips, and cargo companies that were used in them were privatized and turned over to their former operators—many of whom, in interviews with the author, confessed that they did not want to relinquish their former "lifestyle." Arms profiteering offers them adventure, profit, local color, and macho experiences that they are unwilling to give up.[34]

Evasive Tactics: A Shield against Public Scrutiny

At present, private arms networks are supplying much of the light weaponry that is fanning the flames of conflict in the Great Lakes region. These networks include procurers, suppliers, brokers, financiers, shippers, those who expedite transshipment via their territories, and those who acquire the weapons. In their trafficking of arms from production to delivery, these arms networks regularly violate international laws and embargoes, regional sanctions, domestic statutes, and government regulations pertaining to export licensing, import/export activities and customs procedures in countries of origin, transshipment, and final destination.

Well aware that their arms transfers to substate actors and/or pariah governments are in violation of international and local laws, both private and government-sponsored networks have devised intricate covert operations to shroud their activities in a veil of secrecy. "Tried and true" techniques of arms traffickers include the use of fictitious bills of lading, false flight plans, and the transshipment of goods through intermediary countries. Falsified cargo manifests and end-user certificates often list intermediate receivers who are not in fact the final recipients.

Sometimes traffickers camouflage weapons as humanitarian relief supplies in an effort to disguise the sensitive nature of a particular cargo or take advantage of customs loopholes in the supplier and transit countries to conceal the actual destination of an arms delivery. Not atypical of this pattern was a shipment from China to Burundian government forces that listed the cargo as "farm implements."[35] The cargo manifests for several Chinese weapons shipments to the Burundian government (shipped via Tanzania) listed Rwanda and Uganda, not Burundi, as the final destination.[36]

Pilots engaged in illicit arms shipments to the Great Lakes region often file false flight plans, listing final destinations like Swaziland, Gabon, and Nigeria, in order to disguise the true nature or destination of their cargoes. Frequently, moreover, these pilots take indirect routes to their destinations. For example, European traffickers involved in arms shipments to Burundi have flown weapons to Zaire and then on to South Africa before shipping them to clients in the Great Lakes region.[37] Arms traffickers are also known to use "front" companies or organizations, sometimes disguised as relief agencies. One trafficker, previously cited for supplying arms to Renamo rebels in Mozambique, has been operating under the cover of a Christian aid organization in Burundi.[38] To further disguise their operations, traffickers often change their base of operations, the name of their company, their business registrations or license, and the roster of individuals working with them. This was the case, for example, with a number of traffickers who shifted their operations from Zaire to the Belgian port of Ostend in 1996.[39]

Another serious impediment to suppression of the black-market arms traffic is the fact that some of the cargo companies based in Europe, South Africa, and China that have been involved in the shipment of military equipment to governments or substate actors in the Great Lakes area have also been contracted to carry humanitarian relief supplies for some of the international aid agencies.[40] In some cases, arms shipments have been concealed in consignments of humanitarian supplies or identified as such goods in cargo manifests. This has endangered urgent relief programs and provided arms traffickers with a false flag behind which to conceal their deadly cargoes.[41]

The major relief programs of UN agencies, whose air and land transport needs are enormous, are particularly susceptible to manipulation by cargo carriers with double agendas. World Food Program officials, interviewed by the author, have indicated that they are aware that the program's logistical and transport infrastructure has been used as a cover for military assistance and arms transfers from foreign governments and private sources to belligerents in the Great Lakes region and elsewhere, such as Somalia and Sudan.[42]

Efforts to Control Arms Trafficking in the Great Lakes Region

A number of steps have been taken by the international community over the past few years to stem the flow of arms into the Great Lakes region. In May 1994, the UN Security Council imposed an arms embargo on Rwanda. On September 1, 1996, the arms embargo was lifted with respect to the government of Rwanda; however, it remains in effect against the ex-FAR and its allied militias. An international arms embargo against the Burundian government and insurgent forces has been considered by the UN Security Council but not prescribed.[43] The European Union imposed an arms embargo on Zaire in mid-1993, and it remains in place against the DRC. In addition, several supplier states have unilaterally banned arms transfers to various countries in the region for political reasons or because they have policies that prohibit the supply of weapons to nations in conflict. Lastly, a comprehensive trade embargo, covering arms, was imposed on Burundi by neighboring states following the military coup in 1996. (This embargo was lifted in early 1999.)

Advocates in the arms control, human rights, and humanitarian aid community have argued for the strengthening of these measures as well as the establishment of additional controls.[44] At least some of the recommendations made by the community of nongovernmental organizations (NGOs) have been incorporated into UN Security Council Resolutions.[45] One example is UN Security Council Resolution 997 of June 9, 1995, which calls on countries in the Great Lakes region to allow international military observers to monitor the flow of small arms and light weapons into conflict areas. In July 1995, Special Envoy Aldo Ajello was sent to the region by UN Secretary-General Boutros Boutros-Ghali to assess the possibility of deploying observers. Ajello returned lacking the consent of the regional governments, most notably Tanzania, which were unwilling to compromise their sovereignty.[46] Instead, the Security Council decided in September 1995 to establish an International Commission of Inquiry (Rwanda)—commonly known as UNICOI—to investigate the allegations made by human rights groups and other humanitarian agencies. Before its suspension within a year, the Commission had issued three reports (January, March, and October 1996) to the UN secretary-general, though the release of the third report to the public was suppressed until 1998, ostensibly for fear of inciting further unrest in the region. These reports illustrate that international embargoes without effective implementation mechanisms are largely ineffective. UNICOI's valuable and detailed recommendations, which were designed to improve enforcement of the embargo, went unheeded.

The International Commission of Inquiry

From its inception, UNICOI's mandate constrained it from carrying out a successful probe. Before conducting an investigation within a country, UNICOI had to first obtain consent from the government and even then was not granted unimpeded access. This left the UNICOI mission confined to spending most of its time soliciting cooperation from evasive governments and writing letters to acquire what limited evidence states might share. For the most part, governments were intent on protecting their nationals and suppressing information that might be incriminating. In one example, UNICOI repeatedly asked the United States to provide information on a U.S. national living in Kinshasa who was reported to be trafficking arms to Hutu rebels in violation of the international arms embargo, but was refused relevant data.[47] UNICOI had no judicial powers to subpoena witnesses, indict, or even call for the criminal prosecution of suspects against whom it had amassed evidence.

While UNICOI did not contribute much new data in reports to the secretary-general, it did serve to highlight and publicize information on select arms networks and transactions. In certain instances, local media reported on inadequate responses by a number of different countries to UNICOI's requests for cooperation that in turn led to queries in parliaments and further public pressure on national governments to launch their own internal investigations.[48] Although UNICOI may have been meant as a deterrent—by making arms networks aware that there was at least a minimal degree of surveillance—in reality arms trafficking continued at a brutal pace. The most salient aspects of UNICOI's reports are in its recommendations, summarized below.

- The creation of an office that would monitor, implement, and enforce the Rwandan arms embargo, collect evidence of violations, and make regular reports to the Security Council.

- The creation of voluntary regional registers or data banks on movements and acquisitions of small arms, ammunition, and related matériel.
- The establishment, on an ad hoc basis, of commissions of inquiry to investigate reported violations of arms embargoes in the region.
- A request that states producing arms and military matériel take any measures necessary under domestic law to implement the provisions of international arms embargoes and in particular to prosecute any of their nationals who are found to be in violation of such measures, even if they conduct their illegal activities in third countries.[49]

Unfortunately, very little has been done until now to implement these recommendations and others made by NGOs for tightened controls on the flow of arms into the Great Lakes region. The key problem is that no enforcement mechanisms have been established to ensure their effective implementation. Instead, the United Nations has relied on international condemnation and shame to persuade member states to limit their own arms transfers and/or to act against arms brokers operating from within their territory.

Recent Developments

In response to continuing pressure from NGOs to address the problems described above, the UN Security Council adopted a resolution on April 9, 1998, calling for the reactivation of UNICOI.[50] The following week, UN Secretary-General Kofi Annan issued a report on Africa calling for "more effective measures to punish the continent's arms traffickers." Also hopeful is the recent decision by West African states to establish a moratorium on the import, export, and manufacture of light weapons in West Africa (as analyzed in chapter 7 by Joseph Smaldone).

Thus far, the reactivated UNICOI has suffered from lack of funding and continues to be hampered in its work by uncooperative governments. Its first interim report, in August 1998, concluded that there was evidence that the former Rwandan government forces continued to receive weapons, but it provided precious little data on the actual suppliers.[51] While it is too early to tell if sufficient political will can be mustered to provide adequate support for the aforementioned initiatives, clearly they provide mechanisms for future progress.

Recommendations for Further Action

What further steps can be taken to stem the flow of weapons, whether through legal or illegal channels, into the Great Lakes region? Already, certain mechanisms exist or have been proposed that, if simultaneously initiated and robustly enforced, could dissuade the private actors and rogue states from profiting off the afflictions of the region's civilian population. These measures should target the recipients of arms, the states that provide them or facilitate their transshipment, and the international black market in arms.

International and Regional Initiatives

Given the magnitude of the human misery and loss of life in the Great Lakes region, an international arms embargo on the region as a whole would offer the greatest promise. Because, as shown above, the problem is regional in scope, an arms embargo cannot be effectively enforced unless it has a regional dimension. A proposal for an international arms embargo of this sort has been advanced by EU member states; however, the United States and some EU members oppose a regional embargo. While the United States would support an embargo on Burundi, it opposes an embargo on the entire region because of its military support for the current regimes in Rwanda and Uganda; France, on the other hand, has renewed its military cooperation with Burundi and opposes an arms embargo against that country alone. Nevertheless, the Security Council should hold a serious debate regarding the merits of an international arms embargo on the Great Lakes region. And, if an embargo is established, it should be enforced uniformly throughout the region and closely monitored by the international community.

On a number of occasions, the Security Council has considered the deployment of UN or Organization of African Unity (OAU) military observers at key border crossings and airstrips in the Great Lakes area to monitor violations of current embargoes and to deter illicit flows. It would be most effective if such observers were deployed in Burundi, Rwanda, Uganda, Tanzania, Angola, and the DRC. The observers should also be mandated to monitor the activities of armed organizations that operate from the territories of the states in the region. These observers should have the technical capacity for monitoring arms flows and military operations and should not be considered a peacekeeping or an intervention force.

Furthermore, a regional conference on arms trafficking, security, and human rights in the Great Lakes region should be convened under the aegis of the United Nations and the OAU. This measure already has support from the EU parliament, the OAU, and some UN members. At the same time, resources should be provided for a disarmament commission to study ways to undertake the demobilization of subnational military forces and their integration into the national armed forces of the Great Lakes states, along with weapons buy-back and destruction programs.

To prevent the further abuse of aid programs by arms traffickers, UN agencies and related NGOs should put in place and strictly enforce safeguards to prevent traffickers from using UN/NGO transport capabilities for the shipment of arms. They should also abjure the use of cargo operators that also carry military equipment. The same agencies should make lists of contract violators and make them available to other relief organizations to prevent further misuse of the humanitarian "vector" by war profiteers.

National Initiatives

At the national level, individual governments should take unilateral action to prevent their territories from being used as a conduit for arms shipments. They should also stop their nationals from selling weapons or serving as mercenaries on any side of a conflict, regardless of whether the nationals are operating at home or abroad. In doing so, national governments have a number of instruments at their disposal, including, for example, import and export regulations, end-user certification, end-use monitoring, laws and policies on brokering, customs statutes, and other tools of arms control. These tools need to be strengthened and made uniform by both supplier and transshipment countries.

The Need for Further Disclosure

If the violence in the Great Lakes area is to be abated, however, arms flows into the region must be exposed to international scrutiny. As a first step, foreign governments should make public all information on arms transfers to the Great Lakes region since 1993, including types and quantities of weapons, ammunition, military matériel (including dual-use items), and military services. Although activities by both the French government and the Clinton administration in the Great Lakes area have been the subject of inquiries by parliamentary bodies,[52] further scrutiny is warranted. At the same time, the states of the Great Lakes region should establish a regional arms transfer register to which they would submit information on their imports and exports of weapons, ammunition, and military matériel on an annual basis.

Conclusion

While the international community talks endlessly of how to stem ethnic warfare or avert another genocide in the Great Lakes region, there remains a noticeable silence about the way in which weapon transfers influence the likelihood of such outcomes. Even graver still, certain members of the international community continue to supply arms or other forms of military assistance, often covertly, to various parties at war. Others have allowed insurgents to base and arm themselves within their countries.[53] More commonly, private merchants take advantage of friendly government sponsorship, loose restrictions on arms transfers, pliable transshipment countries, poor controls at border points, and/or corrupt officials to operate with impunity in the region.[54]

Weapons will continue to pour into central Africa until curbing arms proliferation is put at the top of the political agenda. Currently, the international community is only at the initial stages of instituting arms control mechanisms in the region. Further coordinated and strategic action is imperative to curtail the weapons flows. While efforts at arms control are complex and the challenges are obviously enormous, no other place in the world is in as dire need of such efforts as the highly militarized and volatile Great Lakes region.

Notes

1. All references to Zaire concern the Zaire under the former President Mobutu Sese Seko and to the period prior to the collapse of his rule in May 1997, after which the country reverted to the name of the Democratic Republic of Congo under its current leader, Laurent Kabila.

2. United Nations Press Release, "Statement by Mary Robinson, United Nations High Commissioner for Human Rights," April 17, 1998; Agence France Presse, "Kabila Regime Worse than Mobutu in Former Zaire: UN," April 15, 1998.

3. See, for example, United Nations Integrated Regional Information Network for Central and Eastern Africa, Democratic Republic of Congo; IRIN Chronology, September 30, 1998; and International Crisis Group.

4. Human Rights Watch Arms Project, *Arming Rwanda: Arms Trade and Human Rights Abuses in the Rwandan War* (New York: Human Rights Watch, January 1994).

5. Human Rights Watch Arms Project, *Arming Rwanda.*

6. Human Rights Watch Arms Project, *Stoking the Fires: Military Assistance and Arms Trafficking in Burundi* (New York: Human Rights Watch, December 1997).

7. Human Rights Watch Arms Project, *Stoking the Fires.*

8. Human Rights Watch Arms Project, *Rearming with Impunity: International Support for the Perpetrators of the Rwandan Genocide* (New York: Human Rights Watch, May 1995).

9. Human Rights Watch Arms Project, *Rearming with Impunity.* For an update, see Kathi Austin, *The Burundi Refugee Situation in Western Tanzania* (Brussels and Washington, D.C.: International Crisis Group, forthcoming).

10. Human Rights Watch Arms Project, *Stoking the Fires.*

11. Human Rights Watch Arms Project, *Stoking the Fires.*

12. Ethnic Tutsi of Rwandan ancestry who migrated to eastern Zaire centuries ago but who were seen as outsiders by Zairean government officials. They were told by authorities to leave South Kivu, Zaire, in October 1996.

13. Author's interview on National Public Radio, *All Things Considered,* April 6, 1997.

14. See, for example, *Washington Times,* "Serbs Blamed in Zaire Atrocities" (Reuters), March, 19, 1997; Olivier Rogeau, "Belgian-American Link to Alien Spy Case; Dreams of Africa and Cash: Networks of Influence," *Le Vif/L'Express,* December 5–11, 1997.

15. See Human Rights Watch Arms Project, *Stoking the Fires;* and "China Sells Jet Fighters, Arms to Mobutu," *Boston Globe,* April 11, 1997.

16. "Rebel Army Consolidates Its Hold over Kinshasa," *New York Times,* May 19, 1997.

17. Human Rights Watch Arms Project, *Rearming with Impunity.*

18. U.S. Arms Control and Disarmament Agency (ACDA), *World Military Expenditures and Arms Transfers, 1995* (Washington, D.C.: ACDA, 1996).

19. See, for example, Saferworld, *Undermining Development: The European Arms Trade with the Horn of Africa and Central Africa* (London: Saferworld, 1998).

20. The primary field research referred to throughout this chapter is that of the author and was conducted during several missions from August 1994 to September 1998 on behalf of the Africa Project at the Institute for Policy Studies, the Human Rights Watch Arms Project, Physicians for Human Rights, and the International Crisis Group.

21. See Reuters, "US Groups Urge Arms Embargo on Burundi," March 20, 1998.

22. This was a constant theme during interviews the author conducted with numerous people during primary field missions in the region.

23. South Africa's Vice President Thabo Mbeki justified South Africa's recent, extensive arms deal with Rwanda. "Rwanda [had] the right to protect itself against such an invasion. Otherwise, we [would] end up with another gigantic blood bath." *De Morgen,* February 11, 1996.

24. As reported by a correspondent for the *New York Times* covering central Africa, there is a "new willingness of African armies to engage in conflicts beyond their borders, which threatens to make armed insurrection, with the help of neighbors, the preferred means of political change on this continent." See "Rebels Backed by Angola, Take Brazzaville and Oilport," *New York Times,* October 16, 1997.

25. The author witnessed such incidents and their aftermath while conducting primary field research in the region. See Human Rights Watch Arms Project, *Stoking the Fires,* pp. 19–20.

26. See "Exodus in Zaire: UN Faces a New Refugee Crisis," *New York Times,* March 3, 1997; "Zaire Rebels Blocking Aid, UN Says," *New York Times,* April 23, 1997; and Physicians for Human Rights, "Investigations in Eastern Congo and Western Rwanda," a report by Physicians for Human Rights, July 1997.

27. Agence France Presse, "Regional Embargo against Burundi Ineffective: EU Envoy," April 10, 1998.

28. Human Rights Watch Arms Project, *Rearming with Impunity* and *Stoking the Fires.*

29. Human Rights Watch Arms Project, *Stoking the Fires.*

30. Author's confidential interviews with U.S. government officials in 1997 and 1998.

31. Human Rights Watch Arms Project, *Stoking the Fires,* pp. 32–33.

32. Human Rights Watch Arms Project, *Stoking the Fires,* p. 33.

33. Human Rights Watch Arms Project, *Stoking the Fires,* p. 32.

34. Author's interviews with traffickers during field research missions to Africa and Europe.

35. *Kenya Daily Nation* (Nairobi), April 26, 1995.

36. Human Rights Watch Arms Project, *Stoking the Fires.*

37. Human Rights Watch Arms Project, *Stoking the Fires,* p. 35.

38. Human Rights Watch Arms Project, *Stoking the Fires,* p. 84.

39. Human Rights Watch Arms Project, *Stoking the Fires,* p. 35.

40. Human Rights Watch Arms Project, *Stoking the Fires,* pp. 101–5.

41. Arms trafficking to the Great Lakes region has, on occasion, received international publicity when governments attempted to interdict weapons shipments that were cloaked as, or combined with, cargoes of humanitarian aid. For example, a Belgium-based company operating under several names but registered in Liberia has attracted such attention. One of the company's aircraft, registered as ELAJO, made frequent flights in 1994 and 1995 to deliver weapons to the former Rwandan military and militias in Zaire in violation of the international arms embargo. In August 1996, this same aircraft was impounded by local authorities in Goma, Zaire, after it was found to be carrying undeclared military uniforms to be off-loaded in Uganda; at the time, the plane was manifested only as carrying relief goods to refugee camps in the area on behalf of the UNHCR, Oxfam, and CARE. See Human Rights Watch Arms Project, *Stoking the Fires,* pp. 101–2.

42. Human Rights Watch Arms Project, *Stoking the Fires,* pp. 101–5.

43. See, for example, United Nations Security Resolution 1040, January 29, 1996; United Nations Security Resolution 1072, August 30, 1996.

44. In January 1994, three months before the genocide, Human Rights Watch published *Arming Rwanda,* which went largely unheeded. *Rearming with Impunity,* published in May 1995 by Human Rights Watch, and *Rwanda: Arming the Perpetrators of the Genocide,* published by Amnesty International in June 1995, highlighted the role of international actors in providing military assistance to the perpetrators of the genocide in Rwanda in 1994 and, later, in exile in eastern Zaire and received widespread international attention because the recipients of the weapons had achieved international opprobrium and the suppliers were in breach of an international arms embargo. In December 1997, Human Rights Watch published *Stoking the Fires: Military Assistance and Arms Trafficking in Burundi.*

45. The original text of the UN Resolutions can be found on the UN Web site under "Resources." See, for example, United Nations Security Council Resolution 918, May 17, 1994; United Nations Security Council Resolution 997, June 9, 1995; United Nations Security Council Resolution 1011, August 16, 1995; United Nations Security Council Resolution 1013, September 7, 1995; United Nations Security Council Resolution 1053, April 23, 1996.

46. Author's discussions with Special Envoy Ajello, October 1996, Bujumbura, and July 1998, Arusha.

47. Human Rights Watch Arms Project, *Stoking the Fires,* p. 33.

48. Joost Hiltermann, "Post-Mortem on the International Commission of Inquiry (Rwanda)," *Bulletin of Association of Concerned African Scholars,* Fall 1997.

49. Recommendations paraphrased by Joost Hiltermann in "Post-Mortem on the International Commission of Inquiry (Rwanda)."

50. United Nations Security Council Resolution 306, April 9, 1998.

51. Interim Report of the International Commission of Inquiry (Rwanda), S/1998/777, August 19, 1998.

52. Agence France Presse, "Inquiry into French Role in Rwanda to Hear Top Military Brass," April 9, 1998, and "French Ex-Minister, Heading Rwanda Probe, Asks for Secret Pacts," April 8, 1998. Several hearings have been held regarding U.S. training to Rwanda and knowledge of the security situation in eastern Zaire; see, for example, U.S. House of Representatives Subcommittee on International Operations and

Human Rights of the Committee on International Relations, December 4, 1996, and Committee on International Relations, July 16, 1997 and November 5, 1997.

53. See Human Rights Watch Arms Project, *Stoking the Fires, Rearming with Impunity*, and *Arming the Perpetrators.*

54. See Human Rights Watch Arms Project, *Stoking the Fires, Rearming with Impunity*, and *Arming the Perpetrators.*

3

Controlling the Black and Gray Markets in Small Arms in South Asia

Tara Kartha

THERE IS LITTLE DOUBT regarding the urgent need to institute practical laws and regulations to deal with the rising incidence of light weapons proliferation in South Asia. Within the region, over 260,000 troops are engaged in fighting insurgent groups armed with weapons that fall into this category,[1] while, within Pakistan, government forces face a dangerous mix of internal arms proliferation and ethnic/sectarian violence that has been described as the "Kalashnikov culture."[2] Terrorism has taken a heavy toll, with a prime minister assassinated in India and numerous political leaders murdered in Sri Lanka. Political instability has followed in the wake of these killings in both countries, while Bangladesh, Bhutan, and Nepal have suffered spillover effects, becoming transit areas for insurgents and arms smugglers and experiencing a rise in armed violence within their own societies.

To a great extent, this regional inundation of light weapons is a result of the heedless and lavish arming of Afghanistan. Nearly 60 percent[3] of an estimated $6 to $8 billion worth of weapons provided to the Afghan *mujahideen* in the 1980s by the United States and China have diffused into Pakistan and, subsequently, into surrounding regions.[4] This supply of weapons to the Afghan factions continues today, with new or recycled actors playing the same bloody game—this time with the difference that

Afghanistan has the distinction of being one of the world's leading producers of opium. The region is no stranger, moreover, to state patronage of armed insurgency. India, Pakistan, and Bangladesh have all armed and trained one another's rebel movements in the past, while the government of Sri Lanka armed its own rebels against the Indian peacekeeping force after mid-1989.[5]

A Rising Curve of Proliferation

In charting the proliferation of small arms and light weapons in South Asia, several factors require mention.

- First, the geographical spread of munitions means that weapons originating in the west (notably Afghanistan) are traveling increasingly eastward. The trafficking in and use of AK-47s and other automatic weapons—largely restricted before 1990 to the Indian states of Punjab and Kashmir—is now evident in five other Indian states, with poachers, smugglers, insurgent groups, and even forest brigands engaging the security forces with these highly lethal weapons.[6]
- Second, there is a marked rise in weapons technology, with 1994 witnessing the first use of rocket-propelled grenades in the northeast of India (where a smoldering insurgency has tied down security forces for many years)[7] and 1995 the first use of shoulder-fired missiles in Sri Lanka.[8] In Pakistan, ethnic violence reached a crescendo at the end of 1995 with the use of rocket-propelled grenades, assault rifles, explosives, and grenades, leaving over 600 dead during a two-month period in one city alone.[9]
- Third, new transit routes and smuggling operations have emerged in the north and east, notably in Nepal and Bangladesh.
- Fourth, areas adjacent to conflict zones are being affected in diverse ways, with some countries (e.g., Bhutan) finding their own malcontents encouraged by neighboring insurgents and others (Nepal and Bangladesh) having their banking systems compromised by the movement of tainted money. A flourishing criminal underworld has developed that links smugglers of guns and endangered species to prostitution rings, drug traffickers, and other such elements.
- Fifth, and most dangerous, is a trend toward cooperation between insurgent groups that facilitates the movement of weapons and points to the possibility of "contract killings" in return for money, weapons, and training. Hence, there is a growing overlap between the gray market (covert arms trafficking by states and state-sponsored entities) and the black market (illegal sales).

Distinguishing between the Gray and the Black

As suggested by this brief introduction, South Asia is suffering from both the gray- and the black-market trade in small arms and light weapons. The *gray market* is taken to mean that element of the arms trade that involves the machinery of the state in some form, notably where the government (or its agents) has either assisted in or turned a blind eye to illicit arms transfers originating from within its own territory or being organized by its nationals operating in other countries. Although gray-market transfers are rarely motivated by profit, quite often the state actors involved in illicit arms trafficking are also involved in drug running, commodities smuggling, financial fraud, high-tech espionage, and other such activities. In this regard, it is worth recalling that the Bank of Credit and Commerce International (BCCI) of Pakistan—the main instrument for laundering drug money during the Zia period—indulged in everything from high-class prostitution to accessing sensitive military-related data.[10]

A second common denominator for many gray-market transfers is the critical role played by certain states in arming extremist Islamic organizations in Asia. Countries such as Iran, Libya, and Sudan have been implicated in transferring weapons to insurgent and terrorist groups in many countries. The Pakistan-based Harkat ul-Ansar, for instance, is cited by U.S. sources as operating in Myanmar, while Islamic extremists in the Philippines are believed to have been supplied by Libya.[11]

By comparison, *black-market* deals are conducted by private organizations and individuals who are motivated primarily by a desire for profit. All along the chain of diffusion, those involved—whether suppliers, brokers, smugglers, or even end users (when they are criminalized insurgents)—are out to make money. At the high end of the spectrum are quasi-legitimate deals in which the state is the primary supplier but plays only a minimal role in the delivery process. Payment may be made in oil, precious gems, or a barter arrangement; false end user certificates, corrupt regulatory officials, and a host of private shipping firms and airlines facilitate movement. At the lower end of the spectrum is the individual arms dealer, who may move large shipments of arms or may be involved only in trafficking the odd dozen firearms that are sold for cash, heroin, or other contraband items.

While the recipients of arms in gray-market transactions normally are dictated by the supplier state, such transfers often employ the same basic networks to move weapons and money as do black-market transactions. The black market may also exhibit "secondary diffusion"—that is, trafficking in weapons that were once part of a gray-market transaction somewhere else.

Light Arms Trafficking in South Asia

Both the gray and the black markets are fed largely by the ongoing war in Afghanistan, which continues to draw in more weapons and fighters from its neighbors. An added complication is the huge narcotics production within Afghanistan, which leads to the so-called weapons-and-drugs nexus. On one level, this is a fairly simple system in which drug production—being an illicit activity—naturally generates a need for armed fighters and weapons for protection. At another level, the nexus is more complex. It is widely believed that profits from the drug trade provide the Pakistani intelligence agencies (notably the Inter-Services Intelligence unit, or ISI) with vast sums of money with which to finance the war in Afghanistan[12] and to continue operations in Kashmir and elsewhere.[13] As a result, the ISI has greatly increased the role it plays among a wide variety of groups, from Afghan refugees in the northwest frontier region to Islamist political parties in Pakistan proper and the *mujahideen* themselves—who, over the years, have sold, bartered, and stashed away large quantities of weapons and narcotics.

Over time, the border between Afghanistan and Pakistan has become at best a notional one, with the expansion of these arms-and-drugs networks into Pakistan and the use of that country's transport, banking, and political systems to exploit the poppy fields that flourish in both countries. According to one Pakistani analyst, "Pakistan is silently and visibly being kidnapped by narco-barons. They can influence and buy anyone at any level in any department. The judiciary, the civil administration, and the police cooperate and coordinate with narco-barons."[14] The resulting process of corruption has been evident since 1992 at the very highest levels,[15] with even the former prime minister's immediate family involved.[16] The vast sums generated by narcotic trafficking are often channeled to insurgent groups in Kashmir and Punjab and to Sindh ethnic groups in Karachi.[17]

From Pakistan, small arms and light weapons have moved eastward, to Kashmir and northeast India. Kashmir has experienced a particularly marked upsurge in violence since 1988 as the smuggling of arms and the insertion of trained fighters from Afghanistan have increased. The annual death toll rose from 390 in 1988 to 2,567 in 1993, while the number of AK-47s seized climbed from 1,474 to 2,424 over the same time period.[18]

The Gray Market

At present, the Pakistan-Afghanistan region remains the largest source of weapons for most of the insurgent/criminal groups in South Asia. Most if not all of Afghanistan's neighbors are heavily involved in supplying arms, ammunition, and technical assistance to particular Afghani factions. The major actors involved in this arms flow are Iran, Pakistan, and the former Soviet republics, with other actors like Saudi Arabia involved in the supply of funds. The northern Afghan warlords find easy access to arms supplies in Uzbekistan and Tajikistan, with spare parts for aircraft coming from Tashkent. The warring Afghan groups are also supported by a number of new air-supply operators (usually with Russian or eastern European crews) that appear to be operating from Sharjah and other Middle Eastern states.[19]

The Talibans' supply and communication lines run directly into Pakistan, thus keeping alive a web of smuggling networks that sustains the clandestine trade in weaponry. Among the poor and illiterate Pashtuns who make up the bulk of the Taliban's "work forces" are many ex-convicts with links to these smuggling networks.[20] One of the Taliban coterie is Mullah Rocketi—so named because of his reported arsenal of shoulder-fired weapons—who was once an arms dealer of note.[21] Though portrayed as a moralizing, "clean-up force" for Afghan society, the Taliban have increasingly been implicated in both weapons smuggling and narcotics production along the Central Asian border. (International monitoring agencies report that, by the end of 1996, 90 percent of opium production in Afghanistan was on lands controlled by the Taliban.[22]) Meanwhile, Pakistani intelligence agencies are reported to have salted away a considerable supply of light weapons, with as many as three million AK-47s still packed and greased in their original boxes.[23]

The gray market is most evident in the Valley of Kashmir in India, where the only regular ingress routes for weapons run through mountain passes from Pakistan and Pakistan-Occupied Kashmir (POK). No weapons are known to be flowing into Kashmir from India, and none have been seized along the Chinese border (which is hardly surprising, given the hostile environment). The presence of well-armed mercenaries—mostly Pakistanis but also including Egyptians, Sudanese, or Libyans now operating openly in the valley—is indicative of outside interest and funding. Clearly, an Afghan-type scenario is intended here: a proliferation of armed groups, the elimination of the "nationalist" cadres, and the employment of drug carriers all suggest that the experience of Afghanistan is being applied. Rebel leaders like Amannulah Khan, the then chairman of the Jammu and Kashmir Liberation Front (JKLF), clearly stated that the uprisings were the result of well-laid plans and that the militants receive arms and training through his organization based in Pakistan.[24] Meetings of senior insurgent leaders with Pakistani intelligence agencies have been extensively documented,[25] and weapons movements continue into both Punjab and Kashmir. The recent discovery of two tunnels—115 and 182 feet long—along the border in Punjab underlines the problems involved in detection and interdiction.[26]

Since late 1993, declining recruitment of militants in Kashmir and Punjab has led Pakistani intelligence agencies and their allies to turn to drug and other contraband smugglers to help ship the arms, in return for which these criminal networks are allowed unimpeded trade in other commodities, principally narcotics. Interviews with captured insurgents confirm this,[27] as well as the fact that all major seizures of arms invariably yield a sizeable quantity of heroin.[28] Accordingly, a thriving contraband market has developed in the region, not so much in Kashmir (where the presence of Indian security forces prevents such open activity) but in other Indian states, such as Gujarat, Rajasthan, Uttar Pradesh, Maharashtra (Bombay), and Punjab.[29]

The Black Market

As noted, there is considerable overlap between the gray and the black markets in small arms and light weapons. An appreciation of the extensive links between criminal syndicates, insurgents, and local political figures surfaced during investigations into one of the worst terrorist attacks in India. On March 12, 1993, twelve blasts tore through India's commercial center of Bombay. Investigation revealed the complicity of a Bombay-based smuggling don (who fled to Pakistan)[30] and the existence of large criminal networks that linked silver-smuggling rings on both sides of the border to former militant gangs that in turn were involved in a range of activities, including bank robberies and kidnapping. A transborder link with fundamentalist Karachi-based organizations was also found with the arrest of the head of the Jammu and Kashmir Islamic Front (JKIF), who revealed that because Kashmiris are readily identifiable in Gujarat (Kashmiris pride themselves on being much taller and fairer than the average plainsman), local criminals had been given special training in the transport of arms and ammunition by Pakistani intelligence.[31]

Elsewhere, the Indian crackdown on Punjab insurgents in the early 1990s had unexpected consequences. Many militants fled the state, with most headed for the largely unpopulated regions of the *Terai* (marshy areas along the Himalayan foothills that border on Nepal). Soon thereafter, a thriving network for narcotics and weapons smuggling emerged in the area, with one tentacle supplying AK-47s to insurgents in the northeast.[32] The fact that insurgents from the remote northeast were tying up with crime syndicates in the northern state of Uttar Pradesh pointed to the fact that weapons coming in from Pakistan are still easier and cheaper to access than those available from other sources.

However, since the mid-1990s, Bangladesh has also become an important transit route for weapons originating further east, as confirmed by at least two major seizures of assault rifles. A large seizure in 1996 occurred near the port of Chittagong when Bangladeshi authorities impounded two vessels carrying more than 500 assault rifles, 80 machine guns, 50 rocket launchers, and over 2,000 grenades.[33] Several large arms shipments to the rebels in northeastern India originated along the Thai-Myanmar border, with Mae Sot proving to be a meeting ground for insurgents of all persuasions.

Singapore and Bangkok have also been calling points for insurgents, while Australia is alleged to have harbored Sri Lankan militants at various times.[34] International cooperation and increased policing were rewarded in 1997 when Thai authorities seized a ship carrying two tons of arms intended for India's northeastern rebels.[35] Another recent operation by Indian forces led to the seizure of U.S. and Chinese weapons of various types, all originating in Cambodia and trafficked through Thailand; Myanmarese nationals were also part of the smuggling ring involved. Most worrying was the possibility that part of the consignment may have been meant for Kashmiri and Sri Lankan insurgents.[36]

Within India, the sale of locally made black-market weapons occurs on the outskirts of most large cities (especially Calcutta, Bombay, and New Delhi), with the market in Uttar Pradesh (which borders on Nepal) being the most active. Known for having one of the country's highest crime rates, Uttar Pradesh bazaars reportedly sell locally made bombs for 35 rupees, .315-bore weapons for 32,000 rupees, and AK-47s for 65,000 rupees.[37] While not sold openly, weapons are available through contacts such as fruit juice sellers and small-time jewelers. According to Indian press reports, such transactions are particularly common at election time, with total sales reaching as much as two million rupees a day. All of the weapons are reportedly brought in from Nepal with the connivance of the local police.[38]

Far larger are the arms bazaars in Pakistan—not just those along the northwest frontier (about which much has been written[39]) but also those in Karachi and Lahore, where weapons *goths* (mainly Pathan-dominated bazaars) operate openly. Most of these arms are derived from the Afghan pipeline, but newer weapons are also flowing in. One route reportedly involves arms that were "lost" in the Tajik conflict by Russian troops; black-market dealers allege that they can access any type of weapon, including tanks, at short notice.[40] In Punjab, there are twenty-five arms outlets in Lahore alone, offering AK-47s for about 16,000 to 18,000 rupees and hand grenades from Vietnamese stocks.[41] The refugee areas of Baluchistan (the Girdi jungle) are also known to be centers of arms smuggling, usually supplying drug traffickers and religious groups. In Karachi, the drop in the price of weapons—AK-47s selling for $3,000 in the 1980s now go for less than $500—reflects their widespread availability.

Criminal syndicates have adopted new and novel methods of arms smuggling, including airdrops. In one such operation, occurring in December 1995 over the Indian state of West Bengal, an Antonov-26 aircraft dropped 300 AK-47s, 20,500 rounds of ammunition, Dragunov sniper rifles, rocket launchers, and night vision glasses.[42] The logistics trail and personnel involved in this particular operation involved at least six countries (Latvia, Bulgaria, Hong Kong, Singapore, Thailand, and the United Kingdom) plus an obscure quasi-religious sect. Another case of arms smuggling, by caravan across the Indo-Pakistan border, involved a Swiss national and an Iranian based in Pakistan.[43] While the gray market continues to provide a majority of weapons to the region, the black market is diversifying in terms of both actors and routes.

Controlling the Traffic in Arms

Given the multiplicity of actors, motives, and routes involved in the arms traffic in South Asia, efforts to control this trade will require the establishment of a comprehensive system of controls at the local, regional, and international levels. Because governments (and their agents) continue to be the primary source of weapons for conflicts in Afghanistan and elsewhere, state policy should be the principal target for these controls. The chaos in Pakistan attests to the fact that nations that act as major transshipment points are themselves at risk from the uncontrolled diffusion of light weapons. Regarding the suppliers, international pressure should be applied on both governments and commercial firms to discontinue covert arms transfers to the factions in Afghanistan.

It is also vital that arms embargoes be implemented on the ground in Afghanistan and other areas of conflict. In the case of Afghanistan, UN inspectors should be deployed along all key surface transport routes and at Kabul and surrounding airports. As with the Great Lakes region of Africa, the aim should be to *reduce* the flow of weapons as much as possible, not to attempt the impossible task of cutting it off entirely.

The severe economic crisis afflicting Afghanistan is, of course, an important factor in sustaining the cycle of conflict. To address this problem, the Organization of Islamic States could be tasked with raising and distributing funds for development programs linked to a weapons buy-back initiative. This could be implemented by the traditional *madrassa* network, which would have the necessary moral backing to implement such efforts.

Other control measures that should be pursued in the region include the following.

Border controls

There can be no real "control" of borders in South Asia, given the difficult and sparsely inhabited terrain of the border regions. What is needed are border development initiatives that would give villagers alternative opportunities for employment. Where a strong "tradition" of smuggling exists (e.g., in the Punjab region) it is worth examining the possibility of legalizing some aspects of the illegal trade into lucrative cross-border commerce, thereby reducing the allure of illicit arms trafficking.

Early warning measures

There is almost always warning of an impending conflict. In Punjab, militants were openly building up their arsenals, as was also the case in Kashmir. But the relatively short time frame between an arms buildup and open conflict (as against the time needed for bureaucratic decision making) makes it imperative that some national semiofficial early warning unit be set up that would include reports from journalists, police, concerned research organizations, and nongovernmental organizations (NGOs), all of whom could publicize their findings on a regular basis. The sluggishness of the official apparatus in almost all of the countries in this area (with the exception of Sri Lanka) makes such a unit necessary to goad authorities into action.

Streamlining national gun laws

Streamlining and implementing national gun-possession laws should remain a major priority. Research indicates that states in conflict tend to loosen arms licensing laws. Pakistan's Interior Ministry, for instance, is accused of having relaxed gun licenses during the period of sectarian violence, to the tune of 92,000 license awards in 1992 alone.[44] Sri Lanka has followed the same policy.[45] India has extremely strict gun laws, but it appears that these are being eroded under the stress of militancy.[46] All states in the region need to elevate their licensing authority to a national rather than a local level, with one central issuing authority whose reports would form part of the Home Ministry's annual report to Parliament.

The above measure would also help satisfy an urgent requirement for accurate data. This is one area that needs to be accorded priority, with some states, such as Nepal, clearly in need of outside assistance. While India and Pakistan do have the requisite bodies, the former has no timely and standardized data collation. Each state has its own vagaries on reporting information, and no ready data are available on weapons seized, stolen, or licensed.

Micro-disarmament

Existing buy-back and weapons collection measures need to be strengthened and new ones established in areas where none exist. There can be no standard formula for disarmament since the response seems to depend heavily on the nature of the conflict. The best option would be to target a particular insurgent recruitment area for accelerated development, to diffuse public discontent, and to guard against young people finding better "rewards" in a militant's lifestyle.

Strengthening the regional convention on terrorism

The "Regional Convention on the Suppression of Terrorism" was signed by a number of South Asian nations on November 4, 1987. This Convention seeks to expedite extraditions and create a regional database and is essentially intended as an umbrella under which national intelligence agencies can cooperate with their counterparts in neighboring states. Although a pioneering initiative, it has failed to accomplish much because of a reluctance on the part of such agencies to share information and also because the necessary enabling legislation has not been adopted by Pakistan. Additionally, states other than Sri Lanka have seen no particular urgency for such a task. While that attitude has since changed, there is still no priority being given to these tasks. Several further steps could be taken:

- The Convention should be expanded in terms of both the scope of issues it addresses and its membership. All of the illicit arms-related activities discussed above should be covered, while membership must of necessity include Southeast Asian states, whose cooperation is vital in tackling all aspects of arms smuggling and money laundering.
- A specially constituted standing body needs to be created to put into effect the provisions of the Convention within a definite time frame, with a small secretariat established to deal with coordination and exchanges of information.
- The Convention should require that all member states furnish the secretariat with annual estimates of arms production, export, and import. States should also provide annual reports on weapons seized and their intended destruction.
- All end-user certificates issued for the export of arms should be cleared with the proposed secretariat. Likewise, standardized procedures should be adopted to certify the induction of weapons (identified by serial number) into the military and internal security forces.
- To keep better track of highly mobile and elusive smugglers and organized crime figures, it is vital that police forces speed up communications and, more important, *habituate* themselves to working with regional partners.

Conclusion

Clearly, there is not going to be an immediate decline in the numbers of weapons flowing into South Asia. However, it is the author's firm belief that given the political will, almost all illegal weapons can be controlled or eliminated over a period of time. This will is apparent to some degree in Bosnia, while it was totally lacking in Afghanistan and Sri Lanka (where covert arming by elements within India continued even as the Indian peacekeeping forces tried to implement a peacekeeping mandate). Once neighbors decide to live in peace, covert arms transaction activities automatically receive a setback.

Regarding gun control, there can no longer be any question of this being merely an issue of domestic politics. When weapons begin to move beyond national borders to affect the security of other states, they must fall under the purview of international security considerations. Henceforth, the infusion of any additional weapons into an area of conflict needs to be deemed unacceptable. Ultimately, recognition of the urgency of instituting some form of controls on light weapons trafficking can come about only when it is accepted that such arms in the wrong hands are the ultimate weapons of civilian destruction and societal decay.

Notes

1. This figure includes 35,000 in Kashmir, around 8,000 in India's northeast, 74,000 troops in Myanmar, 120,000 in Sri Lanka, and 25,000 CIS forces in Tajikistan.

2. See Kenneth J. Cooper, "A 'Kalashnikov Culture,'" *Washington Post*, March 14, 1996.

3. This figure is cited by Christina Lamb, *Waiting for Allah* (London: Hamish Hamilton, 1991), p. 223.

4. Figures for combined aid to all factions vary between $6 billion and $8 billion. This is really immaterial since considerably more would have been financed by narcotics production, which increased sharply from 1988 onward. One meticulous record of these quantities is given by Barnett Rubin, *The Fragmentation of Afghanistan* (New Haven: Yale University Press, 1995).

5. According to the witness Brigadier Bohoran (commanding officer of the 12th Brigade of the Sri Lankan Army) he was told to "ignore" the activities of the Liberation Tigers of Tamil Eelam (LTTE) in the Welioya area, where they received arms and ammunition.

6. AK-47s and other automatic weapons are used by poachers in wildlife preserves (Assam), by opium traffickers (Madhya Pradesh), by ethnic groups aspiring to political dominance (Tamil Nadu), and by Mafia dons in Bihar. Additionally, gunrunning is now solid business in Gujarat, Uttar Pradesh, and Tamil Nadu.

7. See Tara Kartha, "Light Weapons and Militancy—the Case of Assam," Research Paper No. 1, IDSA, New Delhi, July 1995.

8. The Tamil Tigers shot down two Sri Lankan Air Force Avros in April 1995 and one Puccarra shortly after. The missiles were suspected to be SA-7s, though this has not been confirmed. See "LTTE Downs Two AF Planes in 24 Hours," *Island*, April 30, 1995.

9. See *Newsline* (Karachi), December 1995. See also Anthony Davis, "Karachi: Pakistan's Political Time-Bomb," *Jane's Intelligence Review*, July 1996, pp. 321-25.

10. For a detailed analysis of the BCCI operations, see Jonathan Beaty and S. C. Gwynne, *The Outlaw Bank* (New York: Random House, 1993).

11. Personal communication by the author with a Southeast Asian official, March 1997.

12. For detailed discussions on this issue, see Rubin, *The Fragmentation of Afghanistan*, and Lamb, *Waiting for Allah*. See also Tara Kartha, "Diffusion of Light Weapons in Pakistan," *Small Wars and Insurgencies*, vol. 8, no. 1 (Spring 1997).

13. General K. M. Arif, vice chief of army staff during the Zia period, notes the independence and lack of accountability of the ISI. See K. M. Arif, *Working with Zia* (Karachi: Oxford University Press, 1995).

14. Khalid Quayoom, "Baluchistan Provides Drug Route to World Markets," in *Nation* (Karachi), July 15, 1997.

15. For a description of the political nexus, see "Sowing the Wind," the CIA report on narcotics in Pakistan, *The Friday Times* (Karachi), September 3, 1993.

16. For a report on a sting operation by the U.S. Drug Enforcement Agency involving a Pakistani Air Force officer and Mr. Zardari, husband of former Prime Minister Benazir Bhutto, see *Nation* (Karachi), February 24, 1997.

17. *Frontier Post* (Peshawar), August 31, 1993.

18. Government of India, *Annual Report, 1995–96* (New Delhi: Ministry of Home Affairs).

19. See *Jane's Defence Weekly,* January 15, 1994. The arrival of trucks from across the Amyu Darya has also been confirmed by investigative journalists interviewed by the author.

20. See V. D. Chopra, ed., *Afghanistan and Asian Stability* (New Delhi: Gyan Books, 1997).

21. Tara Kartha, "The Weaponisation of Afghanistan," *Strategic Analysis,* vol. 19, no. 10–11 (January–February 1997). For a discussion on the Pakistani-Afghan arms actors, see also Rubin, *The Fragmentation of Afghanistan.*

22. U.S. State Department, *International Narcotics Control Strategy Report* (Washington, D.C.: U.S. Government Printing Office, 1997).

23. Human Rights Watch Arms Project, *India: Arms and Abuses in Indian Punjab and Kashmir* (New York: Human Rights Watch, September 1994), p. 10.

24. *The Times of India,* January 30, 1990.

25. There is a plethora of literature on this aspect, notably Major General Afsir Karim et al., *Kashmir, the Troubled Frontiers* (New Delhi: Lancer, 1994). See also Robert G. Wirsing, *India, Pakistan and the Kashmir Dispute* (London: Macmillan, 1994), pp. 131–38. For an incisive argument, see A. G. Noorani, "Pakistani's Complicity in Terrorism in J&K [Jammuu and Kashmir]: The Evidence and the Law," *Indian Defence Review,* January 1992.

26. *Times of India,* January 27, 1997.

27. For instance, Babbar Khalsa militant Jagtar Singh Hawara, in an interview with *India Today,* February 15, 1996.

28. For more information, see weekly reports of the Narcotics Control Board of India, New Delhi.

29. For an account of smuggling-insurgent links, see Praveen Swami, "The Arms Smugglers," *Frontline,* January 12, 1996, pp. 42-47.

30. See M. Rahman, "Falling into Place, Finally," *India Today,* September 15, 1994, pp. 58–63. Extensive publication of taped conversations between the Memons (the major family involved) revealed links with a Karachi-based smuggler who was reportedly the key contact to intelligence. Later, one of the family fled Karachi and returned to India.

31. The fact that the militant leader Assaddulah and his cohorts had moved in and out of the country through Nepal, and the later seizure of 48 kilograms of RDX explosive in that country, focused attention on the northern borders of India. Assaddulah was arrested in June 1996, and the seizures followed soon after. See *Indian Express,* March 4, 1997.

32. Author's interview with arms smuggler operating in the area, June 1994.

33. Robert Karniol, "Bangladesh Seized Arms Vessel off Its Coastline," *Jane's Defence Weekly,* March 27–April 3, 1996.

34. For details on the Tamil Tiger international network, see Rohan Gunaratne, *Regional Security Implications of the Tamil Insurgency* (London: Bandarnaike Centre of International Studies, International Foundation for Sri Lankans, 1997).

35. *Jane's Defence Weekly,* March 26, 1997.

36. *Times of India,* February 13, 1997.

37. *Statesman,* June 17, 1997.

38. *Asian Age,* April 17, 1996.

39. See, for instance, Henry Kamm, "Pakistani Arms Dealers Hail God and the AK-47," *New York Times,* March 8, 1988.

40. A Russian source identifies military and law enforcement officers as setting up secret exports of guns, even during the Soviet era. See *Nezavisimaya Gazeta* (Moscow), October 27, 1995, pp. 1–2. The media, the Tajik opposition, and members of the government have all charged border guards with deep involvement in the drugs and weapons trade. See also Jeffrey Boutwell, Michael T. Klare, and Laura W. Reed, eds., *Lethal Commerce: The Global Trade in Small Arms and Light Weapons* (Cambridge, Mass.: American Academy of Arts and Sciences, 1995), p. 36.

41. *Frontier Post,* June 30, 1992.

42. Harinder Baweja, "Straining Credibility," *India Today,* March 31, 1996, pp. 58–67. See also R. Prassanan, "Conspiracy," *The Week,* January 7, 1996, pp. 30–39.

43. *Frontline,* April 5, 1996, pp. 33–35.

44. Navaid Hussain, in *Dawn* (Karachi), March 31, 1996.

45. Tara Kartha, "Light Weapon Proliferation: The Case of Sri Lanka"(forthcoming). See also *Island,* March 16, 1997.

46. For instance, surrendered militants in the northeast are allotted armed personal security officers, while some retain their own weapons for "insurance," though only smaller-bore types in both cases.

Part Two

Controlling the Supply of Light Weapons

4

U.S. Policy and the Export of Light Weapons

Lora Lumpe

IN HIS KEYNOTE SPEECH before the 50th General Assembly of the United Nations in 1995, President Bill Clinton focused on the global humanitarian and security threats posed by terrorism, organized crime, and drug trafficking. Citing the facility with which such criminals obtain the weapons needed for their operations, President Clinton urged states to work with the United States "to shut down the gray markets that outfit terrorists and criminals with firearms."

The president's speech marked a turning point in U.S. policy on small arms transfers. Since 1995, efforts have evolved rapidly on several fronts, most notably in the area of seeking to curb the illicit traffic in such arms. In 1996, the administration prompted a change in U.S. law, closing a loophole that previously exempted U.S. citizens brokering arms deals in other countries from U.S. laws and regulations. The administration then supported, in May 1997, a Mexican initiative for "fast track" negotiations through the Organization of American States (OAS) on a convention against the illicit manufacture and trafficking of firearms, ammunition, and related materials. That treaty was signed by the United States and twenty-seven other Western Hemisphere governments on November 14, 1997. And in May 1998 during its meeting in Birmingham, England, the "group of eight" industrialized countries (G-7 plus Russia) agreed to support negotiation of an international agreement to combat illegal arms trafficking. The Clinton administration also played a constructive role in the work of the UN Panel of Governmental Experts on Small Arms and the International Study on Firearm Regulations prepared by the Crime Prevention and Criminal Justice Division of the UN Economic and Social Council (for more, see chapter 9 by Graciela Uribe de Lozano).

At the same time it is pursuing these laudable initiatives, however, the U.S. government annually sells, gives, or licenses for export hundreds of thousands of guns and vast quantities of ammunition. Many thousands of these U.S.-source weapons end up on the black market. In 1996, the U.S. government received approximately 30,000 requests from OAS member states to trace weapons used in crimes. For the most part, these weapons were legally sold, either domestically or abroad, and later retransferred to another party in violation of U.S. law.

The Channels of Supply

There are five principal means by which small arms and light weapons are exported abroad from the United States:

- Government-negotiated sales (Foreign Military Sales, or FMS)
- Free or low-cost transfers of surplus Pentagon arms
- Sales negotiated directly by the arms manufacturer or a middleman (direct commercial sales, or DCS)
- Covert government-run supply operations
- The illegal export of weapons

The legal arms supply channels are described in some detail below, focusing on the magnitude of light weapons transfers, the level of transparency surrounding these channels, and the prevalence of end-user checks in place to safeguard against diversion or misuse. Some general observations are also made about illegal arms exports from the United States and covert government arms supply operations.

Three principal laws and two sets of implementing regulations govern small and light arms exports from the United States. The Arms Export Control Act is the primary law establishing procedures on sales of military equipment and related services. This law stipulates the purposes for which weapons may be transferred (self-defense, regional or collective defense, and internal security) and establishes a process by which the executive branch must give Congress advance notice of major sales valued at $14 million or more, whether the sale is negotiated by the government or directly by the arms industry or a broker. The Arms Export Control Act mandates that foreign government entities gain U.S. government approval before they retransfer U.S.-origin arms to a third party.[1] This law also authorizes the government to engage in covert arms supply operations.[2]

The Arms Export Control Act is implemented by the International Traffic in Arms Regulations (ITAR), which are overseen by the Office of Defense Trade Controls, in the Bureau of Political-Military Affairs at the State Department. The ITAR contain a listing of all categories of equipment considered "munitions." Included in the list are all firearms except for nonmilitary shotguns. Manufacturers or brokers wishing to export such arms must be registered with the Office of Defense Trade Controls, and they must obtain an individual export license from the State Department before making any arms shipment. The ITAR also include a list of proscribed destinations. Currently, twenty-four governments and one insurgent group are ineligible to import any American weapons.[3] The State Department imposed these embargoes for a variety of reasons, including UN Security Council–mandated arms embargoes (which are binding for all UN members), chronic warfare, and/or a determination that the government is a sponsor of terrorist activity. In a few other cases, discussed below, the administration has established a policy prohibiting or restricting transfers of small arms and crowd control equipment to particular destinations because of human rights concerns or concerns about diversion of weapons.

The Export Administration Act governs shipments of dual-use goods—technology with both military and civilian applications.[4] The Bureau of Export Administration at the Commerce Department administers this law through the Export Administration Regulations (EAR), which contain the Commerce Control List of items regulated for export on foreign policy or national security grounds. Included in this list, under the heading of police equipment, are nonmilitary shotguns, shotgun components, shotgun shells, stun guns, and shock batons. Companies wishing to export such items must first obtain a license from the Commerce Department for all entities except those in North Atlantic Treaty Organization (NATO) member countries, Australia, New Zealand, or Japan. Governments deemed by the State Department to be "state sponsors of terrorism" are prohibited from receiving items controlled for export by the Commerce Department, but some other restrictions placed on State Department-licensed arms exports do not apply to those overseen by the Commerce Department.

The Foreign Assistance Act directs the provision of economic and military aid to foreign governments and militaries. This act provides the authority for the president and the Department of Defense to give away stocks of surplus American arms. It includes language barring military aid or arms sales to any country that shows a "gross and consistent" pattern of human rights abuse. The Foreign Assistance Act also contains certain proscriptions on the supply of equipment to foreign police forces, although many of the restrictions have been eroded by U.S. counternarcotics programs over the past several years.

These three laws are amended yearly by Congress, usually through the annual foreign aid and defense authorization and appropriation acts, which set the levels of assistance and weapons procurement for the upcoming fiscal year.[5] The implementing regulations are updated often through notices in the *Federal Register,* the daily bulletin of the executive branch.

Government-Negotiated Foreign Military Sales

Through the Foreign Military Sales program, the U.S. government (represented by the Defense Department) negotiates weapons sales directly with foreign militaries. In addition to the weapons, the Pentagon usually contracts to deliver the goods, provide training in the operation and maintenance of the weapons, supply spare parts, and give performance assurances. The FMS may cover sales of new equipment (procured by the Pentagon from U.S. weapons manufacturers), coproduction of weapons overseas, or sales from surplus Pentagon stocks.

An FMS deal is usually initiated with a request for weapons transmitted from the U.S. embassy in the customer country to the "implementing agency"—the Army or the Defense Logistics Agency in the case of small/light arms. Copies of the request are sent to several relevant government agencies, including the State Department's Bureau of Politico-Military Affairs, the Defense Security Assistance Agency (DSAA) in the Office of the Secretary of Defense, the Arms Control and Disarmament Agency, and the Unified Command responsible for the region where the customer country is located. If no objections are raised, the implementing agency, in conjunction with the DSAA, begins to prepare the contract for the arms package. By law, the administration must notify Congress fifteen to thirty days before offering a sales contract to a foreign customer if the proposed sale is valued at $14 million or more.[6]

In 1997, for example, Congress was notified of the following major light weapons sales:

- In July 1997, the Pentagon disclosed plans to sell the Thai military 37,500 FN M16A2 assault rifles, 4,700 M4 carbines, 2,600 M203 grenade launchers, spare parts, and ammunition at a cost of some $40 million.
- In the same month, the Department of Defense informed Congress of its planned sale of 130 M2 .50-caliber machine guns to Saudi Arabia as part of a much larger ($1.075 billion) sale of light armored vehicles.
- In June 1997, the Pentagon announced the proposed sale of 1,065 Stinger antiaircraft missiles and 213 grip-stock missile launchers to Taiwan as part of a larger $307 million deal.

Because of a law passed in 1996, notifications to Congress of proposed FMS are now printed in the *Federal Register.* The notices are usually published within two weeks of transmittal to Congress, and the *Federal Register* is available on the Internet, meaning that information on some government-negotiated small/light arms sales is widely available to the public prior to finalization of the sales contract.[7] The vast majority of light weapons deals, however, fall below the $14 million notification threshold and receive little or no congressional or public scrutiny.

Until recently, the only source of information on past shipments of government-brokered small arms sales was through submission of a request under the Freedom of Information Act (FOIA), a law directing that the executive branch release all requested information to the public that is not exempt from disclosure (national security and foreign policy reasons are grounds for exemption). Detailed information obtained from the Defense Department in 1994 showed that between 1980 and 1993, the Pentagon transferred nearly 50,000 pistols, over 170,000 rifles and shotguns, nearly 1,000 submachine guns, and more than 12,000 grenade launchers to forty nine countries through FMS.[8] Given the magnitude of the recent light arms sale to Thailand (mentioned above), these figures are surprisingly low but still consequential. Among the data included were the transfers shown in table 4.1.

In response to a subsequent FOIA request for the same information for the period 1994–96, the Department of Defense provided information on which small/light weapons were exported to which countries and the date they were shipped but declined to include the quantity delivered. Thus, while it is impossible to discern the magnitude of the exports, it was shown that during

TABLE 4.1
Foreign Military Sales by the U.S. Government, Selected Countries, 1980–91

El Salvador	1982–91	33,274 M16 assault rifles
	1981–91	3,120 40-mm grenade launchers
	1982–91	267,000 hand grenades
Lebanon	1980–83	38,000 M16 assault rifles
	1983–84	60,000 hand grenades
	1983–84	120,000 81-mm HE (high explosive) mortar rounds
	1983–84	2,944 antipersonnel mines
	1984	4,000 antitank mines
Somalia	1982–87	4,800 M16 assault rifles
Thailand	1980–90	347,588 hand grenades
	1980	185,000 antipersonnel mines
	1980	40,000 antitank mines
Zaire	1988	1,000 M16 assault rifles

Source: Defense Security Cooperation Agency, September 9, 1994.

1994–96, M2 .50-caliber machine guns were delivered to Egypt, Lebanon, and Oman; Bolivia, Bosnia, and Jordan each took delivery of M60 7.62-mm machine guns; Bolivia, Colombia and Tunisia received M249 5.56-mm machine guns; and Egypt, Estonia, Israel, Latvia, and Lithuania all took delivery of M16A1 assault rifles.[9]

A new requirement established in U.S. law in 1996 now requires that the Pentagon report to Congress (and the public) annually on all FMS deliveries, by country and by weapon system, during the preceding year. The first iteration of the report, known as the "section 655 report" after the section of the Foreign Assistance Act that mandates it, was released in September 1997. It lists nearly $12.7 billion of weapons exported in toto through FMS in fiscal year 1996. Among other small arms deliveries, it lists 30,450 rifles and 169 machine guns to Taiwan and 292 machine guns and 39 rifles to Thailand.[10] Detailed information of the sort contained in the section 655 report was provided to Congress throughout the 1970s, but in 1981 the Reagan administration repealed the legislation that mandated it. Reinstatement of this report greatly facilitates congressional and public oversight of U.S. small arms sales policies.

According to a recent report on end-use monitoring of FMS shipments, "whether a minor item, which is readily available commercially [e.g., small arms] or a high technology weapon system, each defense item transfer must be preceded by formal agreement with appropriate end-use and retransfer restrictions."[11] The report goes on to note that the Defense Department's "physical security requirements for transfers to foreign governments of arms, ammunition and explosives are similar to those required by U.S. military forces." Security assistance offices (SAOs), located in U.S. embassies around the world, are charged with the in-country management of weapons sales programs, including oversight of end use. However, there is no indication that any routine or surprise end-use inspections are undertaken to ensure physical control and nontransfer.

Theft of weapons from U.S. military depots is a significant source of black-market arms within and from the United States, and it is reasonable to assume that foreign control of arms sold through the FMS program are equally, if not more, vulnerable to theft and/or diversion. Allegations long persisted, for example, that the Thai government—whether through negligence or official policy—was diverting U.S.-supplied (and other) light arms to Khmer Rouge combatants in neighboring Cambodia. In December 1993, one of several Khmer Rouge arms depots on Thai soil was inadvertently exposed to the press, and U.S.-designed weapons were photographed in the arsenal.[12] The practice apparently continued on an ad hoc basis until recently, although pared down significantly in the past few years. Meanwhile, some of the U.S. M16 assault rifles and other light weapons that flowed into Cambodia have been reexported back through Thailand to rebels fighting the military government in Burma.[13]

Surplus Weapons Grants from the Government

In addition to sales of newly manufactured weapons, the Pentagon gives away or sells at deep discount the vast oversupply of small/light weapons in its post–Cold War inventory. Most of this surplus is dispensed through the Excess Defense Articles (EDA) program. The Foreign Assistance Act defines EDA as weapons or other items owned by the U.S. government that were not procured in anticipation of military assistance or sales requirements. Originally, only the southern-tier members of NATO were cleared to receive EDA, but following the 1990–91 Gulf War, many Middle Eastern and North African states were added; antinarcotics aid provisions expanded EDA eligibility to include South American and Caribbean countries; and the Partnership for Peace program made most Central and Eastern European governments eligible for free surplus arms.

Around 1995, large-scale grants and sales of small/light arms began occurring. Since that time, over 300,000 rifles, pistols, machine guns, and grenade launchers have been delivered to the following countries:

- 158,000 M16A1 assault rifles (principally to Bosnia, Israel, and the Philippines)
- 124,815 M14 rifles (principally to the Baltics and Taiwan)
- 26,780 pistols (principally to the Philippines, Morocco, Chile, and Bahrain)
- 1,740 machine guns (principally to Morocco and Bosnia)
- 10,570 grenade launchers (principally to Bahrain, Egypt, Greece, Israel, and Morocco)

Excess equipment is generally transferred in furtherance of U.S. foreign policy goals, such as narcotics control, military alliance, or encouraging participation in multilateral peacekeeping operations. In addition, there is a budgetary inducement for the military services to unload the surplus weapons rather than bear the expense of storing or destroying them.

Most provisions of law that apply to sales of new weapons also apply to transfers of surplus arms. In fact, EDA are the most transparent of all U.S. arms exports. In 1993, at the urging of the arms industry, the Pentagon created a computer bulletin board on excess weapons sales and grants.[14] When the Pentagon notifies the foreign aid committees of Congress of upcoming EDA weapons transfers (required thirty days prior to shipment, no matter the value of the equipment, whether grant or for sale), the information is posted on the bulletin board. In addition, the section 655 report itemizes all grant EDA offered to each country during the preceding fiscal year.

That report also lists surplus weapons provided during the preceding year under special presidential authority to "draw down" U.S. military equipment to meet emergency needs. The Foreign Assistance Act provides permission for the president to transfer, on a grant basis, up to $150 million of military articles from U.S. stocks annually.[15] The executive branch has used this provision increasingly in recent years, particularly in support of counternarcotics efforts. In addition, Jordan and Bosnia have taken delivery of large quantities of surplus light arms under this emergency authority. The law requires the president to notify Congress of any planned drawdowns of equipment and also to notify Congress on completion of delivery.

Section 623 of the Foreign Assistance Act requires the Department of Defense to supervise the end use of weapons provided under grant aid programs. This function is delegated to SAOs located in overseas embassies. According to an August 1997 report on end-use monitoring, "As part of their normal duties, SAOs are responsible for observing and reporting on utilization by the host country of defense articles and defense services, including training." Again, however, there was no indication in the report that this observation or reporting is routinely, or even occasionally, occurring in most recipient countries.[16] The State Department, however, does appear to conduct some end-use checks of small arms provided under the special drawdown authority in support of drug control operations. During 1995, the U.S. embassy in Bogota inspected M16A1 rifles, M60 machine guns, M9 pistols, shotguns, M79 grenade launchers, 60-mm mortars, and ammunition that had been shipped to Colombian forces.[17]

In addition to concerns about the repressive nature of some of the governments taking delivery of weapons through this program (discussed below), the precedent of exporting rather than destroying surplus small arms is potentially dangerous. Several other countries have (or had) large surplus arms holdings. The Federal Republic of Germany, for example, inherited the entire military of the German Democratic Republic; many former Soviet republics inherited arsenals in excess of their ability or desire to field soldiers. Liberal transfers of excess arms by the United States, for economic or diplomatic gain, may be used as justification by these and other states for similar actions, contributing to a further proliferation of guns.

Some past U.S. transfers of surplus light weapons have come back to haunt U.S. policymakers. Beginning in the 1950s, the Department of Defense gave or sold nearly 2.5 million World War II-era military pistols, rifles, and carbines to some forty governments around the world. South Korea, Vietnam, Turkey, Pakistan, Cambodia, and the Philippines were the largest recipients of the weapons—M1911 .45-caliber pistols, M1 carbines, and M1 Garand rifles. Now the pro-gun lobby in the United States is seeking to force the executive branch (through an act of Congress) to allow U.S. citizens to import these old-model but still quite lethal weapons—referred to as "curios and relics" by the National Rifle Association (NRA). The Departments of Defense, State, Justice, and Treasury, along with the White House, are firmly opposed to allowing these weapons into civilian circulation.

Industry-Direct Arms Sales

Despite the large quantities of small/light arms sold through FMS and given away through surplus programs, the vast majority of such weapons are exported from the United States through direct commercial sales negotiated between U.S. companies or brokers and foreign buyers. The foreign customer may be a government entity (e.g., interior ministry, justice ministry, ministry of defense, or national police), a corporation or person using the weapons for private security or sport, or a gun vendor. The DCS must be approved by the State Department's Office of Defense Trade Controls or the Commerce Department's Bureau of Export Administration, depending on the equipment. State Department-licensed sales are subject to the same congressional notification procedure as are FMS (i.e., for sales over $14 million). Commerce Department-licensed sales are not subject to any prior congressional scrutiny.

In general, when the customer is a government entity, the choice of whether to use the government-to-government channel or to deal directly with the arms manufacturer or broker is up to the purchaser. Most public and policy attention focuses on government-negotiated FMS since that program is much more visible and has accounted for the majority of U.S. arms exports in dollar terms over the years. Arms export licenses approved by the State Department's Office of Munitions Control (later renamed the Office of Defense Trade Controls) totaled some $2 billion to $3 billion annually during most of the Cold War, with much of this believed to comprise small/light arms. By the mid-1980s, however, license approval averaged $10 billion annually, and since the 1990–91 Gulf War, licenses have shot up to an average of more than $25 billion a year. State Department officials are quick to point out that DCS license approvals do not represent final sales; they estimate that about a quarter to half of the licenses approved will result in actual exports. Still, this represents a dramatic increase in the value of industry-negotiated arms sales.

The growing popularity of direct sales is due to the fact that the commercial route is quicker and sometimes cheaper and entails less oversight than do government-negotiated sales. In addition, both the Commerce and the State Department are much less transparent about the deals they are licensing than the Pentagon is about sales it is negotiating.[18] Many foreign customers have viewed this secrecy with favor.

State Department–Licensed Small Arms

The section 655 report now makes it possible to tally the vast quantities of small arms, light weaponry, and ammunition that the State Department is clearing for export. The report for 1996 lists in great specificity some $590 million of small arms and ammunition that the State Department authorized manufacturers to export directly to foreign countries.[19] It is possible to quantify the value of licenses granted for ammunition and ammunition-manufacturing equipment, carbines, grenades/grenade launchers, machine guns, submachine guns, pistols, M16 rifles, other rifles, and so on to each recipient country. It is important to note, though, that this information concerns only licenses that have been approved by the State Department, not the actual delivery of items. These licenses are valid for four years.

Because the State Department previously refused to release any information about small arms sales it has licensed,[20] it is not possible to determine relative changes in the volume of exports or licenses over time. However, in mid-1994 the State Department's Office of Defense Trade Controls reported that it had experienced a recent noticeable increase in the number of applications for firearm and ammunition exports.[21] Data obtained by congressional investigators showed that during 1989–93 the State Department granted 1,600 export licenses for over $100 million of pistols, revolvers, and rifles to eight Latin American countries (see table 4.2).[22]

Around this same time, according to a State Department bulletin, foreign governments requested that the United States be more careful in licensing small arms and ammunition for export. Concerned about the quantity of firearms entering their countries and the possibility for diversion to terrorists, drug traffickers, and criminals, governments requested that the U.S. government demand more extensive documentation for license applications. As a result, the State Department modified the regulations governing firearms ex-

TABLE 4.2
Export Licenses Granted by the U.S. State Department to Eight Latin American Countries, 1989–93

Country	Value of Licenses	Number of Licenses	Number of End-Use Checks
Argentina	$47,747,115	686	7
Brazil	$3,957,533	343	2
Colombia	$643,785	39	0
Costa Rica	$556,274	117	0
El Salvador	$891,916	61	3
Guatemala	$6,766,983	141	3
Mexico	$34,362,973	108	3
Peru	$11,704,189	137	3
Total	$106,630,768	1,632	21

Source: U.S. Senate Committee on Governmental Affairs, *A Review of Arms Export Licensing,* Senate Hearing 103–670, p. 37.

ports in several ways. First, a firm and specific purchase order must be submitted with a license application. Second, a "nontransfer and use" certificate is required for export applications for fifty or more handguns or rifles or for 100,000 or more rounds of ammunition. Third, an import authorization issued by the importing government is now required as well.[23]

In 1990, the State Department initiated a global end-use monitoring program known as Blue Lantern. The program, required by an act of Congress,[24] is administered by overseas diplomatic posts under the direction of the Office of Defense Trade Controls. Embassy personnel verify directly with local authorities and foreign firms or persons the bona fides of proposed transactions. They also perform some random spot checks. Some 3,000 cases have been initiated since the program began (on an estimated 50,000 licenses granted annually). Investigations are triggered when someone included in the State Department's watch list applies for an export license or when other key flags indicating high-risk transactions are raised. These include requested equipment that does not match the known requirements or inventory of the foreign end user (including requests for spare parts), insufficient information about parties to the transaction, or involvement of a foreign broker in a third country. But, as shown in table 4.2, information revealed through a congressional hearing showed that the State Department conducted only twenty-one checks on 1,600 licenses granted for gun exports to Latin American countries during 1989–93.

Nevertheless, according to an August 1997 report, the State Department believes that the Blue Lantern program has effectively disrupted several "gray arms market transactions" and had an important deterrent effect in dissuading bogus imports.[25] In 1996, thirty-one cases referred to Blue Lantern resulted in export license denial; nearly half of these cases were in Latin America, and most of the remainder were in Europe.[26] As a result of one recent investigation, the U.S. government instituted a ban on firearms exports for commercial purposes to Paraguay, and sales to the government and police are now subject to a high degree of scrutiny.[27] According to a U.S. embassy official in Asunción, "The diversion of arms and munitions from Paraguay to neighboring countries (chiefly Brazil) is becoming a major regional issue. The Blue Lantern program provides us with a mechanism for measuring and controlling U.S. commercial exports to Paraguay."[28] The program also reportedly heightened British officials' awareness of the need to monitor more closely commercial U.S. small arms exports to the United Kingdom and uncovered two cases of fraudulent orders in Bolivia—one concerning sniper rifles allegedly for the government and the other involving phony import permits issued by the ministry of defense.[29]

A recent State Department inspector general report agrees that the program is becoming more aggressive and effective but acknowledges that it is still implemented unevenly at different embassies. In particular, the report cites communication problems between the embassies and Washington, D.C., frivolous investigation requests, and sloppy or nonexistent record keeping on investigations. The inspector general took several recommendations from embassy personnel; one of these would waive Blue Lantern checks for certain U.S. munitions list items, including handguns or "other sporting armaments."[30]

Maintaining control over licensed manufacture in foreign countries of U.S.-design small/light arms is another area of concern. In 1988, the General Accounting Office (GAO) disclosed that South Korean industry had violated the terms of a license by Colt for the manufacture of M16A1 assault rifles, producing them in excess of the permitted quantity and exporting the rifles without U.S. government approval. The State Department classified the names of the third-country recipients, but a member of Congress disclosed in a hearing that they were "hostile." The Pentagon maintained that the exported rifle, known as the K-2, is a "Koreanized" version of the M16 but with enough modification that it could be considered "indigenous" and, therefore, exempt from U.S. government export controls. Other countries that have produced M16A1 assault rifles under license are Canada, the Philippines, Singapore, and Taiwan. Chartered Industries of Singapore now produces an M16 clone that it exports widely.

Commerce Department–Licensed Exports of Shotguns

The Commerce Department is also secretive about what precisely it is licensing for export to which particular entities in foreign countries, but it is possible to glean some data. In response to a request under the FOIA about shotgun exports licensed during 1991–93, the department released country-specific data on the quantity and dollar value of licenses approved for the commodity category that includes shotguns (as well as shotgun components, shotgun shells, stun guns, and shock batons). According to this information, over $100 million in exports of these items was approved during the three-year period. At an average price of $200 per shotgun, this translates into roughly 500,000 guns approved for export during this three-year period.

Although it is impossible to know with certainty, since this information is not released, the bulk of these licenses were probably for 18″ or 20″ Mossberg, Maverick, and/or Winchester 12-gauge shotguns, shells, rifle scopes, and sights. Smith & Wesson, E. I. Dupont de Nemours, Bausch and Lomb, Olin Corporation, Valor Corporation of Florida, and U.S. Repeating Arms are some of the principal U.S. manufacturers and exporters of these weapons and components.

Shotgun exports have apparently increased in recent years as well. In fiscal year 1995, the Commerce Department approved 1,301 licenses, valued at over $75 million—nearly as much as it had licensed during 1991–93.[31] The following year, Commerce signed off on over $67 million in shotgun exports while rejecting just under fifty applications (valued at nearly $3 million) for shipment to entities in Vietnam, Nigeria, Indonesia, and other countries.[32] Taken together, these figures represent foreign sales of approximately 700,000 12-gauge shotguns in 1995–96. These figures actually underrepresent total sales since U.S. manufacturers and middlemen do not need a license to export crime control items to destinations in NATO member countries, Australia, Japan, and New Zealand.

The guns are exported both to private dealers for commercial resale and to ministries of justice, interior, or defense for use in the importing country. Section 6(n) of the Export Administration Act imposes controls on the export of police equipment principally because of human rights concerns. According to a recent Commerce Department report, "Applications for licenses will generally be considered favorably on a case-by-case basis, unless there is evidence that the government of the importing country may have violated internationally recognized human rights and that the judicious use of export controls would be helpful in deterring the development of a consistent pattern of violations or in distancing the United States from such violations."[33] The document goes on to say that the State Department's annual *Country Reports on Human Rights Practices* will be consulted in making licensing decisions. Information on which states received high levels of gun export licenses from the Commerce Department in 1995–96 is not publicly available, but several recipient countries during the 1991–93 period had records of severe human rights violations, high levels of armed violence, or a history of diversion. Among the countries of greatest concern on these grounds are Guatemala, Israel, Pakistan, Paraguay, Peru, Thailand, Saudi Arabia, and Venezuela.

The Commerce Department's Bureau of Export Administration (BXA) performs no dedicated end-use monitoring on exports of shotguns, components, and ammunition. The BXA's Office of Enforcement Support is responsible for preventing and investigating export control violations. It has over 140 staff, half of whom are special agents, located in headquarters in Washington, D.C., and in eight field offices around the country. These agents are empowered to make arrests, carry firearms, execute search warrants, and seize goods about to be illegally exported. The enforcement office also examines export license applications to assess risk of diversion, but the focus is on major strategic weapons—especially technologies used in nuclear, chemical, or biological weapons or missiles. In 1996, the Commerce Department, through the Office of Enforcement Support and Foreign Commercial Service staff in overseas embassies, conducted 427 prelicense checks and 234 postshipment verifications (on tens of thousands of export licenses granted annually). Two cases closed during that year dealt with illegal exports of light weapons.[34]

Covert Government Arms Supply

Clandestine U.S. government operations are another way in which small/light arms are exported from or by the United States. The National Security Act of 1947 authorizes covert political and military operations, including secret arms supply. The president must first make a "finding" that the operation is vital to U.S. national security. Section 505 of the act requires the Central Intelligence Agency (CIA) or other government agencies engaging in such activities to notify the congressional committees responsible for oversight of U.S. intelligence community activities of any arms supply operation undertaken valued at $1 million or more.

During the 1970s, and particularly during the Reagan administration, covert arms supply operations run by the CIA (or the National Security Council) were a major source of small/light arms to insurgent groups around the world. Some of this weaponry was manufactured in the United States; some, in an effort to hide U.S. support of the operation, was not. Because these programs are classified, little is known with any precision about the frequency, magnitude, and specifics of covert arms supply. Information is sketchy even for the most public of these operations, which armed, trained, and financed guerrillas fighting communist-backed state forces in Nicaragua, Angola, and Afghanistan.

As discussed in chapter 3 by Tara Kartha, the classified operation to arm various *mujahideen* factions fighting in Afghanistan to liberate the country from Soviet invaders began in 1979. Before it ended in 1991, the CIA had shipped via Pakistan an estimated 400,000 AK-47 assault rifles; an undisclosed quantity of Stinger portable antiaircraft missile launchers and missiles; vast quantities of Italian-made antipersonnel mines; 60,000 archaic rifles, 8,000 light machine guns, and over 100 million rounds of ammunition from Turkey; 40 to 50 Oerlikon Swiss-designed antiaircraft guns; mortars from Egypt; Blowpipe surface-to-air missiles from the United Kingdom; and 100,000 rifles from India.[35]

Covert U.S. aid to insurgents in Angola began in 1974 and continued until 1992. It is estimated that during the 1970s, the CIA provided some $300 million in aid, most of it through neighboring Zaire and much of it in the form of light weaponry. Former CIA operative John Stockwell wrote that in the early phase of the operation (1970s), the CIA provided 7,771 7.62-mm rifles, 12,215 .30-caliber carbines, 4,210 66-mm light antitank weapons, and 410 grenade launchers.[36] It is not publicly known how many weapons were transferred to the National Union for the Total Independence of Angola (UNITA) and President Sese Seko Mobuto in Zaire when the operation was intensified by the Reagan administration in the mid-1980s.

The recycling of weapons transferred through the CIA or the White House covert pipeline is a major contributor to continuing violence and instability today in Central America, South Asia, and southwestern Africa. Because of the secret and unaccountable nature of these transactions, they feed directly into the global black arms market.

It is generally believed that the use of covert military supply operations has greatly diminished in the 1990s, and yet calls for armed destabilization of the regimes in Iran and Iraq persist. Most recently, it has been reported that the CIA is considering plans for covert support to Iraqi Kurdish and Shi'ite groups to sabotage the Iraqi economy and propel the overthrow of President Saddam Hussein.[37] Ongoing covert arms supply to forces opposing the Sudanese regime is reported as well.

Illegal Exports

In part, the Clinton administration's recent focus on the illicit arms traffic was spurred by the concerns of the Mexican government about the proliferation of illegal U.S. weapons in the hands of Mexican drug traffickers and other criminals. According to the Bureau of Alcohol, Tobacco and Firearms (BATF), Mexico is one of the leading recipients of illicitly exported U.S. weapons. Guns flow from and through the United States to Mexico in several ways, one method being the transshipment of weapons.[38] In March 1997, for example, federal agents opened two crates in a "left cargo" hold at the Otay Mesa border crossing near San Diego and uncovered the largest illegal shipment of arms ever intercepted in the United States en route to Mexico. The weapons—thousands of unassembled grenade launchers and parts for M2 automatic rifles—had been sitting unclaimed for two months. The shipment had originated in Vietnam, where the United States left behind large quantities of weapons, including M2 automatic rifles.[39] Before the arms returned home, they were well traveled, having gone from Ho Chi Minh City to Singapore to Bremerhaven, Germany, through the Panama Canal and up to Long Beach, California, where the weapons entered the United States in two large, sealed containers.[40] The contents were falsely represented as hand tools and strap hangers, but U.S. Customs at Long Beach did not inspect the cargo since the shipment was "in-bond"—that is, the items were simply transiting the United States to another country, in this case Mexico. In-bond cargo containers typically remain sealed as they move from ship to truck to border. According to a Customs source, "In the normal course of business, no one would have ever opened them. [The arms] were discovered through a fluke."[41] (The shipment was held up at the border because the Mexican freight forwarder that was commissioned to get the crates to Mexico City did not have an address for the purchaser.)

The in-bond system is built on trust and on the Customs Department's lack of resources. Customs has fewer than 135 inspectors at the port of Long Beach, the nation's busiest port.[42] Nevertheless, the Customs Department has successfully thwarted a number of illegal arms export efforts, many of them involving small arms shipments. For example, in 1997 several defendants were indicted for attempting to export illegally fifty-three AR-15 rifles from the United States to Colombia. In another case in 1997, Customs blocked an attempt to import surface-to-air missiles from Bulgaria for transshipment to Colombia. Customs also successfully prosecuted a former Venezuelan secret service agent for the unlawful shipment of 120 firearms to Venezuela between 1993 and1995.[43] Unfortunately, there is no way to know what percentage of the illegal trade is being intercepted.

Large and relatively well-organized arms shipments, like the one intercepted in San Diego in March 1997, are thought to be unusual. A more routine way of smuggling arms across the border is the *hormiga* (ant) run: repeated trips across the border with one or a few guns. A legally eligible, or "straw," purchaser buys a few weapons (often cheap .22- and .25-caliber pistols, "38 specials," and 9-mm pistols) from gun stores in El Paso and other U.S. border towns and hands them over to the trafficker, who smuggles them across the border, generally either on foot or in the trunk of a car. This process is repeated countless times a year, as smugglers make repeated trips to gun stores and shows, particularly in Florida, Texas, and California.[44]

Some legal constraints are now in place, but a lack of investigative and regulatory resources reduce their efficacy. The so-called Brady bill mandates a national system of background checks prior to gun purchases. Before that system was up and running in November 1998, a mandatory five-day waiting period prior to purchase was in effect. In addition, a rule recently enacted by the Clinton administration requires purchasers to show that they have lived for at least three months in the state where they are buying a gun. And the 1994 assault weapons ban curbs purchases by civilians of automatic and semiautomatic weapons (see chapter 6 by Natalie Goldring).

The Firearms Owners Protection Act of 1986 (sponsored by the NRA) requires that multiple sales be reported to the BATF and local law enforcement agencies so that they can monitor multiple gun purchases and investigate if they suspect criminal intent. Currently, however, only three states—Virginia, Maryland, and South Carolina—have laws that prevent people from buying more than one gun a month. In all other states, straw purchasers can buy significant quantities of guns and ammunition from gun dealers at one time and pass them on to smugglers for clandestine shipment. A 1991 BATF report describes a number of such transactions, including a 1989 case in which three Arizona residents purchased ninety-three assault rifles and twenty-two handguns for a well-known Mexican narcotics trafficker who then smuggled them into Mexico.[45]

Military depots in the United States are another likely source of supply. In 1993, the GAO found that small arms parts were routinely stolen from a number of U.S. military repair shops and warehouses. The parts were then sold to gun dealers or to walk-in customers at gun shows around the United States. The GAO investigators were able to purchase military small arms parts at thirteen of the fifteen gun shows they visited. They were able to buy everything needed to convert a semiautomatic AR-15 rifle into a fully automatic M16 as well as 30-round M16 magazine clips still in their original packages.[46] Given the paucity of end-use checks performed on U.S.-supplied arms, it is reasonable to assume that theft from Mexican depots contributes to the black market in arms as well.

Conclusion

The United States continues, as during the Cold War, to be a major exporter of light weaponry around the world, and by all available evidence, legal exports of shotguns, small arms, and ammunition have been increasing in recent years. Because other governments are not open about their light weapons shipments, it is not possible to rank the place of the United States in the global small arms trade; however, given the sheer magnitude of U.S. licenses and sales—in 1996, the State Department approved $590 million of small arms exports, the Commerce Department approved $75 million of shotgun exports, and the Department of Defense gave away 50,000 assault rifles and over 10,000 grenade launchers—it is reasonable to speculate that the United States dominates the market (as it does the market for larger weapons systems).

In the 1990s, the threat perceptions of the United States have shifted dramatically. No longer facing a global nuclear confrontation with the Soviet Union and its allies, civil and regional wars (and the chaos they spawn), drug trafficking, international terrorism, and other forms of transnational crime are now considered among the most serious threats. The Clinton administration has identified a link between the illegal traffic in arms and several of these threats, but it has yet to acknowledge the link between massive legal U.S. light arms exports and the illegal traffic. Other governments understand this connection, and they have been pressing the United States to be more restrictive and careful in its supply. Initiatives such as the 1997 OAS treaty, when ratified and fully implemented, should help curb illicit gunrunning, but there is more that the Clinton administration could be doing to reinforce its stated goal of shutting down the gray market in arms.

Embargo Light Arms to Repressive Regimes

Several of the countries currently receiving large quantities of arms through surplus programs or buying weapons through commercial channels are engaged in conflict or have extremely poor human rights records. Bahrain, for example, has received significant quantities of free machine guns, ammunition, and grenade launchers in recent years. At the same time, government forces have fired live ammunition and tear gas into crowds of demonstrators demanding a restoration of the parliament, which the ruling family dissolved in 1975. In addition to some measure of representative democracy, protestors are demanding freedom of speech, the release of political prisoners, and the return of deported dissidents. Israel, the leading beneficiary of U.S. military and economic aid, used U.S.-supplied arms in its deadly 1996 assault in Lebanon, in which an ambulance and a UN refugee camp were apparently targeted as they were thought to be shielding Hezbollah guerrillas. Under surplus grant arms programs, Israel has received nearly 75,000 M16A1 rifles, 2,500 M203 grenade launchers, and large quantities of ammunition. Morocco, also a major recipient of U.S. surplus small arms, is governed by a highly repressive monarchy that has illegally occupied the western Sahara for twenty years and long thwarted a negotiated peace process. And, according to the State Department's 1996 human rights report, the Colombian police and armed forces were responsible for "widespread human rights abuse" in 1995, including political and extrajudicial killings, kidnappings, and torture.[47] Colombia is a major recipient of grant surplus arms for counternarcotics purposes.

Small arms—and assault rifles in particular—have long been the principal symbol of state repression used by police, internal security forces, and allied militias to crush opposition movements, eliminate dissidents, and terrorize populations. The Christmas 1997 massacre in Chiapas of forty-five unarmed civilians, carried out by government-affiliated paramilitary forces with high-powered AK-47 assault rifles, is one of countless examples. In addition to being immoral, transfers of such tools to repressive governments likely encourage insurgent forces to seek countervailing arms through the black market—the principal source of supply open to them. The Clinton administration has, in at least two recent cases, announced a policy of barring sales of small arms to U.S. friends or allies on human rights grounds. In February 1994, the State Department announced that it would deny licenses for the transfer of small or light arms and lethal crowd control items to Indonesia. Later that year, Congress passed law codifying this ban until certain human rights conditions are met. The ban is still in place.

According to a July 1997 State Department report to Congress on Turkey's use of U.S.-supplied weapons, "U.S. policy is to restrict the sale of arms that clearly could be used to repress a civilian population, such as small arms and violent crowd-control devices."[48] But the report goes on to note that Turkey now produces the majority of its own pistols, rifles, and handheld automatic weapons. And Turkey's paramilitary Jandarama and the Turkish National Police—the forces most prominently cited in the commission of gross human rights abuses in Turkey—have purchased M16 and AR-15S assault rifles and M203 grenade launchers through State Department-licensed commercial sales. According to the State Department report, "In July 1995, in Tunceli province, following the death of several of their comrades, members of these special teams went on a rampage, indiscriminately firing on shops and residential buildings and attacking individuals at random."[49] The State Department said that no resources are available generally to monitor the end use of U.S.-supplied weapons in Turkey to ensure that they are not being used in the commission of gross abuses but that "mission personnel have seen some of this equipment, which is still in service." Despite the stated policy and lack of oversight, the State Department continued to authorize small arms exports in 1997.

A comprehensive ban on small arms exports—those overseen by the Departments of Commerce, State, and Defense, as well as intelligence agencies—should be implemented on all repressive forces, as identified by the State Department in its annual *Country Reports on Human Rights.*

Provide More Transparency

As evidenced in this chapter, there is an increasingly high level of transparency around U.S. small and light arms exports, yet compiling this information from the various sources is time consuming and difficult. Moreover, some key information is still withheld from the public. In particular, the section 655 report should include information on which State Department-licensed arms are actually shipped abroad in addition to listing those items licensed for export. The State Department needs this information in a computerized and searchable form in order to facilitate and improve end-use verification of weapons exports it is authorizing. In addition, increased transparency would allow the nongovernment community as well as congressional staff to play an important role in aiding the administration's efforts to curb the illicit arms traffic by providing oversight through research and questioning of discrepancies in the data. This information is also important to aid and relief workers who might be working in a region where a sudden influx of guns has occurred. Transparency around such shipments could prove to be an early warning indicator of pending violence and instability. On a more positive note, increased openness about weapons shipments could serve as a confidence-building measure among forces within a state or among states in a region, potentially heading off some purchases spurred on by "fear of the unknown." Finally, the U.S. government and/or nongovernment groups could use the example of relative openness by the U.S. government in its small/light arms exports to press for similar transparency by other exporters.

Controlling the Domestic Gun Market Is Vital to U.S. National Security

Given that drug traffickers and terrorists have been identified as a major post–Cold War threat, the United States must do more to prevent such criminals from obtaining lethal firepower in the United States. The Brady bill (requiring a five-day waiting period and criminal check prior to gun sales) and the ban on sales of assault rifles have complicated business for gunrunners. Also needed is a national law limiting customers to one gun purchase per month. Such a measure would, according to BATF findings, help curb the multiple-gun straw purchases that often end up on the black market.

Take the Issue Seriously

Finally, a policy of reflexive approval of large shipments of light arms to security forces and private actors in friendly states around the world should give way to a new, more restrictive norm. In short, in light of the increased security threat posed by the illicit traffic in arms (as stated by the Clinton administration), the issue of light arms proliferation in general should be viewed more seriously. As part of this recognition, there is perhaps a need for the administration to press Congress for increased resources for Customs and Commerce Department special investigations and routine inspections. In addition, rather than relegating light arms to the back burner, as is currently the case at the Commerce Department, or removing them from end-use coverage entirely, as is under consideration by the State Department, these agencies need to undertake more frequent "end-use" inspections of small/light arms shipments to ensure that legal transfers are not being diverted into the black market.

Notes

1. See section 3 of the Arms Export Control Act, available from the U.S. Government Printing Office (1976). This provision technically refers only to government-negotiated arms transfers, but the State Department has interpreted it to apply to commercially negotiated sales as well. The law will likely be modified soon to make this coverage explicit.

2. Section 40(h) of the Arms Export Control Act references covert arms supply operations authorized under title V of the National Security Act. Section 505 of that act requires the administration to notify congressional intelligence oversight committees of clandestine arms exports valued at $1 million or more.

3. As of January 1998, the governments of Afghanistan, Armenia, Azerbaijan, Belarus, Burma, China, Cuba, Cyprus, Haiti, Iran, Iraq, Liberia, Libya, Nigeria, North Korea, Rwanda, Somalia, Sudan, Syria, Tajikistan, Vietnam, Yemen, Yugoslavia (Serbia and Montenegro), and Zaire (now called the Democratic Republic of Congo) are unable to import munitions from the United States, as is UNITA in Angola. See the State Department's embargo reference chart at http://www.pmdtc.org/country.html. Not all of these destinations are prohibited from importing police equipment, including shotguns, licensed by the Commerce Department.

4. Technically, this law lapsed in 1994, but it continues to be implemented un-

der emergency powers of the president. Congress will likely rewrite and reinstate the law soon.

5. Both the Arms Export Control Act and the Foreign Assistance Act, as most recently amended, are published annually by the congressional foreign relations committees. The joint committee print, entitled *Legislation on Foreign Relations,* is available for purchase from the U.S. Government Printing Office.

6. Fifteen days' prenotification is required for NATO allies and "major non-NATO allies," such as Israel, Egypt, Jordan, Argentina, Australia, New Zealand, Japan, and South Korea. For all other countries, Congress has thirty days to review proposed sales.

7. The *Federal Register* is available online through the U.S. Government Printing Office home page at http://www.access.gpo.gov/su docs/aces/aces140.html

8. Defense Security Assistance Agency, September 19, 1994; information obtained under the Freedom of Information Act (FOIA) by the Federation of American Scientists.

9. Office of the Assistant Secretary of Defense, November 8, 1996. Some of the deliveries reported here were sales or grants of Excess Defense Articles; FOIA, Federation of American Scientists.

10. U.S. Department of State and U.S. Department of Defense, "Foreign Military Assistance Act Report to Congress, Fiscal Year 1996," September 1997.

11. The White House, "End-Use Monitoring of Defense Articles, Defense Services and Related Technology," August 18, 1997. This report is required annually by section 40A of the Arms Export Control Act, which Congress added in 1996 because of concerns about inadequate end-use monitoring of government-negotiated arms exports.

12. Craig Etcheson, "Punish Thai Military over Khmer Rouge Aid," *The Asian Wall Street Journal Weekly,* June 27, 1994, and "Wimon Promises 'Stricter Controls,'" *The Nation* (Bangkok), December 10, 1993.

13. Philip Shenon, "Cambodia Arms Flow back to Thailand," *New York Times,* March 7, 1993.

14. The EDA bulletin board can be reached by dialing 703-604-6470 on a computer modem. The telephone number, for assistance, is 703-604-6615.

15. See section 506 of the Foreign Assistance Act.

16. The White House, "End-Use Monitoring of Defense Articles, Defense Services and Related Technology," August 18, 1997, p. 2.

17. U.S. Department of State, Bureau for International Narcotics Control and Law Enforcement, "End-Use Monitoring Report," February 1997, p. 12.

18. The Commerce and State Departments cite section 12(c) of the Export Administration Act as blocking the release of information on sales they are licensing, even for items long ago shipped abroad. This section of law states that "information obtained for the purpose of consideration of, or concerning, license applications . . . shall be withheld from public disclosure unless the release of such information is determined by the Secretary to be in the national interest." The provision presumably is intended to safeguard sensitive business information about deals in the works, but why the information would remain proprietary after the sale has been won and the commodities have been shipped is not clear.

19. U.S. Department of State and U.S. Department of Defense, "Foreign Military Assistance Act Report to Congress, Fiscal Year 1996," September 1997.

20. A request under the Freedom of Information Act in 1994 for information on

small arms exports licensed by the State Department during 1980–93 yielded nothing. The State Department claimed that section 12(c) specifically exempted the information from disclosure. (See note 18.)

21. U.S. Department of State, *Defense Trade News,* vol. 5, no. 3 (July/October 1994), p. 6.

22. U.S. Senate Committee on Governmental Affairs, *A Review of Arms Export Licensing,* Senate Hearing 103–670, p. 37.

23. U.S. Department of State, *Defense Trade News,* vol. 5, no. 3 (July/October 1994), pp. 6, 13.

24. See section 38 of the Arms Export Control Act, available from the U.S. Government Printing Office.

25. The White House, "End-Use Monitoring of Defense Articles, Defense Services, and Related Technology," August 18, 1997.

26. The White House, "End-Use Monitoring of Defense Articles, Defense Services, and Related Technology," August 18, 1997, p. 5.

27. A Blue Lantern check found a false order for firearms by the national police in Paraguay. The fraudulent documents misspelled the name of the chief of police and provided an identification number that referred to a traffic accident rather than a purchase order. U.S. Department of State, "Congressional Presentation Document for Foreign Operations for Fiscal Year 1999," p. 1160.

28. U.S. Department of State, Office of Audits, "Review of Department of State Export Controls and Watchlist Process," Memorandum Report 6-CI-023, September 1996, p. 6.

29. U.S. Department of State, Office of Audits, "Review of Department of State Export Controls and Watchlist Process," Memorandum Report 6-CI-023, September 1996, p. 7.

30. U.S. Department of State, Office of Audits, "Review of Department of State Export Controls and Watchlist Process," Memorandum Report 6-CI-023, September 1996.

31. U.S. Department of Commerce, Bureau of Export Administration, *Export Administration Annual Report 1995,* and *1996 Report on Foreign Policy Controls,* March 1996, p. III-8.

32. U.S. Department of Commerce, Bureau of Export Administration, *Export Administration Annual Report 1996* (manuscript copy), January 1997, p. III-9.

33. U.S. Department of Commerce, Bureau of Export Administration, *Export Administration Annual Report 1996* (manuscript copy), January 1997, p. III-7.

34. U.S. Department of Commerce, Bureau of Export Administration, *Export Administration Annual Report 1996* (manuscript copy), January 1997, pp. II-95–111.

35. Chris Smith, "Light Weapons and Ethnic Conflict in South Asia," in Jeffrey Boutwell et al., eds., *Lethal Commerce: The Global Trade in Small Arms and Light Weapons* (Cambridge, Mass.: American Academy of Arts and Sciences, 1995), pp. 62–64.

36. Lucy Mathiak, "Light Weapons and Internal Conflict in Angola," in Boutwell et al., eds., *Lethal Commerce,* pp. 81–97; John Stockwell, *In Search of Enemies* (New York: W. W. Norton, 1978), pp. 265–68.

37. Tim Wiener, "CIA Drafts Covert Plan to Topple Saddam," *New York Times,* February 26, 1998.

38. U.S. Department of the Treasury, Bureau of Alcohol, Tobacco and Firearms, *International Traffic in Arms,* Report to Congress (1993).

39. The M2 is a World War II-era rifle, identical to the M1 used by the Mexican police, except that it has a small selector switch that converts it into a fully automatic weapon.

40. Valerie Alvord, "Illegal Weapons Were Well-Traveled," *San Diego Union Tribune,* March 21, 1997.

41. Valerie Alvord, "Two Truckloads of Illegal Arms Found," *San Diego Union Tribune,* March 14, 1997.

42. Anne-Marie O'Connor and Jeff Leeds, "U.S. Agents Seize Smuggled Arms," *Los Angeles Times,* March 17, 1997. A recent congressional hearing that was focused on the adequacy of the Customs Department's $2.1 billion budget noted that Customs has just 167 people in its investigative unit in Los Angeles, less than half the number in each the New York and Florida branches. Jeff Leeds, "Customs Staffing Disparity Seen to Favor East," *Washington Post,* October 20, 1997.

43. U.S. Department of Justice, Export Control Enforcement Unit, "Significant Export Control Cases," September 5, 1997.

44. As of July 1997, there were 108,591 federally licensed firearms dealers in the United States. Of these, 1,860 were in Arizona, 7,138 in California, 955 in New Mexico, and 7,922 in Texas. According to the Bureau of Alcohol, Tobacco and Firearms, most of the U.S.-origin firearms traced to crimes in Mexico during 1994–97 came from Houston, Tucson, Phoenix, El Paso, and Dallas.

45. U.S. Department of the Treasury, Bureau of Alcohol, Tobacco and Firearms, Firearms Division, "International Traffic in Arms," report to Congress (1991), p. 132.

46. U.S. General Accounting Office, "Small Arms Parts: Poor Controls Invite Widespread Theft," Report GAO/NSIAD-94-21 (1994).

47. U.S. Department of State, "Colombia," Country Reports on Human Rights Practices for 1995 (1996).

48. According to the report, "The U.S. has not sold violent crowd-control devices to Turkey in several years. Arms sales are reviewed on a case by case basis." U.S. Department of State, "U.S. Military Equipment and Human Rights Violations," submitted to Congress on July 1, 1997, p. 3.

49. U.S. Department of State, "U.S. Military Equipment and Human Rights Violations," submitted to Congress on July 1, 1997, p. 6.

5

The European Union and the Light Weapons Trade

Paul Eavis and William Benson

IN RECENT YEARS, the European Union (EU) and its fifteen member states have increasingly been turning their attention toward addressing the problems associated with the widespread proliferation and use of light weapons in conflict-prone regions. Such concerns have largely focused on tackling the illicit trade in light weapons and culminated in June 1997 with EU-wide agreement on the Programme for Preventing and Combating Illicit Trafficking in Conventional Arms. In 1998, during its presidency of the EU, the United Kingdom was successful in securing agreement among EU member states on an EU Code of Conduct on arms exports, and it also began exploring ways of taking the EU Programme forward in Southern Africa.

Background

The EU and its fifteen member states have a significant role to play in both restricting the supply of light weapons and stemming their proliferation in conflict-prone regions. Member states continue to be significant exporters of light weapons, accounting in 1995 for 33 percent of total arms exports compared to 54 percent for the United States and 11 percent for Russia (see table 5.1).

In addition to the light weapons that are exported directly from the EU,

TABLE 5.1
The Major EU Arms Exporters (1995)

Country	Arms Exports ($m)	% EU Exports	% Global Exports
Belgium	130	1.4	0.4
Denmark	20	0.2	0.1
France	2,200	23.1	6.9
Germany	1,200	12.6	3.8
Italy	150	1.6	0.5
Netherlands	230	2.4	0.7
Spain	80	0.8	0.3
Sweden	310	3.3	0.7
United Kingdom	5,200	54.6	16.3

Source: U.S. Arms Control and Disarmament Agency, "World Military Expenditures and Arms Transfers" (Washington, DC: U.S. Arms Control and Disarmament Agency, 1997).

significant further quantities of arms are either smuggled through EU territory or brokered by EU nationals and companies. A recent study into the illicit trade from the EU to sub-Saharan Africa found that the countries most seriously implicated were Belgium, France, and, to a lesser extent, the United Kingdom.[1] The vast majority of allegations relating to Belgium involved Belgian ports and airports being used as transit points or Belgian-based companies and individuals brokering deals. France is alleged to have supplied arms to Rwanda and the former Zaire throughout the 1990s in contravention of the EU and UN arms embargoes. Similarly, arms manufactured in both Britain and France have been seen in use throughout Sudan.

Member states are also well placed to exert influence over the export policies of central and eastern European nations, themselves significant exporters of light weapons. Many of these countries currently hold associate membership in the EU, and full membership should be made contingent on the implementation of more rigorous arms export controls. As a first step, applicant EU member states have announced that they share the objectives set out in the Code and the EU Programme on Preventing and Combating Illicit Weapons.

The vast number of light weapons already in circulation in regions of conflict, however, means that supply-side initiatives to tackle the problem will not be enough on their own. Although it is undoubtedly important to prevent a further influx of weapons into regions of instability and conflict, it is also necessary to look at policies and strategies to reduce the availability and demand for weapons on the ground. As the largest single public donor of humanitarian aid and the second-largest multilateral donor of development assistance, the EU has an important role to play in funding initiatives to remove weapons from society once conflicts have ended through demobilization and reintegration schemes and through the destruction of surplus weapons. Additionally (and while not the focus of this chapter), the EU and its member states have a role to play in addressing the root causes of conflict and insecurity that drive the demand for light weapons in the developing world. Such commitments have been articulated in a series of policy statements by the EU.[2]

Challenges for Control

In reviewing EU export control policies on light weapons, it is important to remember that the EU is essentially a group of fifteen member states, each with its own foreign and security policies. This can make the coordination of export controls difficult. For example, whereas France continued to export arms and provide military assistance to Rwanda in the early 1990s, other countries, such as Germany, imposed a de facto arms embargo on the region. Similarly, while Portugal imposed an arms embargo on the Suharto regime in Indonesia and Sweden refrained from signing new contracts with the regime, other countries, such as the United Kingdom, continued to export arms to Indonesia.

These policy differences are further complicated by differences in the regulatory mechanisms governing the export of light weapons. Different member states apply different controls to different weapons. For example, Finland controls "nonmilitary" firearms (such as single-shot hunting rifles, shotguns, pistols, and revolvers) under a separate legal framework from the bulk of military exports. The capability for sustained fire is the factor determining whether a weapon belongs under military or nonmilitary controls. Similarly, in Italy a specific provision in the law exempts "sport and nonautomatic weapons" from the export licensing process. These items fall under the authority of the police (as opposed to the foreign ministry); the export of such items is therefore subject to less rigorous scrutiny.

These differences are compounded by the absence of a common EU munitions list. Although the Wassenaar Arrangement control lists have been adopted by all EU member states, they do not contain certain important categories of light weapons, such as those set out in PL5001 of the U.K. Military List.[3] This group contains items such as electroshock batons, stun guns, and electric shock dart guns.

End-use certification requirements also vary from state to state. The use of false end-use certificates is not uncommon, and there is little in current certification requirements that would prevent irresponsible end users using arms for proscribed purposes. The "BMARC scandal" that came to light in 1995 (U.K.-supplied naval cannon were found to have been reexported from Singapore to Iran in the late 1980s) is a good example of the fact that current systems of ensuring end use are insufficient and subject to abuse. However, some countries, such as Belgium, Austria, and Italy, do have mechanisms for following up such end-use assurances and verifying the delivery of arms in the recipient country through their embassies and diplomatic services. The majority of EU states, however, continue to rely on written end-use assurances alone.

There are also wide variations in measures taken by EU states to address the problem of arms brokering from their territory. Such problems were highlighted in the United Kingdom, where it emerged in November 1996 that the U.K. firm Mil-Tec brokered the sale of arms from Albania and Israel to the former Rwandan government both before and during the genocide of 1994. Despite the scandal that ensued and an interdepartmental report that called for brokering to be tackled, the issue remains unaddressed in both the United Kingdom and the majority of EU states. The exceptions are Sweden and the Netherlands, which require the licensing of brokers; Italy, where brokering activities are regulated by the police; and Belgium, which is in the process of legislating to curtail the activities of brokers.

Levels of parliamentary transparency in arms exports vary widely among EU member states. Some states, such as Italy and Belgium, have statutory provisions for the reporting of arms exports to national parliaments; others, including the United Kingdom and the Netherlands, have developed customary procedures of providing information to Members of Parliment (or a committee of MPs) on a regular basis. The rest either provide information on an ad hoc basis (e.g., in Finland and Germany information is given in response to parliamentary questions) or have stringent commercial confidentiality provisions that restrict both the level and the detail of information revealed and the audience to whom it is reported. Sweden is unique among EU member states by providing prior notification of arms exports to a parliamentary committee. The Swedish Export Control Council is notified each month, by the government, of proposed arms exports; the members can ask for specific details and, where there are concerns, raise objections to individual exports.

Finally, there are also differences in domestic gun control and ownership laws throughout the EU. For example, in the United Kingdom, the private ownership of all handguns was recently banned, following a massacre of schoolchildren in the town of Dunblane, Scotland (see chapter 6 by Natalie Goldring). Finland, by contrast, has one of the highest ratios of firearms licenses in the world, with 50 percent of households possessing at least one firearm, or one for every four people.

EU Efforts to Address Light Weapons Proliferation

For many years, very little was done to control the export of light weapons as a specific category of weapon. Light weapons, for the most part, traditionally have been addressed within the same policy agenda as other forms of military exports and, as such, have been subject to the same processes of control.

A particular problem for coordinating EU action in this area has been article 223 of the Treaty of Rome, which the EU member states interpret as meaning that policies relating to the production and export of arms and munitions remain within the competence of individual member states. This means that efforts to coordinate policies can take place only at the intergovernment level; the European Commission and the EU Parliament are excluded from the decision-making process.

In June 1991 and 1992, however, member states agreed on eight criteria governing arms exports, among which were the internal and regional situation of the purchasing country, the purchasing country's human rights record, the country's attitude to terrorism, and the effect that the purchase of arms would have on the country's economy. These criteria formed the basis of the EU Code of Conduct, which was agreed to on May 25, 1998 (see below).

In addition, member states have also agreed on common EU arms embargoes. Such embargoes have been imposed on Bosnia Herzegovina, Croatia and the Federal Republic of Yugoslavia (1996), Burma (1991), China (1989), Nigeria (1995), Serbia (1998), Sudan (1994), and the former Zaire (1993).

Aside from these initial efforts to coordinate export controls, the EU has also been involved in removing weapons from societies in developing countries through support for capacity-building programs (such as support for customs and police forces) and demobilization and reintegration programs.

In recent years, however, the issue of light weapons has been moving up the policy agenda among EU member states. In 1997, during its presidency of the EU, the Netherlands secured agreement on the EU Programme for Preventing and Combating Illicit Trafficking in Conventional Arms. Many EU member states are now keen to ensure that this program is implemented. In this regard, a number of EU governments, including the Dutch and the U.K. governments, are interested in supporting a regional moratorium on the import of arms agreed to by states in the Sahara-Sahel. Germany is promoting the issues of postconflict reconstruction and disarmament, as evidenced by its resolution in the UN General Assembly on promoting micro-disarmament,[4] and the Belgian government is interested in light weapons issues, particularly as they relate to postconflict disarmament and sustainable development.

The EU Code of Conduct on the Arms Trade

The idea of a Code was first put forward by a number of nongovernmental organizations (NGOs)[5] in 1994. The aim was to develop and elaborate on eight common criteria that the Council of Ministers agreed to in 1991 and 1992. The objectives of the NGO Code initiative were to promote a common restrictive interpretation of the criteria and to encourage accountability and transparency.

In February 1998, a draft proposal for a Code of Conduct was tabled by the United Kingdom, together with France, and after three months of discussion in the EU working group on arms export issues (COARM), a Code was formally agreed to in June 1998 at the General Affairs Council.

The Code is made up of two parts: (1) guidelines governing arms exports and (2) operative considerations that contain, inter alia, basic procedures for notification and consultation between member states on granting export licenses and provisions for an annual review of the implementation of the Code. The eight criteria of the Code governing arms exports are as follows:

- Respect for the international commitments of the member states, in particular the sanctions decreed by the UN Security Council, agreements on nonproliferation and other subjects, and other international obligations
- Respect of human rights in the country of final destination
- The internal situation in the country of final destination as a function of the existence of tensions or internal armed conflicts
- The preservation of regional peace, security, and stability
- The national security of the member states and of territories whose external relations are the responsibility of an EU member as well as that of friendly and allied countries
- The behavior of the buyer country with regard to the international community, particularly in terms of its attitude to terrorism, the nature of its alliances, and respect for international law
- The existence of a risk that the equipment will be diverted within the buyer country or reexported under undesirable conditions
- The compatibility of the arms exports with the technical and economic capacity of the recipient country, taking into account the desirability that states should achieve their legitimate needs of security and defense with the least diversion for armaments of human and economic resources

While the Code is an important initiative in that it represents a first step toward the development of a common, responsible approach to arms exports by the EU member states, the agreement falls short of the essential standards for an effective Code set out by NGOs, which would allow the Code to meet its stated aims of "setting high common standards in the management of and restraint in conventional arms exports."[6]

The guidelines attempt to clarify circumstances under which licenses should be denied, although they are unlikely to provide for a consistent approach. For example, in a welcome development, the Code states, under the human rights guidelines, that "member states will not issue an export license if there is a clearly identifiable risk that the proposed export might be used for internal repression." Yet, under criterion 6, member states are required only to "take into account" the record of the buyer country with regard to its international commitments, including international humanitarian law applicable to international and noninternational armed conflicts. In other words, member states may still, for strategic reasons, consider authorizing arms transfers despite likely breaches of international humanitarian law even though, under article I of the Geneva Conventions, states have a responsibility to "respect and ensure respect" for international humanitarian law.

As for the notification and consultation mechanisms, member states will have to inform one another when they refuse an export license. If one member state wishes to take up a license that another has turned down, it must consult only with the country that issued the denial. If the member state subsequently wishes to go ahead with granting the license, it must inform only the member state that issued the denial. This is the first time that EU countries will be required to exchange information on arms exports to specific end users, and as such it represents a welcome development. However, if the Code is to facilitate the development of a common approach to arms exports among the member states, full multilateral consultations will be necessary.

Another major weakness of the Code is that it fails to provide any mechanisms for parliamentary and public scrutiny over arms exports, which is necessary for the proper regulation of the arms trade. While the Code requires member states to produce a national annual report on their arms exports, it is stressed that this will take place in confidence. Moreover, while a consolidated report is to be produced by the fifteen, and while nothing in the text of the Code precludes its publication, agreement to do so must be unanimous. It is unlikely that some member states will agree to this. If the aims of transparency and accountability are to be realized, the member states will need to adopt common, rigorous systems of parliamentary scrutiny over their arms exports, including prior notification of sensitive exports to a parliamentary committee (as occurs in Sweden and the United States). The member states should also publish the reports on their national arms exports as well as the consolidated report on the implementation of the Code.

The Code's operative provisions also state that "EU member states will work for the early adoption of a common list of military equipment covered by the Code, based on similar national and international lists." As of September 1998, the Austrian government was reportedly developing such a common list. Until this process is completed, national lists will form the basis of denial notification and consultation, "incorporating, where appropriate, elements from relevant international lists." Utilization of national and international lists for any length of time could lead to a gap in the application of controls on the part of some member states. The member states should, moreover, ensure that the agreed-to EU Code control list contains (1) all types of major conventional weaponry, all types of small arms and light weapons, police and paramilitary equipment, and military and paramilitary training equipment and services and (2) a list of prohibited equipment—such as antipersonnel mines, death penalty equipment, leg irons, electroshock equipment, and so on—whose sole or primary practical use results in serious abuses, such as breaches of humanitarian law and international human rights standards.

Further measures are also needed if the effectiveness of the Code is not to be undermined. Despite concerted pressure from the nongovernment sector, the EU Code contains no reference to the need to control the activities of arms-brokering agents; the need to control licensed production of military, paramilitary, and security equipment; or the need for common EU controls governing end use. The absence of even a reference to these issues is a major disappointment. The member states should, therefore, seek to address these omissions at the earliest opportunity by agreeing to common strict EU controls on the activities of international arms-brokering agents, on end-use certification and monitoring, and on licensed production.

Finally, it is disappointing that the member states have agreed to adopt the Code only as a council declaration (under the Common Foreign and Security Policy of the EU). This means that the Code will be politically but not juridicially binding. This raises some important questions as to the effectiveness of the implementation of the Code in view of the fact that a politically binding agreement was insufficient to ensure a common approach among the member states under the eight common criteria on arms exports agreed to by the Council of Ministers in 1991 and 1992.

Stemming the Illicit Trade in Light Weapons

Moves to address legal exports alone, of course, will not be sufficient, as a large proportion of European arms exported to regions of tension are either reexported in breach of end-use assurances or brokered or trafficked by individuals and companies based within the EU or by EU nationals without actually touching European soil,[7] thus the importance of the EU Programme for Preventing and Combating Illicit Trafficking in Conventional Arms. Although the initiative focuses solely on the "illicit trade" and addresses trafficking of *all* types of conventional weaponry, it has particular relevance for the trafficking of light weapons.

The Programme combines measures to combat the illicit trafficking of arms through EU member states with demand-side measures, such as providing for assistance toward building local capacity and in removing arms from society. While the EU Programme has given an important indication of the EU's willingness to address the problems caused by the widespread availability of light weapons, there is now a clear need for the further development and implementation of the agreement.

In terms of tackling the illicit supply of weapons from the EU, the Programme urges enhanced cooperation and coordination among intelligence, customs, and other law enforcement agencies and calls on member states to improve the exchange of information and data on arms trafficking. To this end, the U.K. government hosted a meeting of customs and intelligence officials in February 1998 that sought to highlight areas for potential cooperation and to develop best practice in combating illicit trafficking.

Similarly, in 1997 the Belgian government set up an interministerial coordinating committee for combating illicit weapons transfers. The aim of the committee is to provide for structured coordination between government departments and to improve information flows. A similar initiative is also being explored in the Netherlands.

In order to tackle the illicit trade, it is important that EU member states act to control the activities of arms-brokering agents. As mentioned above, the issue of brokering remains unaddressed in a number of EU states. As part of a coordinated program to close down "gray market" trading networks, EU members should enhance cooperation on policing and regulating the activities of arms brokers. Such measures could include a compulsory registration system for arms traders, as is the case in Sweden.

Finally, the traceability of light weapons should also be improved. At present, there is no coherent system that enables identifying the source of arms confiscated or found in embargoed regions, thus reducing the ability to identify and address failures of control systems. In November 1997, the Organization of American States agreed to a convention that provides for measures to "tag" weapons both at the point of production and when they are imported into member states. A similar system could be implemented in the EU. Technologies now exist to tag weapons and ammunition cheaply and in a way that is hard to remove or tamper with, and the implementation of such a system, if complemented by a database, would allow for the exchange of information between national authorities when needed.

Capacity Building and Removing Weapons from Society

The EU Programme also identifies a number of areas where coordinated EU action could actively reduce the number of weapons in circulation or reduce the demand for light weapons.

First, the EU (and EU member states) have a role to play in building the capacity of "recipient" states to inhibit and reduce flows of light weapons within and across their territories. Such measures could include training and resources to strengthen customs and border controls and expertise to help ensure the secure collection and destruction of "surplus" or confiscated arms and ammunition. Some EU states are already pursuing such programs. The United Kingdom has been involved in training the police in Ethiopia, and the Netherlands contributed to the UN Development Programme (UNDP) activities in Mali. Elsewhere, other EU member states have been involved in broader capacity-building projects. Austria, for example, has contributed to improving the judiciaries of developing countries. Despite such individual action, however, coordination and concerted action across the EU remain rudimentary.

Similarly, because light weapons flows are regional phenomena, they cannot be effectively tackled at a national level alone; little can be done while neighboring states promote or ignore destabilizing activities (such as light weapons trafficking). Coordinated action at the subregional level is therefore needed. While this is widely accepted in principle, it is difficult to effect in practice. The EU (and EU member states) should aid in the development of subregional institutions and structures through the provision of resources (technical and capital) and expertise. To this end, in May 1988 the U.K. government sponsored a conference in South Africa with a view to exploring, with EU and regional governments, ways and means of implementing the EU Programme in southern Africa. The conference developed the southern Africa regional Action Programme on Light Arms and Illicit Arms Trafficking to tackle the proliferation and trafficking of light weapons. The plan included elements to strengthen regulations and controls on accumulations and transfers of arms, to promote the removal and destruction of surplus arms from society, and to enhance transparency, information exchange, and regional consultation.

The EU Programme also urges member states to "promote the integration of former combatants into civilian life." Indeed, this is one area where both the EU Commission and EU member states have been actively involved in the general process of peace building. The EU has supported demobilization and reintegration programs (DRPs) in a number of countries, including Eritrea, Ethiopia, and Uganda.[8] In Uganda, the EU and its member states funded 63 percent of the total costs of the demobilization program; in Eritrea, the EU and its members funded 80 percent of the external assistance granted for the reintegration of former combatants. These programs are often implemented through NGOs working on the ground, as in Rwanda and Ethiopia, where efforts to demobilize child combatants and reintegrate former combatants into civil society have been undertaken in coordination with the Save the Children Fund and Oxfam, respectively.

As noted by Nat Colletta in chapter 13, reducing the size and political power of the armed forces in developing countries can substantially increase economic and political stability, reduce the risks of the recurrence of armed conflict, and enhance a country's long-term development prospects. However, despite the fact that EU member states are contributing to such schemes, there are considerable problems in the provision of such assistance: much of the aid that is disbursed is short term, when effective reintegration of former combatants requires sustained support. Additionally, aid is often ill coordinated with other bilateral or multilateral donors and is often subject to delays. The DRPs could, therefore, be better coordinated with other national and multilateral donors and could be more coherent with other instruments of foreign policy. In order to demonstrate the dividends of peace to demobilized soldiers, DRPs could also emphasize the creation of training and employment.

Finally, the EU Programme acknowledges that EU states have a role to play in assisting "recipient" states in removing destabilizing accumulations of weapons from societies. Accordingly, the EU could press for disarmament to be included in all UN mandates to ensure that surplus weapons (including light weapons) are "mopped up" after periods of conflict or instability. The EU member states could also assist in what the UN secretary-general referred to as "micro-disarmament initiatives," such as buy-back, turn-in, or exchange schemes.

Conclusion

Two broad conclusions can be drawn from an examination of EU policies toward tackling light weapons proliferation. First, despite recent initiatives, such as the EU Code and the EU Programme for Preventing and Combating Illicit Trafficking in Conventional Arms, relatively little has been done in practice to specifically target and prevent the export (both legal and illicit) of light weapons from the EU. Measures that do focus on light weapons tend to do so predominantly within a "domestic gun control context."

Second, while member states have supported DRPs, there has been a marked reluctance on the part of EU member states and the European Commission to use development assistance for security purposes, such as support for the police and security forces. While a few states have provided assistance for disarmament or buy-back schemes or have contributed toward building the capacity of institutions on the ground, such efforts are by no means uniform throughout the EU. Since countries with high levels of insecurity or violence cannot make effective use of economic or social development assistance, it is important that the EU and its member states incorporate a "security first" approach into development assistance programs.

The EU Programme is reviewed on an annual basis. It is important that EU member states agree on a clear set of principles in this area as soon as possible and embark on a program of identifying and overcoming institutional obstacles to implementing them within the Commission, EU member states, and international aid institutions of which EU states are members.

Notes

1. Saferworld, *Undermining Development: The European Arms Trade with the Horn of Africa and Central Africa* (London: Saferworld, February 1998).

2. The 1996 Commission communication "EU and the Issues of Conflict in

Africa: Peacebuilding, Conflict Prevention and Beyond" (sec. [96] 332) states that development assistance should seek to foster "structural stability," described as a situation "involving respect for human rights, viable political structures, and healthy social and environmental conditions, with the capacity to manage change without resort to violent conflict." The Resolution of the Council on Coherence (June 1997; 8631/97) also recognized that development assistance, if targeted at the root causes, can make an important contribution to the prevention of violent conflict. Further details are provided in Saferworld/Oxfam, *Partnership 2000: The Future of EU-ACP Relations and Conflict Prevention* (London: Saferworld/Oxfam, September 1997).

3. Contained in the U.K. Export of Goods (Control) Order (London: HMSO); see Paul Eavis, "EC Regulation," in DELTAC, *Worldwide Guide to Export Controls*, 1996–97 edition, February 1997 update (London: Export Control Publications, 1997).

4. *Consolidation of Peace through Practical Disarmament Measures*, A/C.1/51/L.38, October 30, 1996 (New York: United Nations).

5. The Code was developed by Saferworld, BASIC, and the World Development Movement and is supported by more than 600 NGOs across Europe.

6. See also *Proposals for an Effective EU Code of Conduct on the Arms Trade* (London: Saferworld, BASIC, Oxfam, and Amnesty International, 1998).

7. Saferworld, *Undermining Development: The European Arms Trade with the Horn of Africa and Central Africa* (London: Saferworld, February 1998).

8. For a further discussion of the issues involved, see *Demilitarisation, Reintegration and Conflict Prevention in the Horn of Africa* (London: Saferworld, May 1998).

6

Domestic Laws and International Controls

Natalie J. Goldring

ALTHOUGH LARGELY NEGLECTED by analysts and policymakers until quite recently, light weapons proliferation is a pervasive and continuing problem. Light weapons have probably been used for most of the recent killing in conflicts, despite the regular involvement of both light and major conventional weapons.[1]

This chapter addresses one aspect of the light weapons problem, presenting the preliminary results of a project to develop strategies that would overcome domestic obstacles to the control of light weapons.[2] It demonstrates that it will be difficult, if not impossible, to control the illicit international market in light weapons without monitoring and controlling domestic access to weapons. In the United States, for example, two key obstacles to light weapons control are the government's failure to enforce controls on light weapons transfers (for more on this issue, see chapter 4 by Lora Lumpe) and the activities of "pro-gun" groups, such as the National Rifle Association (NRA).

The first section of the chapter discusses issues related to the domestic control of light weapons. The focus is on domestic issues in the United States, supplemented with brief overviews of recent initiatives on domestic gun control in the United Kingdom and Australia. The section provides several examples of how the U.S. government has helped create the problems it now faces (such as armed drug lords) through inadequate controls on light weapons transfers.

To have effective international controls, it will be important to enforce existing laws governing the sales of weapons and to provide sufficient resources to control national borders. It will also be important for the United States to work with other governments on efforts that recognize and deal with the interrelationship between drug trafficking and gun trafficking.

The second section provides a brief update on recent international efforts regarding light weapons. It summarizes the results to date of three UN efforts focused on small arms and light weapons: the UN Disarmament Commission's work on illicit transfers, the UN Economic and Social Council's (ECOSOC) study on firearms regulations, and the UN Panel of Governmental Experts on Small Arms. It also provides information on the 1997 Organization of American States (OAS) convention on illicit weapons.

The third section focuses on the ways in which pro-gun organizations such as the NRA have actively opposed controls on light weapons and small arms while arguing disingenuously that they oppose illegal weapons transfers. The NRA in particular is devoting extensive resources to opposing international controls in addition to its traditional campaigns to block domestic gun measures, be they safety measures or actual controls on weapons purchases.

The fourth section presents preliminary policy options, including prospects for increasing transparency or access to information, improving oversight, and strengthening measures to actually control light weapons. Long-term success in linking domestic and international control will likely depend on developing a new norm that supports limitations on the production, sale, and transfer of light weapons. But just as the absence of domestic controls will tend to undermine international restraint efforts, the presence of domestic controls may increase the likelihood of successful international restraint efforts.

Domestic Control of Small Arms and Light Weapons

National laws governing small arms and light weapons vary widely from country to country. For example, while the United Kingdom and Australia have recently taken significant gun control initiatives, the same weapons are still widely available in many other countries, such as the United States. This section provides a brief update on recent changes in gun laws in the United Kingdom and Australia but concentrates on U.S. gun laws. This is not because U.S. laws are typical but because U.S. weapons production and weapons exports constitute such a major part of the world weapons market.

Increased Domestic Control in the United Kingdom

Two recent laws have significantly increased domestic control of small arms and light weapons in the United Kingdom. Together, these two laws have banned private ownership of handguns. The first law, sponsored by the Conservative government of John Major in February 1997, banned the private possession of handguns greater than .22 caliber. This law was spurred in large part by the massacre in Dunblane, Scotland, in March 1996 in which sixteen children and one teacher were killed in just a few minutes by a lone gunman.

The February 1997 law affected some 80 percent of handguns in the United Kingdom. It required that .22-caliber handguns be stored in gun clubs and provided stricter standards for firearms ownership certification. Owners of prohibited weapons were required to hand them in by October 1, 1997. Virtually all of the weapons turned in as a result of the February law will reportedly be destroyed. According to a press account in the *Daily Telegraph,* "Nothing will be excepted from destruction apart from Glock 17s, which the police use themselves, and any items of historic interest."[3] As noted by Alun Michael, minister of state, Home Department, "The vast majority of these firearms are being destroyed under local arrangements in each police force area once the claimant has received compensation from the Home Office Firearms Compensation Section. Some forces have begun destroying firearms where the related claim has already been met, though no central record of actual destruction is being kept. None of the surrendered firearms will be sold either within the United Kingdom or abroad. A small minority of firearms may be retained by police forces for training purposes and some by museums for public display."[4]

Following his election in May 1997, Prime Minister Tony Blair reiterated his government's support for a total ban on handguns, and indeed such a ban was passed both by the House of Commons and the House of Lords and received royal assent on November 27, 1997.[5] In addition to banning all handguns not included in previous versions of the legislation, the bill revoked the right of gun owners to keep their guns on club premises. As of September 1998, more than 160,000 weapons had been turned in under the new firearms laws.[6]

The estimated cost of implementing the two laws is £166 million. While the handover of illegal weapons appears to have proceeded fairly smoothly, the compensation scheme has been controversial, with one lawsuit arguing that there have been unreasonable delays in compensating gun owners.[7] As of mid-February 1998, the government estimated delays at nearly six months.[8] By August 1998, the government did not expect all claims to be settled until 1999.[9]

Increased Domestic Control in Australia

In April 1996, just six weeks after the Dunblane massacre in Scotland, another lone gunman killed more than thirty-five people in Port Arthur, Australia. The next month, Australian state and territory police ministers held a special meeting and reached agreement on a nationwide program to ban semiautomatic and pump action firearms and to implement a buy-back program for the prohibited weapons.[10] Their intent was to create uniform national laws in contrast to the diverse laws in effect in the states and territories at the time.

The new laws are quite far reaching. They include bans on several types of rifles and shotguns, the introduction of comprehensive registration systems for all firearms, implementation of required permits and a twenty-eight-day waiting period for firearms purchases, safety training and storage requirements, and compensation and amnesty arrangements.[11] Some individual states are now trying to weaken these laws; the twenty-eight-day waiting period is under special pressure. Prime Minister John Howard remains committed to the uniform laws, however, and according to a press account, he "guaranteed" they would remain in force.[12]

A key part of the implementation of the new laws is a gun buy-back and amnesty program to collect weapons prohibited as the result of the new legislation. For much of the Commonwealth this program was in operation for twelve months, ending September 30, 1997 (it ended earlier in South Australia).[13] By the end of the buy-back period, more than 640,000 weapons had been handed in and destroyed.[14] Total compensation is estimated at $A300 million. As an incentive to participate, gun owners were given 110 percent of the fair market value of their weapons.[15] Controversy continues over the extent to which business owners will be compensated for losses resulting from the new laws.[16]

The government set a useful precedent in requiring that all weapons collected from the buy-back be destroyed. The only exceptions are weapons of particular historical interest, which may be purchased by museums, and non-military-style weapons, which can be consigned to dealers for overseas sale. In the latter case, however, if the weapons are not sold within one year, they must be returned to the buy-back program and destroyed.

U.S. Legislation Governing Light Weapons

In the United States, a few key laws contain the main provisions affecting light weapons: the Gun Control Act of 1968, the National Firearms Act of 1934, and the Arms Export Control Act of 1976. Authority for dealing with light weapons issues is often divided among different departments and agencies. For example, the Treasury Department's Bureau of Alcohol, Tobacco and Firearms (BATF) deals with the import provisions of the Arms Export Control Act, while the Department of State is in charge of the export control provisions.

The BATF's activities are constrained both by resources and by law. The BATF does not have design approval, standard setting, or recall regulatory powers. According to the Violence Policy Center, "America's gun manufacturers have near carte blanche to manufacture virtually any product they wish. As long as the firearm is not fully automatic, uses ammunition that is .50 caliber or less and has a barrel of a set minimum length, there are no federal restrictions."[17]

As of January 1998, there were roughly 5,000 licensed firearms dealers in California alone.[18] With limited numbers of BATF agents—reportedly just sixty-five in all of southern California, for example—enforcement is challenging at best. In addition, licensed firearms dealers are only subject to a surprise inspection once per year, and BATF agents go to gun shows only when they are investigating a specific case.[19] This further restricts BATF's enforcement capabilities.

Despite these huge obstacles to effective enforcement, BATF's task has become somewhat easier as a result of the passage of the Violent Crime Control and Law Enforcement Act of 1994. This act significantly increased the cost for a federal firearms license and set more rigorous standards for license applicants. Since the passage of this law, the number of licensed firearms dealers in the United States has dropped from roughly 250,000 to fewer than 100,000.

Potential Enhancements to U.S. Legislation

Legislation introduced in the 105th and 106th Congresses has taken a variety of approaches to enhancing gun control. Some legislation would extend state laws to the national level, other bills focus on public safety issues related to weapons, and still others are specifically designed to close loopholes in existing law. Two key types of bills are the proposed "one-gun-a-month" laws and the proposed bans on domestic production of weapons that do not meet the standards for imported weapons (such weapons are sometimes referred to as "junk guns" or "Saturday night specials").

The NRA has opposed both types of bills, claiming they violate Americans' Second Amendment rights to bear firearms. In addition, the NRA claims that opponents of junk guns are denying Americans affordable weapons for self-defense, challenging the technical assessments of junk guns as being of low quality. As noted below, the NRA's opposition to these two bills exemplifies the contradiction between the NRA's consistent policy positions in opposition to gun control and its claim that it actively opposes illicit weapons transfers.

The one-gun-a-month bills would strengthen restrictions on weapons purchases by extending provisions currently in effect in several states to the national level. This would establish a national policy of preventing purchasers from buying more than one gun per month. Designed to prevent gunrunners from purchasing multiple weapons in states with lax gun laws and then transporting them and reselling them on the black market in states with more restrictive gun laws, the law would reduce the monetary incentive for domestic gun trafficking and make international gunrunning less viable.

Although a few states have enacted one-gun-a-month laws, a national limit is needed to make the controls effective. Otherwise, prospective gunrunners can simply arrange to make their purchases in neighboring states. According to Senator Frank Lautenberg (D-NJ), one of the main sponsors of one-gun-a-month legislation, "A one-gun-a-month law would take a bite out of gun-running without imposing any burden on hunters and other law-abiding gun users. After all, who but gang members, drug dealers, and other criminals needs more than 12 guns a year?"[20] A recent study showed the importance of national limits, finding that roughly 25 percent of all guns acquired outside the state where they were used in crime came from just four states: Florida, Georgia, South Carolina, and Texas.[21]

Public safety issues are addressed by the proposed American Handgun Standards Act, S. 193. This bill would ban domestic manufacture of all U.S.-made handguns where the same type of weapon is prohibited for import (because they do not meet minimum safety standards for weapons size, design, and performance).[22]

Saturday Night Specials are low-quality handguns whose barrels measure less than three inches. The overall length of pistols is less than six inches). A "junk gun" is a handgun lacking essential safety features. Both are produced by six manufacturers in southern California, the "Ring of Fire" producers.[23] According to news reports, by 1993 these companies produced eight out of the ten types of handguns that were most frequently confiscated in California. In addition, few of their weapons would meet the criteria for import into the United States. Every weapon made by two of the companies would fail to do so, as would nearly every weapon from three of the others. In 1992, these companies produced nearly 700,000 handguns, or roughly one-third of all handguns manufactured in the United States that year.[24]

According to the Senate bill, "The disparate treatment of imported handguns and domestically produced handguns has led to the creation of a high-volume market for junk guns, defined as those handguns that fail to meet the quality and safety standards required of imported handguns."[25] According to Handgun Control, Inc., "Whatever name is attached to them, these handguns are not useful for sport or self-defense because their short barrels make them inaccurate and their low quality of construction make them dangerous and unreliable. They are, however, favored by criminals because of their low cost and easy concealability."[26]

Difficulty in Enforcing Existing U.S. Laws

Several vignettes regarding U.S. weaponry highlight the difficulty of ensuring adequate controls over light weapons. These problems seem to stem from both insufficient political will and inadequate financial resources. These vignettes focus on the United States because the magnitude of such problems seems to be greater with respect to U.S. weapons.

One major problem is the failure to verify that weapons reach the intended recipients. Between 1989 and 1993, the Department of State's Office of Defense Trade Controls verified end-user certificates for only 21 of 1,632 applications for small arms transfers to eight Latin American countries.[27]

Another significant problem is lax border controls. According to Brazilian diplomats, in one set of drug raids in Brazil, officials captured one hundred weapons that originated in the United States. Of these, one weapon had been transferred legally, and the other ninety-nine had been transferred illegally.[28] In a September 1996 article, Justice Minister Nelson Jobim said, "In the international arena, one of the serious problems that we have to confront is that of the smuggling of heavy weapons from the United States, especially the AR-15 rifle, either through triangle operations through countries bordering Brazil, or directly through sea or air routes, especially those originating with Miami."[29]

Mexican officials have long maintained that thousands of U.S.-made weapons flow south each year.[30] According to the Mexican federal attorney general's office, in 1994 the Mexican police seized more than 16,000 pistols and 6,000 machine guns, rifles, and shotguns, the majority of them manufactured in the United States.[31] While Mexico maintains strict laws on gun ownership, lax U.S. regulations have made cross-border gunrunning profitable. The existence of 6,000 legal gun shops in the four states bordering Mexico is also of concern to Mexican officials.[32] While at first the United States appeared to ignore Mexico's requests for increased U.S. border control, a U.S.-Mexico declaration on drug trafficking issued during President Bill Clinton's visit to Mexico in May 1997 included a provision to increase cooperation to curb cross-border firearms trafficking.[33]

The interrelationship between drug trafficking and gunrunning also makes it difficult to ensure adequate controls over small arms and light weapons. The report from the Mexican federal attorney general's office cited above provided evidence that guns and drugs frequently follow the same transportation routes, with guns going south while the drugs go north.[34] According to the Mexican ambassador to the United States, Jesus Silva-Herzog, "Our preliminary information is that most of the illegal gun trafficking from the U.S. goes to narcotics traffickers."[35] This interrelationship is also shown by the places in which guns are priced in terms of kilos of cocaine. In an article on the drugs/guns connection in Mexico, a Clinton administration official blamed lax U.S. laws rather than weak enforcement, saying, "Since the United States doesn't have very tight gun control laws, there is only a limited amount of things we can do."[36]

In Colombia, according to data from the Judicial and Investigative Police Directorate, more than 15,000 weapons were seized in operations during the first six months of 1997. An estimated 80 percent of these weapons were made in the United States.[37] There, too, the interaction between drugs and guns is strong. National Police Director General Rosse Jose Serrano said, "It is a mixture of guerrillas and drug traffickers; no longer is there a difference. One does not know if the drug trafficker is a guerrilla or if the guerrilla is a drug trafficker. The line is blurred now; it is a brotherhood community."[38]

In addition to the weapons flows resulting from inadequate enforcement of existing laws, "leftover" weapons also pose significant problems. For example, the United States left an estimated 1.8 million small arms in Vietnam, including nearly 800,000 M16 rifles, more than 850,000 other rifles, and 90,000 .45-caliber pistols. The U.S. military left roughly 300,000 additional small arms in Cambodia, including more than 150,000 M16A1 rifles and more than 100,000 other rifles.[39] These weapons are now recirculating around the world. A major weapons seizure in California in the spring of 1997 reportedly consisted of weapons parts initially shipped from U.S. stockpiles left in Vietnam.[40] The capture included parts for M2 carbines, M79 grenade launchers, and M16 rifles.[41]

International Efforts to Deal with Light Weapons

Ironically, the attention of gun groups to international initiatives dealing with light weapons issues has brought international attention to panels whose work normally would garner little notice. The brief summary provided here (for more detail, see chapter 9 by Graciela Uribe de Lozano) gives the context for discussion of domestic initiatives and policy options.

Arguably, the most significant international efforts dealing with light weapons have taken place under UN auspices. In addition to discussions about light weapons in the 1994 and 1997 expert reviews of the UN Register of Conventional Arms, important work on light weapons has been taking place within three key venues: the UN Disarmament Commission, the ECOSOC Commission on Crime Prevention and Criminal Justice, and the Panel of Governmental Experts on Small Arms.[42] Key regional efforts, such as those of the OAS, are also moving forward.

Each of these groups has reached consensus on important principles that are likely to aid efforts to control the international trade in light weapons. Perhaps most important, they have been willing to set standards, such as including in all UN peacekeeping missions a mandate to destroy weapons that remain when conflicts end. They have also agreed on ways to improve national and regional controls on small arms and light weapons, such as improving the monitoring of customs regulations and border controls. They have not been as successful in increasing access to information on light weapons transfers at the regional and global levels. Nonetheless, their work has advanced the issue considerably and provides many useful precedents for future action.

The first effort was in the UN Disarmament Commission, which adopted guidelines for international arms transfers in the spring of 1996 that focused mainly on the illicit trade. They recommended that states institute a variety of national measures to combat illicit trafficking, including strengthening national laws and regulations, establishing effective import and export licensing procedures, providing adequate numbers of customs officials, and defining which weapons are legal for civilians and which can be held by military personnel. International initiatives outlined by the Disarmament Commission included establishing verifiable end-user certificates, cooperating on border control and law enforcement, complying with UN arms embargoes, developing common legislative and administrative import and export controls, and participating in the UN Register of Conventional Arms.[43]

A second effort is taking place through the ECOSOC Commission on Crime Prevention and Criminal Justice. At its May 1997 meeting in Vienna, the Commission adopted a resolution on "firearm regulation for the purpose of crime prevention and public safety." The resolution recommended continued UN data collection and dissemination on firearms regulation and urged member states to institute a variety of measures, including regulating firearm safety, licensing firearm businesses, and marking firearms at the point of manufacture and import.[44] The U.S.-based NRA submitted a statement declaring that the conclusions of the firearms survey were "incomplete and inconclusive" and that "its conclusions are not supported and its recommendations are not warranted at this time."[45] This statement was never introduced as a formal resolution, indicating that the NRA was unable to convince even a single country to support its position.[46] In April 1998, the Commission agreed to develop an international instrument to combat illicit manufacturing and trafficking in firearms, firearms parts and components, and ammunition, largely through improved methods of identification and tracing.[47]

The third effort is that of the UN Panel of Governmental Experts on Small Arms with a mandate covering the types of small arms and light weapons being used in conflicts being dealt with by the United Nations, the nature and causes of excessive and destabilizing transfers of small arms and light weapons, and ways and means to prevent and reduce excessive and destabilizing accumulations.[48] The panel's report emphasized destroying surplus weapons and weapons remaining after conflicts end, including halting the practice of storing surplus weapons in poorly guarded warehouses.

In particular, the report recommended that all peacekeeping missions include a mandate to destroy weapons remaining when conflicts end. The panel also endorsed improving border controls and training for customs officials, continuing and expanding regional buy-back programs, studying problems associated with ammunition, and evaluating the feasibility of marking weapons at the time of manufacture and restricting manufacture and sales of small arms and light weapons to government-authorized manufacturers and dealers. There was significant emphasis in the small arms panel's report on controlling illicit weapons transfers. The panel's effort was endorsed by the UN General Assembly, which also authorized the UN secretary-general to initiate a study of issues related to ammunition, consider an international conference on the illicit weapons trade, and establish another group of government experts in 1998 to report on the implementation of the panel's recommendations and to present supplemental recommendations. In 1998–99, the Group of Governmental Experts on Small Arms (renamed from the previous Panel of Governmental Experts) is holding a series of plenary meetings and regional workshops and is expected to submit its report to the secretary-general in August 1999.[49]

At the regional level, the OAS has been setting a strong example with its Inter-American Convention Against the Illicit Manufacturing of and Trafficking in Firearms, Ammunition, Explosives and Other Related Materials, signed in Washington, D.C., on November 14, 1997. Signatories to the OAS convention will be required to mark weapons at the time of manufacture and import and will have to tighten border controls to prevent illicit transfers. The convention also emphasizes the importance of information sharing and communication and prevents exporting states from authorizing the transfer of firearms until the recipient state issues an import license. State parties must share information collected and are encouraged to cooperate fully on all technical and legal matters.[50]

Although many of these provisions are significant, the convention does not seek uniform domestic legislation. The preamble even makes specific reference to national sovereignty, and the agreement itself avoids any reference to a national registry of gun owners, even though earlier drafts required states to establish domestic registries.[51] Much of this omission can be attributed to pressure from the NRA as well as the reluctance of the Clinton administration to change U.S. domestic gun legislation; a central registry of gun owners would be illegal according to current U.S. law.[52] Other U.S. laws could also interfere with implementation of the convention since enforcement is on a government-to-government level. If other governments inquire about licenses issued in the United States, they may be unable to obtain the information; current U.S. law protects proprietary information contained in State and Commerce Department licenses. In addition, as noted above, weak U.S. laws still allow "straw purchases" in most states, facilitating gunrunning.

The Role of Pro-Gun Organizations

The gun industry's apprehension regarding new initiatives on light weapons stems from the fact that an increased recognition of the significant relationship between domestic and international flows of such weapons will increase the pressure for domestic gun control. In response to recent efforts at international light weapons control, the gun organizations have taken two sets of steps: they have worked toward strengthening their own international links, and they have directly attacked both proposals for light weapons control and the organizations sponsoring those proposals.

Past Efforts to Strengthen International Gun Connections

Although there has been significant press attention to the World Forum on the Future of Sport Shooting Activities, which held its first general meeting in Nuremberg, Germany, on March 13, 1997, such international efforts are not new. In 1992, a representative of the Sporting Shooters Association of Australia addressed the NRA at its annual board meeting, seeking its help with setting up a world conference dealing with firearms laws "with the primary objective of protecting the rights of firearms owners wherever they are threatened." According to press reports, the NRA board endorsed the proposal for such a conference. As a result, the International Conference on Firearms Legislation (ICFL) was established.[53] Its first meeting took place in August 1993 in Australia and included twelve representatives from groups in the United States, Canada, South Africa, New Zealand, and Australia.[54] The group continued to meet during the early to mid-1990s in locations as diverse as Australia, the United States, and South Africa, although only limited information is available about their gatherings.

The World Forum on the Future of Sport Shooting Activities

The March 1997 meeting of gun organizations and firearms manufacturers from twelve countries in Nuremberg established a new international organization, the World Forum on the Future of Sport Shooting Activities. The registered office for the World Forum is in Brussels, Belgium, and its secretariat is based in Rome. Its founding members include the NRA and the Sporting Arms and Ammunition Manufacturers Institute (SAAMI), which is based in Connecticut.[55] The NRA is widely known, but SAAMI is not, even though it is a highly influential organization. SAAMI sets standards for the manufacture of both sporting weapons and ammunition. While these standards are voluntary, an estimated 90 percent of all U.S. firearms and ammunition producers adhere to its standards.[56]

Few details are available concerning this new organization; gun organization representatives refused to provide information about scheduled meetings or organizational plans. In fact, one NRA representative, Oregon lawyer Thomas Mason, cited lawyer-client privilege in refusing to answer inquiries. This is ironic, given Mason's repeated criticism of the UN small arms panel and other UN bodies for not holding open meetings and not inviting pro-gun organizations to brief these groups.

According to a news release from the Sporting Shooters Association of Australia (SSAA), "The Forum will facilitate the exchange of information, the reaching of consensus positions and actions by the member associations or the Forum itself in those situations which warrant it."[57] The SSAA also said that the group would "receive at regular intervals representatives from all over the world who are active in target shooting, hunting and firearms collection, to discuss subjects of common interest and in particular regulatory efforts currently harming sports shooting."[58]

According to *Gun News Digest,* by June 1997 the coalition had twenty-one participating organizations.[59] The U.S. contingent is apparently the largest, with at least six groups; other groups were generally from countries with significant gun industries, including Belgium, France, Germany, Italy, the Netherlands, and the United Kingdom.[60] The World Forum will "work jointly to establish a presence during discussions of global gun control to insure that correct and unbiased information is available to international decision makers."[61] A one-paragraph NRA account of the group's June 26, 1997, meeting in Brussels indicated that the World Forum is expected to apply for nongovernmental organization (NGO) status at the United Nations and stated that "among the many challenges the Forum now faces are efforts by the United Nations to promote international gun control schemes as well as proposed gun bans that could put an end to the shooting sports in several nations."[62] The group's existence and activities remain under wraps despite a pledge that "adhering to the principles of openness and inclusiveness, the Forum will offer its cooperation, solutions and alternatives to various decision-making authorities."[63]

In March 1998, World Forum members again met in Nuremberg on the anniversary of the Dunblane massacre. According to a press release from this meeting, the World Forum now has more than two dozen members. An indication of the gun groups' attention to international issues is that one of the World Forum's four subcommittees will deal with "UN and Legislative Issues."[64] Press reports are unclear about the scope of the effort and the nature of sponsorship of the World Forum organization. According to one report, the annual budget of the group will be $200,000.[65] This budget seems low for a group that has already held two large international meetings and is setting up international operations. The budget is far less than the NRA has reportedly earmarked for its anti–gun control activities at the United Nations. Even if this seemingly low figure is correct, this budget would almost certainly need to be supplemented by in-kind contributions from the group's members.

The NRA: Taking the Lead in Attacking International Efforts at Light Weapons Control

A significant recent activity of gun groups has been attacking international efforts at light weapons control. The gun groups seem to be quite concerned about all three UN efforts described in the previous section of this chapter, though their activities related to the UN small arms panel have received the most notice in the press. The NRA has generally led the gun groups' attack, regularly writing on the theme of "global gun grabbers."[66]

When the UN small arms panel published its report in the summer of 1997, the NRA publicized its results widely, citing certain provisions as particularly troublesome. These include the panel's support for destroying small arms left over when conflicts end, exploring the marking of firearms at the time of manufacture, and studying the possibility of restricting the production and trade of small arms to manufacturers and dealers. According to the NRA, "This panel's recommendations provide an alarming example of what international gun control bureaucrats at the UN want to pursue."[67]

Publications of the NRA frequently emphasize the possibility that UN efforts to control light weapons could strengthen national gun control efforts in the United States. For example, a January 1997 paper that NRA representatives tried to present to the UN small arms panel stated, "One view, with which we clearly do not agree, is that the availability of firearms in one jurisdiction affects other jurisdictions."[68] The NRA's approach is simply to suggest that the views of other countries or organizations are irrelevant to U.S. policy. At the ECOSOC firearms' panel meeting in Tanzania in November 1997, for example, the NRA representative repeated his message that, "with all due respect to the main supporter of this effort, *non-hunting societies should not seek to impose their values on hunting societies*" (emphasis in original).[69] Tanya Metaksa, former executive director of the NRA's Institute for Legislative Action, was particularly outspoken on these issues. In 1996 she wrote to Senator Jesse Helms (R-NC) to propose that Congress deny funds to UN activities related to "small arms used by the civilian population in the United States." In this letter, she addressed the UN Disarmament Commission's recommendations that national controls over light weapons be harmonized, arguing that "any 'harmonization' would inevitably mean tightening controls on the loosely regulated U.S. gun business, and would be opposed by the National Rifle Association and other U.S. pro-gun organizations."[70] In the same letter, she quoted Andrew Molchan, director of the National Association of Federally Licensed Firearms Dealers, who said, "It's politics as usual, the Colombians blaming their internal problems on American law. . . . The domestic arms trade is irrelevant to what's happening internationally."[71]

While the NRA is by no means shy about attacking President Clinton's gun control positions, it has also been quick to blame other governments for UN initiatives. The British, Japanese, and Canadian governments have all come under direct attack, but the NRA's most violent attacks have been on the Japanese government. An NRA fax alert assessing the ECOSOC regional firearms workshop in Tanzania focused largely on the Japanese government: "In fact, through the UN, the government of Japan *actually paid the expenses* for 23 of the 28 governments who sent representatives to the Africa conference" (emphasis added).[72] The NRA either did not know or chose to ignore the fact that such sponsorship is common, especially when the regional participants come from countries with few resources.

Evidently, the NRA has also found such attacks useful as a fund-raising strategy. A direct-mail letter in the fall of 1997 from Metaksa to supporters of the NRA's Institute for Legislative Action focused on the ECOSOC study. Interestingly, although the NRA has been arguing that it is an international organization, the letter focused solely on the consequences of the study for gun owners in the United States. The letter stated that the consideration of a UN declaration of principles on firearms would likely be followed by an international treaty, meaning that

> we are just two steps away from an international treaty that could cost you and your family your rights and your guns—*without even a full vote by Congress!* . . . As I write, a multi-national cadre of gun-ban extremists is lobbying the United Nations, demanding that this Declaration include a virtual *worldwide ban on firearms ownership*. . . . Would you be forced to get a government license to keep a gun in your home? Would you be forced to register all the firearms you now own? Would your handguns, semi-auto hunting rifles and pump shotguns be outlawed, and subject to government seizures, like we have witnessed in Australia and Great Britain? What would happen if the UN demands gun confiscation on American soil? (emphasis in original)

In an April 1998 article, Metaksa suggested that "a treaty becomes domestic law in America, not by a vote of the whole Congress, but by a vote of the Senate only. Who can guarantee that sometime in the future we won't have an anti-gun Senate that would adopt such a treaty?"[73] She does not mention that treaty ratification requires a two-thirds vote of the Senate.

Joining the Chorus: Other Gun Groups Also Attack International Control Efforts

Several other gun groups have joined the NRA in these efforts to counter the initiatives at controlling light weapons. One such group, the Second Amendment Foundation, expressed its fears that the UN Panel of Governmental Experts on Small Arms "could turn into a real problem by promoting a treaty on arms smuggling that would require signatory nations to regulate the market."[74] After the release of the small arms panel's report, they echoed the NRA's conclusions about the report, using virtually identical language.[75] In *The Gottlieb-Tartaro Report*, the foundation also attacked NGOs working on light weapons, accusing them of "fronting for an array of ultra-wealthy foundations that want to make the world safe for big money—which means taking guns away from everybody."[76]

Other gun groups have also joined the NRA in blaming governments in Japan and Canada for UN efforts to promote light weapons control. For example, the American Firearms Council has published an article titled "Japan Pushes UN Gun Control Plan."[77] Some groups blame both the Clinton administration and foreign governments: "The Clinton romance with global gun control fully blossomed when he gave his support to a new United Nations gun ban plan. We're not talking about sightings of black helicopters everywhere, but the real thing: a U.N. gun control initiative hatched in Tokyo."[78]

Gun Owners of America has characterized the United Nations as "a tourniquet that is slowly being drawn around gun owners' necks" and a front for domestic gun control in the United States. They have even gone so far as to recommend U.S. withdrawal from the United Nations to avoid what they see as dangerous momentum toward global gun control. Referring to the work of the UN Commission on Crime Prevention and Criminal Justice, they say that "these other countries were not sneaking in the back door of U.S. sovereignty—our own government was hiding behind the U.N. to carry out the civilian disarmament they did not think they could get away with by themselves."[79] Not surprisingly, they are also hostile to suggestions of any links between domestic gun control and international control of small arms and light weapons: "Pretty soon we will be told that we need a 'one-gun-a-month' rationing scheme to stop the flow of guns not just to poor crime-racked Washington, DC, but to drug-lord oppressed Colombia."[80]

Policy Options

This section analyzes three sets of options and strategies to make the connections between domestic gun control and international control over small arms and light weapons. The first deals with the prospects for increasing transparency or access to information on light weapons flows, the second with improving oversight, and the third with measures to actually control light weapons.[81]

Long-term success in linking domestic and international control will likely be dependent on the development of a new norm that supports limitations on the production, sale, and transfer of light weapons. While it will be easiest to attain short- and medium-term successes in improving transparency and oversight, and it may be possible to implement some control measures in the near term, the most demanding policy changes will probably require such a new global norm.

Increasing Transparency

"Transparency" generally refers to openness or ease of access to information. One important way to improve available information on light weapons is to obtain and publicize information about countries' relevant policies and laws. This proposal assumes that openness ("sunshine") favors restraint—

that public scrutiny leads to more care in decision making. Once the contents of these laws are better known, analysts will be able to assess which laws have been most (and least) effective. The strongest and most effective provisions can then be used as models for efforts by other countries or as the basis for regional or global standards (see also chapter 11 by Ed Laurance).

Increased transparency would also result from marking all small arms and light weapons at the time of manufacture. This practice of establishing a "weapons biography" could help in tracking light weapons and limiting the illicit trade. States could also establish databases of authorized manufacturers and dealers. Marking firearms at the time of manufacture is a key provision of the new OAS convention on illicit weapons.

Another way of increasing transparency is by using country case studies to produce regional or global overviews. Individual case studies can provide detailed information about one or two countries, including key actors, the extent of domestic controls over imports and exports, and the dynamics of weapons flows. By building an inventory of such cases, analysts could then prepare regional or global assessments of links between domestic and international factors. Such analyses should include problems and opportunities associated with past attempts to control light weapons while also suggesting better routes for the future.

Establishing or Improving Oversight

"Oversight" generally refers to the process of monitoring the establishment and enforcement of laws, regulations, or processes affecting a particular issue. This process may be controlled by groups such as bureaucracies, legislatures, and regional or international organizations.

Strengthening national oversight

In some countries, it may be necessary to begin by establishing or strengthening national laws providing for oversight of the light weapons trade. If countries lack administrative procedures for documenting production, imports, and exports of light weapons, they may not have access to the information necessary to participate in regional or global regimes.

Countries can improve oversight by enforcing existing laws governing weapons manufacture and sale, licensing, and storage. Oversight can also be improved by providing sufficient resources to monitor and police national borders. In the United States, some states are currently increasing their oversight in the absence of strong national standards. For example, Massachusetts is using consumer protection laws to regulate handguns, an activity that is prohibited on the federal level.

It is also important to learn from prior successes and failures. Comparative case studies of successful buy-back or turn-in programs can be used as the basis for policy recommendations to improve future oversight. Similarly, in-depth critiques of failures may help prevent similar problems in other countries.

Strengthening regional and international cooperation

Attention to regional and international processes is a prominent feature of many recent documents, including the May 1997 resolution of the ECOSOC firearms panel, the UN small arms experts group report, and the OAS convention. Strengthening regional and international cooperation is a common theme in all of these endeavors. One way to do so is by harmonizing national measures at the regional and international levels. Similarly, requiring suppliers and recipients to verify that weapons are reaching the intended recipients will help highlight where improving regulatory mechanisms is most likely to be useful.

The illicit weapons trade is most often a multinational or regional problem. Some countries are primarily transshipment points, while others are key origin or destination points. But all are important links in illicit weapons transfers. Attacking all aspects of the problem simultaneously is often impossible. Determining weak links in the chain, such as frequent and predictable routes for illicit transfers, may be more effective at less cost. Imposing stronger penalties at the national level for illegal possession of weapons and for smuggling is also likely to reduce the international trade in illicit weapons.

Controlling Light Weapons

While there are many ways to link domestic and international control of light weapons, they take a few basic forms. Most proposals are intended to limit the quantity or quality of weapons available by controlling production, access and availability, or transfers. Countries can break the supply line of especially dangerous weapons by ending production, as is now occurring with antipersonnel land mines. They can also do so by destroying weapons gathered through amnesty or buy-back programs, surplus weapons, and weapons that remain when conflicts end.

This chapter focuses largely on the *supply* of light weapons. A crucial way to control *demand* for light weapons is conflict prevention. In this regard, regional confidence- and security-building measures can be quite useful, as can efforts to prevent destabilizing accumulations of weaponry. Once conflicts begin, it may be necessary to declare and enforce bans on weapons transfers to all parties to the conflict. Conflict prevention and conflict management programs are a necessary complement to the proposals that follow.

Improving domestic control

The direct relationship between lax U.S. gun laws and illicit trafficking in U.S. weapons suggests that to control light weapons internationally, it will be necessary to control them nationally. It will be difficult, if not impossible, to control the illicit market in light weapons without monitoring and controlling domestic access to weapons. The credibility of the efforts described below would be enhanced if governments simultaneously eliminated covert aid and transfers.

As described earlier, laws limiting purchasers to one gun per month are already being implemented in several states in the United States; proposed legislation would implement a similar plan on the national level.[82] Such legislation has already decreased gunrunning in the affected states; national legislation would make it more difficult to obtain the large quantities of weaponry that make illicit trafficking financially attractive. Coupled with enforcement of existing guidelines governing the domestic sale of weapons, this could make it much easier to limit the international trade in these weapons.

For those who live in countries with strict gun control legislation, "one gun a month" may seem like a weak control measure. However, such a policy would represent a significant change from existing U.S. practice. At present, in almost every state in the United States, an authorized purchaser can buy literally dozens of weapons at one time; the sale or transfer of such weapons to criminals or unauthorized purchasers thus becomes relatively simple.

Destruction

A promising way of reducing the availability of light weapons is to control and destroy weapons that are turned in as part of buy-back or amnesty programs or are no longer needed because of military force reductions. At present, such weapons are often kept in poorly guarded police facilities or warehouses, and inventories are often not carefully maintained. Press reports regularly document weapons thefts in many countries, involving motivations ranging from simple greed to responses to instability.[83]

Destroying surplus stocks and turned-in weapons, or at least establishing better controls, can also decrease the damage caused by these weapons. To ensure that weapons are permanently taken out of circulation, destruction of weaponry can also be incorporated into other efforts to control light weapons flows. For all destruction efforts, it will be important to keep careful records and to make them public. This will assure those who give up their weapons that the weapons will actually be destroyed.

Selective bans and embargoes

Another option is to ban the production and sale of entire categories of weapons that are especially indiscriminate in their effects. Efforts to ban land mines and blinding weapons are under way; there has been particular success with the campaign to ban antipersonnel land mines. As described above, both the United Kingdom and Australia have recently banned certain categories of small arms and light weapons in response to civilian killings (ironically, the United Kingdom and Australia neglected to include the particular types of weapons used in the other country's massacre). Banning both weapons production and transfers (rather than only transfers) would also reduce the feeling in developing countries that light weapons control is being used to deprive them of adequate defenses.

Other options focus on limiting rather than barring whole types of weapons. While these approaches may be more readily implemented because they are less severe, they may also be more difficult to monitor and verify. A total ban is more readily verified than more modest limits because any weapon of the prohibited type is by definition a violation of the ban.

Yet another approach is to limit ammunition as a means of helping to break the cycle of violence. Because light weapons often last for decades, the world could still be awash in them decades from now, even if all production and transfers of light weapons were stopped today. But ammunition is rapidly consumed in conflict. It is unattractive for smuggling since it has relatively high weight and relatively low dollar value. Reliable (safe) ammunition is also difficult to produce. Ammunition also has a significantly shorter shelf life than the weapons in which it is used. For these reasons, limitations on ammunition supplies may be more feasible than limitations on the weapons themselves. Senator Daniel Patrick Moynihan (D-NY) has frequently proposed a graduated tax on ammunition, with sporting rounds taxed quite lightly, progressing to much higher taxes on ammunition used primarily for nonsporting purposes.

However, the little information that is currently available on ammunition is widely dispersed. In accepting the UN small arms panel report, the General Assembly endorsed a study of explosives and ammunition, and both private groups and governments are working on the issue.[84] This should help answer questions about the technical aspects of ammunition, the nature and structure of the ammunition industry, and the prospects for control.

Conclusion

Many of these recommendations are mutually reinforcing. For example, both destroying surplus weapons and destroying weapons when conflicts end will help get weapons out of circulation, ending the "recycling" process. Increasing domestic oversight helps prevent the diversion of weapons; doing so while also strengthening regional and global cooperation on illicit weapons helps restrict the available market for such weapons.

There has been significant progress in national, regional, and global fora on these issues in recent years. One key to future progress will be joint action by NGOs working on a variety of issues, including humanitarian aid, disarmament, gun control, and development; NGOs, journalists, and the public can effectively pressure sometimes reluctant governments to construct and implement higher standards for light weapons manufacture, storage, and transfer. Continued progress also depends on sharing information effectively, maintaining active contacts with international government organizations working on these issues, and finding governments willing to take the lead in organizing regional and global efforts.

Notes

1. Examples of major conventional weapons in use in recent conflicts include tanks and ships in Albania; combat aircraft, armor, and artillery in Chechnya; aircraft and attack helicopters in Colombia; artillery, heavy infantry fighting vehicles, and combat aircraft in the former Yugoslavia; tanks, armored vehicles, and fighter aircraft along the Ethiopia/Somali border; mortars and heavy artillery in Liberia; armored personnel carriers and artillery in Yemen; and aircraft in Zaire. For more information about the interaction between light and major conventional weapons, see Natalie J. Goldring, "Bridging the Gap: Light and Major Conventional Weapons in Recent Conflicts," paper prepared for the annual meeting of the International Studies Association, Toronto, March 18–21, 1997.

2. Portions of this chapter are based on Natalie J. Goldring, "Overcoming Domestic Obstacles to Light Weapons Control," in James Brown, ed., *Arms Control Issues for the Twenty-First Century* (Albuquerque, N.M.: Sandia National Laboratories, 1997). The author gratefully acknowledges the contributions to these chapters of current and former British American Security Information Council (BASIC) staff members Susannah Dyer, Joel Johnston, Katherine Joseph, Christine Kucia, and Geraldine O'Callaghan.

This chapter is largely a product of BASIC's Project on Light Weapons, an international research, public education, and advocacy program. Through a series of international workshops and extensive work with analysts and activists worldwide, the Project on Light Weapons has developed a research and policy agenda on the light weapons trade. BASIC's research and publications now focus on the most promising approaches developed in its initial work, including (1) the destruction of light weapons in disarmament and demobilization efforts and (2) technical issues, such as ammunition and high-technology light weapons as well as the issue of illicit light weapons trafficking. Current national and international attitudes toward gun possession and gun control also make this an opportune time to emphasize the connections between domestic gun control and international control of light weapons flows. The author is continuing her research and analysis on this issue in her new role as executive director of the Program on General Disarmament at the University of Maryland.

3. Boris Johnson, "Tears as Sportsmen Lay down Their Arms," *Daily Telegraph,* September 15, 1997, p. 34.

4. *Hansard,* House of Commons Written Answers, Firearms Surrender Compensation, col. 42, November 17, 1997.

5. Fred Barbash, "Britain Votes to Ban Handguns; House of Commons Fulfills Blair Vow by Extending Law," *Washington Post,* June 12, 1997, p. A01.

6. Reuters, "Total Ban on Handguns Comes into Force in Britain," January 26, 1998; BBC News Online Network, "Public Give up 160,000 Guns after Dunblane," September 3, 1998 (available at http://news.bbc.co.uk/hi/english/uk/newsid%5F 164000/164402.stm).

7. Philip Johnston, "Gun Cash Delay to Be Investigated," *Daily Telegraph,* March 9, 1998.

8. Philip Johnston, "Gun Owner Can Sue Home Office over Late Compensation," *Daily Telegraph,* February 19, 1998.

9. BBC News, "Gun Owners up in Arms over Compensation," August 9, 1998 (available at http://news.bbc.co.uk/hi/english/uk/newsid%5F147000/147948.stm).

10. Australian Firearms Buyback, "Our Most Frequently Asked Questions" (available at http://203.2.143.13/questions/questions.htm).

11. Australian Firearms Buyback, "Successful Implementation of the Laws" (available at http://203.2.143.13/legislation/success.htm). Further information on the Australian Firearms Buyback Program is available at http://203.2.143.13.

12. Margo Kingston, "Gun Laws to Stay PM," *Sydney Morning Herald,* March 12, 1998.

13. Australian Firearms Buyback, "Firearms Reform—Debated Nationally for Many Years" (available at http://203.2.143.13/legislation/history.htm).

14. Australian Firearms Buyback, "National Tally" (available at http://203.2. 143.13/tally/tally.htm).

15. Geraldine O'Callaghan, interview with Rebecca Peters, March 1998.

16. Robert Wainwright, "Gun Dealers Primed up for Class Action over Low Compensation," *Sydney Morning Herald,* July 17, 1998 (available at http://www.smh. com.au/news/9807/17/text/pageone9.html).

17. Violence Policy Center, "Firearms Industry Fact Sheet," 1997 (available at http://www.vpc.org/fact_sht/industfs.htm).

18. Data on licensed firearms dealers are from the Regulatory Office, Bureau of Alcohol, Tobacco and Firearms, U.S. Treasury Department, January 1998.

19. Jeff Brazil and Steve Berry, "Crackdown on Assault Weapons Has Missed Mark," *Los Angeles Times,* August 24, 1997.

20. U.S. Senate, "The Anti-Gun Trafficking Act of 1997," *Congressional Record,* March 18, 1997. The current version is S. 407, the "Stop Gun Trafficking Act of 1999."

21. Fox Butterfield, "Report Links Crimes to States with Weak Gun Control," *New York Times,* April 9, 1997.

22. See the summary of "Hot Guns: 'Ring of Fire' " (available at http://www.pbs. org/wgbh/pages/frontline/shows/guns).

23. Handgun Control, Inc., "Saturday Night Specials/Junk Guns" (available at http://www.handguncontrol.org/gunlaw/B2/b2snsqa.htm).

24. See Frontline, "Hot Guns: 'Ring of Fire': A Hazardous Consumer Product"; "Ring of Fire: Guns and Crime"; and "Ring of Fire: Companies and What They Make" (available at http://www.pbs.org/wgbh/pages/frontline/shows/gun/ring/).

25. U.S. Senate, "The American Handgun Standards Act of 1999," *Congressional Record,* January 19, 1999.

26. Handgun Control, Inc., "Key Legislative Issues for the 105th Congress," updated November 10, 1997.

27. Senate Committee on Governmental Affairs, *A Review of Arms Export Licensing,* cited in Michael Klare and David Andersen, *A Scourge of Guns* (Washington, D.C.: Federation of American Scientists, 1997), p. 66.

28. "Brazil-U.S. Counternarcotics Cooperation: Fighting the Illegal Trade of Weapons," statement of Brazilian embassy officials at a roundtable discussion hosted by BASIC, March 20, 1996.

29. "Brazil: Minister Views Efforts to Control Weapons Smuggling," an FBIS Daily Report translation of an article by Justice Minister Nelson Jobim titled "The Fight against Weapons Trafficking," FBIS-TDD-96–029-L, September 28, 1996.

30. Clifford Krause, "Harried over Drugs, Mexico Presses Own Peeve: U.S. Guns," *New York Times,* March 19, 1997, p. A12.

31. Pierre Thomas and John Ward Anderson, "Mexico Asks U.S. to Track Guns Being Imported by Drug Cartels," *Washington Post,* November 5, 1996, p. A13.

32. Howard LaFranchi, "Mexicans Too Have a Problem Border: Awash in U.S. Guns," *Christian Science Monitor,* April 11, 1997.

33. Stuart A. Powell, "Clinton Gains Pledge from Mexico," *San Francisco Examiner,* May 6, 1997, p. A2.

34. Thomas and Anderson, "Mexico Asks U.S. to Track Guns Being Imported by Drug Cartels," p. A13.

35. George Gedda, "Mexicans Also Have Cross-Border Smuggling to Complain About," Associated Press, May 3, 1997.

36. Krausse, "Harried over Drugs, Mexico Presses Own Peeve: U.S. Guns," p. A12.

37. "Colombia: Report on Weapons, Increasing Violence," *Santa Fe de Bogota Samana,* in FBIS Daily Report, FBIS-TDD-97–271, September 28, 1997.

38. "Colombia: Police Chief on Cali Arms Cache, Trafficker-Guerrilla Links," *Santa Fe de Bogota Inravision Television,* in FBIS Daily Report, FBIS-TOT-97–020-L, February 26, 1997.

39. Edward C. Ezell, *Small Arms Today,* 2nd ed. (Harrisburg, Pa.: Stackpole Books, 1988), p. 444.

40. Valerie Alvord, "Illegal Weapons Were Well-Traveled: Mexico-Bound, They Went Round the World to San Diego," *San Diego Union Tribune,* March 21, 1997.

41. Valerie Alvord, "Selected Gun Parts a Riddle Waiting to Be Unraveled," *San Diego Union Tribune,* April 6, 1997. For additional detail, see also Lora Lumpe, "U.S. Policy and the Export of Light Weapons" (chapter 4 in this volume).

42. Some of the material in this section and in the section on policy options is drawn from Natalie J. Goldring, "Developing Transparency and Associated Control Measures for Light Weapons," paper presented at the April 1997 workshop for the 1997 review group of governmental experts on the UN Conventional Arms Register, Tokyo. The paper also presents and assesses several proposals to increase the transparency of light weapons transfers, primarily within the UN context.

43. "Guidelines for International Arms Transfers in the Context of General Assembly Resolution 46/36H of 6 December 1991," reprinted in "Review of the Implementation of the Recommendations and Decisions Adopted by the General Assembly at its Tenth Special Session: Report of the Disarmament Commission," A/51/182, July 1, 1996, pp. 64–69.

44. "Firearm Regulation for the Purpose of Crime Prevention and Public Safety," E/CN.15/1997/L.19, April 30, 1997.

45. "Statement submitted by the National Rifle Association of America, Institute for Legislative Action (Roster), a Nongovernment Organization in Consultative Status with the Economic and Social Council," April 28–May 9, 1997.

46. For additional detail on gun groups' involvement in ECOSOC activities, see the section "The Role of Pro-Gun Organizations."

47. United Nations Economic and Social Council, "Measures to Regulate Firearms for the Purpose of Combating Illicit Trafficking in Firearms," July 28, 1998 (available at http://www.prepcom.org/low/pc2/pc2a31.htm).

48. For further information about the small arms panel, see Natalie J. Goldring, "UN Small Arms Panel Makes Progress," *BASIC Reports*, no. 56, February 11, 1997, and "After Discord, Consensus on UN Small Arms Report," *BASIC Reports*, no. 59, August 25, 1997.

49. "Interview with Dr. Owen Greene on UN Efforts to Control Small Arms," *BASIC Reports*, no. 65, August 4, 1998.

50. "Inter-American Convention Against the Illicit Manufacturing of and Trafficking in Firearms, Ammunition, Explosives and Other Related Materials," AG/RES.1 (XXIV-E/97), adopted by the 24th Special Session of the General Assembly, Organization of American States, Washington, D.C., November 13, 1997.

51. "Draft Convention Against the Illicit Manufacturing and Trafficking of Firearms, Ammunition, Explosives and Other Related Materials," prepared by a group of experts in Cancún, March 6–7, 1997, and submitted by the Rio Group to the Organization of American States.

52. Kate Joseph, interview with an official of the Mexican mission to the OAS, November 7, 1997.

53. Editorial, *Australian Shooters Journal*, August 1992.

54. Editorial, *Australian Shooters Journal*, September 1993.

55. Peter H. Stone, "From the K Street Corridor," *National Journal*, April 12, 1997, p. 712.

56. Interview with Jim Baker, SAAMI, March 17, 1998, cited in Rachel Stohl, "Deadly Rounds: Ammunition and Armed Conflict," BASIC Research Report 98.4, May 1998.

57. News release, Sporting Shooters Association of Australia, April 4, 1997.

58. Editorial, *Australian Shooters Journal*, May 1997.

59. "World Forum Seeks to Save Sport Shooting," *Gun News Digest*, Fall 1997, p. 20. The organization's growth is apparently slowing; in April 1998, the NRA claimed that twenty-four organizations were members. Tanya K. Metaksa, "Gun Owners Branded 'A Threat to Mankind,'" April 1998 (available at http://www.nra.org/poli tics 96/0498tar.html).

60. Philip Alpers has identified thirteen members of the group: the American Shooting Sports Council, Firearms Importers Round Table, National Shooting Sports Foundation, National Rifle Association, Safari Club International, Sporting Arms and Ammunition Manufacturers Institute, International Shooting Union, International Practical Shooting Confederation, International Metallic Silhouette Union of France, British Shooting Sports Council, Sporting Shooters Association of New Zealand, Sporting Shooters Association of Australia, and the Associazione Nazionale Produttori Armi e Munizioni. For further information, see Philip Alpers, "An Armed Planet Is a Polite Planet: The Gun Lobby Goes Global," forthcoming, 1999.

61. "World Forum Seeks to Save Sport Shooting," *Gun News Digest*, Fall 1997, p. 20.

62. "World Forum on the Future of Sportshooting Activities Established," NRA-ILA Fax Alert, vol. 4, no. 28, July 11, 1997.

63. Tanya K. Metaksa, "Gun Owners Branded 'A Threat to Mankind,'" *American Rifleman*, vol. 146 (April 1998), p. 4.

64. The press release is available at http://www.ssaa.org.au/forum1.html.

65. Peter H. Stone, "From the K Street Corridor," *National Journal*, April 12, 1997, p. 712.

66. Letter from Tanya K. Metaksa, executive director of the NRA's Institute for Legislative Action, to Senator Jesse Helms, January 11, 1996 (available at http://www.saf.org/cgi-bin/wwwwais; search for "Metaksa and Helms"). (Note that the website incorrectly dates letter as 1995.)

67. "UN Panel Recommends Studying Gun Licensing," in *NRA Grassfire*, January 1998 (available at http://www.nra.org/pub/ila/test_1997/97–11-25_grassfire_bigger_ban).

68. "Statement of the National Rifle Association of America, Institute for Legislative Action, before the United Nations Panel of Government Experts on Small Arms," January 21, 1997. Despite the title, this statement was not presented before the panel.

69. "Statement of Thomas L. Mason, National Rifle Association of America (NRA)," United Nations Regional Workshop on Firearm Regulation (Africa), Arusha, Tanzania, November 6, 1997.

70. Letter from Tanya K. Metaksa, executive director of the NRA's Institute for Legislative Action, to Senator Jesse Helms, January 11, 1996; see note 66.

71. Andrew Molchan, director of the U.S. Association of Federally Licensed Firearms Dealers, quoted in a letter to Senator Jesse Helms from Tanya K. Metaksa, executive director of the NRA's Institute for Legislative Action, January 11, 1996; see note 66.

72. "Firearms Owned by Civilians Are the Target," NRA-ILA Fax Alert, November 26, 1997 (available at http://www.nra.org/pub/ila/test_1997/97–11-26_faxalert_civilian_firearms).

73. Tanya K. Metaksa, "Gun Owners Branded 'A Threat to Mankind,'" *American Rifleman*, vol. 146 (April 1998), p. 4.

74. "Global Gun Control? Global Fighters for Gun Rights," *The Gottlieb-Tartaro Report*, no. 24, December 1996 (available at http://www.saf.org/pub/rkba/gtreport/gt-report_024.html).

75. "The United Nations Wants Your Guns," *The Gottlieb-Tartaro Report*, no. 35, November 1997 (available at http://www.saf.org/pub/rkba/gt-report/gt-report_035.html).

76. "World Gun Control Groups Tout Efforts as 'Arms Control,'" *The Gottlieb-Tartaro Report*, issue 38, February 1998 (available at http://www.saf.org/pub/rkba/gt-report/gt.report_038.html).

77. "Japan Pushes UN Gun Control Plan," *The American Firearms Council Journal*, vol. 1, no. 1 (Summer 1996).

78. Tanya K. Metaksa, "The Clinton War on Guns," *American Rifleman*, April 1996 (available at http://www.nra.org/politics96/bcwar.html).

79. Gun Owners of America, "News Flash: Rep. Ron Paul Moving to Eliminate Gun Control Bureaucracy—Amendment Would Remove U.S. from U.N. jurisdiction," June 4, 1997 (available at http://www.gunowners.org).

80. Larry Pratt, "The United Nations: Pressing for U.S. Gun Control," June 1997 (available at http://cgibin1.erols.com/crfields/op9705.htm).

81. Some of the measures described below have been developed in part through discussions among participants and advisors of BASIC's Project on Light Weapons. Several of these recommendations have subsequently been taken up by the UN Panel of Governmental Experts on Small Arms.

82. U.S. House of Representatives, "Twelve Is Enough Anti-Gunrunning Act," *Congressional Record,* January 7, 1997.

83. Dana Priest and Roberto Suro, "Probe of Black Market in Weapons Widens," *Washington Post,* October 18, 1997.

84. See Rachel Stohl, "Deadly Rounds: Ammunition and Armed Conflict," BASIC Research Report 98.4, May 1998; and Canada, Department of Foreign Affairs and International Trade, *The Role of Ammunition Controls in Addressing Excessive and Destabilizing Accumulation of Small Arms* (Ottawa, April 1998).

Part Three

Regional Efforts to Control Light Weapons

7

Mali and the West African Light Weapons Moratorium

Joseph P. Smaldone

THE PROLIFERATION OF SMALL ARMS and light weapons, especially through illegal trafficking, has become a widespread affliction in sub-Saharan Africa, contributing to rising crime, domestic violence, internal and international conflicts, large-scale humanitarian crises, and socioeconomic catastrophes. Increasingly, African states are taking the initiative to combat these threats to national and regional security. On October 31, 1998, heads of state and government of the sixteen-member Economic Community of West African States (ECOWAS), meeting in Abuja, Nigeria, made history by declaring a three-year renewable "moratorium on the importation, exportation, and manufacture of light weapons in ECOWAS member states," to become effective the next day. This much-anticipated decision capped a five-year effort that began when the president of Mali, Dr. Alpha Oumar Konare, requested assistance from the UN secretary-general in addressing the proliferation of small arms in the subregion.[1]

This chapter examines and assesses the origins, progress, and prospects for this little-known but unprecedented and promising local arms control initiative as it has emerged and evolved in the process of national reconciliation and peace building in Mali after a period of armed rebellion and near civil war. In so doing, it aims to contribute analytically to the understanding of the role of arms control in the prevention, management, and resolution of conflict and as an integral part of the security-development equation.

Introducing Mali

The Republic of Mali is a large, landlocked, sparsely populated country in the heart of the West African bulge. Its 1.24 million square kilometers embrace an area about twice the size of Texas or France, and its 7,243 kilometers of boundaries abut seven neighbors whose territories stretch to the Mediterranean, the Atlantic, and the Gulf of Guinea. The country's 9.8 million people are concentrated around and south of the Niger River bend, the great riverine arc around which West Africa's historical empires have risen and fallen. Indeed, Mali's historical namesake, the empire of Mali, ruled much of the territory of the modern state and surrounding areas at its zenith in the fourteenth century.

However, modern-day Mali, which gained its independence from France in 1960, is one of the poorest countries in the world. Geography has dictated much of its fortunes. Mali's three main geographical zones encompass a large inhospitable desert tract in the north, a semiarid Sahel region in the middle, and a small wooded grassland savanna in the south. Continued desertification, deforestation, and soil erosion have reduced Mali's arable land to only 2 percent of its territory. The national economy, as well as the livelihood of 80 percent of Malians engaged in subsistence agriculture and livestock production, depend utterly on the vagaries of rainfall. In 1995, Mali's gross national product (GNP) was only about $2.5 billion, and its $259 per capita GNP ranked 148th in the world. Modern economic infrastructure is severely limited, with small local industries concentrated on food processing. Its export earnings, largely from primary products, are low, while foreign aid dependence and external debt are high. Demographic pressures add to the country's parlous conditions. Given geographic and economic constraints, Mali's 3.2 percent population growth rate adds to its burdens. On the other hand, high infant mortality, a life expectancy of only forty-six years, and a 31 percent literacy rate sap its human potential.

About 90 percent of Mali's population is Muslim, and 80 percent share a common language, Bambara. However, like most sub-Saharan African states, Mali exhibits serious internal divisions and disparities. Ethnolinguistic composition is mixed. About half the population is classified as Mande (including Bambara, Malinke, and Sarakole), 17 percent Peul (Fulani), 12 percent Voltaic (including Senufo, Mossi, and Bobo), 6 percent Songhai, 10 percent Tuareg and Moor, and 6 percent other smaller groups. Mali's three main geographical zones also constitute demographic, socioeconomic, and political divides. To be sure, in the present, as in the past, these zones continue to shift, but at any given time they broadly define different human populations, cultures, modes of livelihood, and salient political constituencies.[2]

Background to Conflict and Its Resolution

The remote and harsh desert zone of northern Mali has been the most sparsely populated, backward, and neglected area of the country, under both French colonial rule and national governments ruling from Bamako in the Mande heartland in the south. This area, historically populated principally by the nomadic and itinerant Tuareg (Berber descent) and Moors (Arab descent), experienced severe droughts in the mid-1970s and mid-1980s, with devastating consequences for the region and its inhabitants. The northerners lost their livestock, their livelihoods, and their very identities. Many emigrated to Libya, where they were inducted into Mu'ammar Gadhafi's Islamic Legion or otherwise inspired to liberate their kinsmen at home. These natural and human catastrophes in northern Mali, aggravated by external political forces and mismanagement and marginalization by a succession of one-party and military regimes at home, gave rise in mid-1990 to the so-called Tuareg problem, or Tuareg rebellion, in Mali and neighboring Niger.

The incumbent Malian government of Moussa Traore reacted harshly toward the northern rebels, who fought under the banner of various fronts and movements and against other dissident elements throughout the country. Traore's regime succeeded only in alienating itself and precipitating a military coup in March 1991. Lieutenant Colonel Amadou Toumani Toure formed a collective presidency that ruled through a largely civilian government and began a phased transition to democracy. A new constitution was adopted in January 1992, and in June 1992, Konare assumed office as the country's first elected president and head of Mali's Third Republic.

The democratic transition of 1992 involved a nationwide consultation and reconciliation process, the centerpiece of which was the April 1992 Pacte National signed by the transitional government and an umbrella group of Tuaregs. However, after some hopeful developments in 1993, the political situation deteriorated, and in 1994 a civil war nearly erupted between the northerners and an armed countermovement of sedentary peoples (Ganda Koy). The north desperately needed both development and security, but $200 million in aid commitments to the region were blocked because of local insecurity. Accordingly, the political leadership undertook a "security first" approach to national reconstruction. During 1994–97, domestic peace was gradually restored by means of a remarkable series of local, intercommunal, national, and international meetings and negotiations, together with equally innovative reconciliation and reintegration programs. In May 1997, President Konare won reelection to a second and final five-year term in a mismanaged and politically damaging electoral process, but peace, always tenuous, seems to be holding.

A recently published UN study of the Malian peace process by Robin-Edward Poulton and Ibrahim ag Youssouf, *A Peace of Timbuktu,* has characterized its essential ingredients as "six different courses of action which together prevented the outbreak of civil war. These were (1) the building of civilian-military relations, (2) discreet mediation by both national and international figures, (3) the decentralization of governance, (4) the promotion of reconciliation through civil society, (5) the process of disarmament and demobilization [of ex-rebels], and (6) assistance for the re-integration of former rebel combatants." In their estimation, "these aspects of the Malian peace process provide a model which may inspire peacemaking elsewhere."[3]

The details of the "Malian model," including military demobilization, disarmament, and reconstruction, are well documented in the UN study. These included training and absorbing 2,000 ex-combatants, a UN Development Programme (UNDP)–sponsored socioeconomic reintegration program for the remaining 9,500, and the dramatic "La Flamme de la Paix" (Flame of Peace) of March 27, 1996, at which 3,000 weapons collected from the former rebels were burned in Timbuktu at a ceremony attended by President Konare and other West African and international officials. However, that UN study discusses only briefly Mali's proposal for a moratorium on the import, export, and manufacture of small arms as an integral part of its effort to expand "shared democratic space" within West Africa.[4] It is this small arms moratorium that is the subject of the remainder of this chapter.

Small Arms Proliferation: Searching for a Solution

Arms control has been an integral part of the Malian peace process from the beginn[illegible]s an adjunct to domestic pacification through elaboration of participa[illegible]y political structures, invigorated civil society, healthy civil-military relations, and demobilization/disarmament of ex-combatants, Mali proposed and promoted the establishment of a subregional moratorium on small arms. Recognizing that the illegal proliferation of small arms was one of the factors contributing to political instability, in October 1993 President Konare asked the UN secretary-general to help define the extent of the problem and ways to address it. An in-house UN study concluded that the problem was subregional and had to be addressed as such; however, a subregional approach proved difficult in the short run because of prevailing political and security conditions in neighboring states. It was therefore decided to conduct the project in two phases: (1) an initial pilot project in Mali and (2) a follow-up phase in neighboring states when conditions permitted. The first phase was carried out in Mali in August 1994 and the second during February–March 1995 in

Burkina Faso, Chad, Côte d'Ivoire, Mauritania, Niger, and Senegal. Algeria participated in the project, but only through discussions in New York.

Former Organization of African Unity (OAU) Secretary-General William Eteki-M'Boumoua led the UN missions to the participating countries, supported by staff from various UN agencies. Each cooperating government set up a national commission on the proliferation of small arms to coordinate with the UN mission and provide for its local administrative and logistical needs. In each country, the UN team undertook a wide-ranging review of the security situation, including relevant legal documents, the sources of domestic conflict, the nature and extent of refugees and displaced persons, banditry, "self-defense" (vigilante) measures, issues related to the proliferation of weapons (its scale and nature; sources such as smuggling, thefts from army/police stocks, and illegal sales; misuse of traditional weapons; and national weapons control legislation and practices), the roles of security forces and other agencies such as customs services, and ongoing efforts by the governments to remedy these problems. In carrying out its mandate, the UN team met with relevant government ministers and their staffs, nongovernmental organizations (NGOs), UN agencies, and foreign diplomatic missions.

The mission concluded that insecurity at every level (personal, local, national, and subregional) was impeding development and driving the demand for firearms; illicit small arms proliferation was a serious problem, but there was inadequate information on its magnitude; virtually all countries lacked the human and material resources to improve their security conditions and needed external assistance to do so; and arms control measures could succeed only after the security conditions had improved. Hence a security-first strategy was required to address personal security concerns, without which neither development nor arms control could proceed. The mission concluded further that international "security assistance" should be directed not to the armed forces but to the police, national guard, gendarmerie, and customs—those agencies whose actions most affected personal security. Finally, the mission concluded that a neutral authority should oversee the provision of external assistance regardless of source.

The mission made two sets of recommendations. The first, addressed to the participating countries themselves, could be undertaken on their own with little or no outside help (e.g., improve internal controls and procedures, tighten national legislation, and enhance training of security forces). The second set, addressed to the United Nations itself, called for coordination with the UNDP with a view to its taking the lead for the United Nations under its mandate to support human security and good governance and to coordinate with and solicit support for this security-first approach from interested donor countries. The mission specifically recommended promoting a subregional approach, ensuring arrangements for monitoring and supervision and aid in standardizing legislation and customs procedures, technical training, and developing confidence-building measures. It also envisioned a subregional workshop to review and validate the conclusions and recommendations of the advisory mission and to explore the possibility of a subregional arms register.[5]

Unveiling the Small Arms Moratorium

The subregional workshop envisioned by the UN mission materialized in the form of the international Conference on Conflict Prevention, Disarmament, and Development in West Africa, held in Bamako during November 25–29, 1996. Jointly organized by the UN Institute for Disarmament Research (UNIDIR), the UN Department of Political Affairs, and UNDP, in collaboration with the government of Mali, the conference was attended by delegations from twelve West African states and representatives of other governments, international organizations, and NGOs. Most of its work was accomplished in three workshops. Workshop 1 discussed the idea of a code of conduct of civil-military relations, updating and strengthening national legislation and policies concerning illicit arms, establishing national and regional information systems, and developing policies for controlling small arms in West Africa. Workshop 2 dealt with security issues, such as the demobilization of former combatants, disarmament, and border control. Workshop 3 had wide-ranging discussions on all aspects of the subregional security situation and possible remedies, including arms control.

In its concluding document, the conference urged the creation of formal coordination mechanisms between the subregion's national commissions; a permanent system of information exchange; coordination with other subregional organizations, such as ECOWAS and members of the Accord de nonagression et d'assistance en matiere de defense (Accord on Nonaggression and Assistance in Defense Matters, or ANAD); and establishment of a subregional register of arms and arms transfers.

It was at this conference that Mali's foreign minister officially unveiled the proposed subregional moratorium on the import, export, and manufacture of light weapons. Attendees expressed keen interest in this proposal and urged Mali to sensitize subregional leaders on the concept and to submit it through diplomatic channels for consideration by other African states. The conference also called for a subregional ministerial-level meeting to study the possibility of adopting such a moratorium and for establishing a dialogue between concerned West African governments and the Vienna-based Wassenaar Arrangement on Export Controls for Conventional Arms and Dual-Use Goods and Technologies (a thirty-three-nation suppliers' forum, established in 1996 to promote transparency, responsibility, and restraint in the international transfer of arms and sensitive dual-use technology).[6]

The Moratorium Concept

Mali's proposed West African small arms moratorium, as elaborated at the November 1996 international conference in Bamako and in subsequent diplomatic communications, was conceived as an important measure to implement the 1994–95 UN advisory missions on the proliferation of light weapons in the subregion, and the three related UN General Assembly resolutions subsequently passed. It was to be a declaratory confidence-building measure, a political "act of faith" rather than a treaty or legally binding convention. It envisioned a grace period during which the problem of illegal weapons in circulation could be addressed and the recommendations of the UN advisory missions implemented.

The scope of the moratorium would cover the import, export, and manufacture of all light weapons procured by governments or private persons and parties under their jurisdiction. It excluded "weapons of war" used by the armed forces and allowed for possible exceptions. Participation would be open to any interested African country on a voluntary basis whenever it was prepared to undertake the requisite commitments. Its initial one- to three-year duration could be extended by agreement among participating governments. Finally, several supplementary measures that had been recommended by the UN advisory missions were proposed for consideration by participating governments, either unilaterally or collectively. The details of these and other provisions of the moratorium and its supporting measures were to be negotiated among interested subregional states.[7]

Diplomatic Efforts

Over the next several months, the United Nations and Mali undertook intensive diplomatic efforts to carry out the mandate of the Bamako conference. In February 1997, representatives of UNIDIR, UNDP, and the UN Department of Disarmament Affairs briefed Friends of the Chair of the Wassenaar Arrangement in Vienna on the moratorium proposal. The Friends welcomed the UN briefing, conveyed to the chairman and the thirty-three member states of the Wassenaar Arrangement the interest of the West African states in conducting a dialogue on security cooperation with supplier states in support of the proposed moratorium, and urged direct contacts between West African states and individual Wassenaar members to promote their aims.[8]

For its part, Mali briefed the OAU Secretariat, headquartered in Addis Ababa, Ethiopia, characterizing the proposed moratorium as an important precursor and test case for the OAU's Early Warning System (EWS), a computer-based information system being developed for the OAU's Mechanism for Conflict Prevention, Management and Resolution, to enable OAU decision makers to monitor, evaluate, and respond to emerging conflicts. In February 1997, the Mali delegation to the OAU Council of Ministers meeting organized briefings on the margins of the ministerial in Tripoli for the OAU secretary-general and delegations of ten West African states, Algeria, Burundi, and Rwanda. Mali also circulated its moratorium proposal formally as an aide-mémoire to interested African governments through diplomatic channels and invited them to a ministerial consultation in Bamako in conjunction with the Week of Peace celebration during March 24–28, 1997, to commemorate the first anniversary of the Flame of Peace. In short, within a few months of the unveiling of the moratorium proposal in November 1996, the combined efforts of the United Nations and Mali succeeded in putting the moratorium proposal before high political levels in West Africa, within the wider context of OAU conflict prevention and resolution initiatives, and among the world's major arms suppliers.[9]

The Week of Peace: Launching the Moratorium

Mali's Week of Peace, March 24–28, 1997, jointly sponsored with UNDP, UNESCO, and the UN Department of Political Affairs, featured two events: the Forum on the Culture of Peace in Mali and the Flame of Peace anniversary commemoration in Timbuktu. Mali's foreign minister presided over a committee-level ministerial negotiation of the moratorium text with representatives of Algeria, Burkina Faso, Guinea, Liberia, Mali, Mauritania, and Senegal and observers from UN agencies, the OAU, the ANAD secretary-general, the University of Yaounde (Cameroon), the U.S. Arms Control and Disarmament Agency (ACDA), the Wassenaar Arrangement, the Norwegian Institute of International Affairs, and France.

The committee identified multiple causes of light weapons proliferation in the subregion and recommended greater international assistance for the peace process, several measures to combat arms proliferation (essentially those of the UN advisory missions), and, significantly, implementation of the proposed moratorium. The ministerial consultation also recommended diplomatic efforts to explain and promote support for the proposed moratorium and the establishment of the Programme for Coordination and Assistance on Disarmament and Security (PCADIS), a five-year UNDP-sponsored and -staffed technical mechanism to support and administer the moratorium, which would become effective on its declaration by one or more states. Finally, the Bamako consultation urged the adoption of associated measures to strengthen the ability of participating governments to control illicit light weapons trafficking and the consideration of the establishment of a subregional arms register to cover procurement of weapons for the armed forces. Among the measures recommended to address illicit arms trafficking were an intensive subregional training program for police forces, cross-border hotlines between security authorities to facilitate cooperation among neighboring states, strict licensing of weapons to individuals and a register of those authorized to possess them, and development of an education program for civilians.[10]

Promoting the Moratorium: Recent Developments

From mid-1997, support for the proposed moratorium grew steadily. In June 1997, Mali's presidential delegation to the OAU summit in Harare conducted "sensitization" consultations with other delegations. The UNDP prepared a formal implementation plan and conducted a low-key but effective international campaign to secure political, technical, material, and financial support for the five-year $6.88 million budget for the administration and Secretariat, which was renamed the Programme for Coordination and Assistance on Security and Development (PCASED). By April 1998, at least three governments had publicly pledged substantial financial support, including Norway's $2.5 million and the United Kingdom's $500,000, and five others had expressed their intention to make contributions.[11]

The emergence and conjunction of several other international initiatives to address small arms proliferation and illegal arms trafficking also helped to highlight Mali's bold proposal, to enhance its visibility on the global level, to secure its place in a wider context of multilateral arms control efforts, and to boost its momentum and prospects. In June 1997, the European Union (EU) approved the Programme for Preventing and Combating Illicit Trafficking in Conventional Arms, including assistance to recipient countries to improve their ability to institute weapons control measures and to remove surplus arms from general circulation. The EU also agreed on the Common Position on Prevention and Resolution of Conflicts in Africa (for more on this, see chapter 5 by Paul Eavis and William Benson).[12]

Mali's efforts received further endorsement and encouragement from the UN and the Wassenaar Arrangement. The report of the UN Panel of Governmental Experts on Small Arms, released in August 1997, referred specifically to Mali in two of its recommendations, calling for the application of small arms moratoria elsewhere and for international assistance to such efforts:

> The United Nations should adopt a proportional and integrated approach to security and development, including the identification of appropriate assistance for the internal security forces initiated with respect to Mali and other West African States, and extend it to other regions of the world where conflicts come to an end and where serious problems of the proliferation of small arms and light weapons have to be dealt with urgently. The donor community should support this new approach in regard to such regions of the world.
>
> The United Nations should encourage the adoption and implementation of

> regional or subregional moratoriums, where appropriate, on the transfer and manufacture of small arms and light weapons, as agreed upon by the States concerned.[13]

Moreover, at the December 9–10, 1997, Plenary Meeting of the Wassenaar Arrangement in Vienna, participating states welcomed and encouraged the proposed West African small arms moratorium and held a preliminary discussion on how the Arrangement might respond to such initiatives.[14]

Meanwhile, on the diplomatic front, in the early fall of 1997, President Konare urged West African heads of state to declare the moratorium effective in their countries by the end of the year and, at the December 16–17 ECOWAS summit in Lome, Togo, he pressed again for expedited announcement and adherence to the proposed moratorium. During early 1998, there was some speculation that Mali might declare the moratorium unilaterally—to lead by example and spur others to follow suit—but Mali continued to pursue its initiative through diplomatic channels, primarily within ECOWAS, aiming for a joint West African declaration. On March 12, 1998, the ECOWAS ministerial meeting in Yamoussoukro, Côte d'Ivoire, instructed the Secretariat to prepare a draft text for declaration of the moratorium at the ECOWAS summit then planned for July 1998.

UNIDIR's publication of *A Peace of Timbuktu* provided another opportunity to promote Mali's initiative. UN Secretary-General Kofi Annan's statement at the March 18, 1998, ceremony in Geneva to launch the book lauded it for showing "how disarmament can help create the conditions—the security—in which development can take place and take root." Annan observed that the consolidation and preservation of peace in Mali and West Africa depended on the success of efforts to stem the proliferation of arms and that "one possible step which I would strongly support is a subregional moratorium on the trade in small arms." He also urged concerned states to explore the possibility of negotiating an African variant of the November 1997 OAS convention on illegal arms trafficking and concluded by pledging "to do my utmost to ensure that the Malian model is brought to the attention of governments and policy makers around the world."[15]

President Konare's April 1998 visit to Norway, the country that made the largest donations to Mali's peace process, gave significant political impetus to West African adherence to the moratorium, consideration of regional applications of such moratoria elsewhere, and donor contributions to PCASED. On April 1–2, the Norwegian Initiative on Small Arms Transfers (NIAST) and the UNDP sponsored two events in Oslo to coincide with President Konare's visit: the International Conference on the Proposed Moratorium for Small Arms Transfers for West Africa, and the Seminar on Regional Moratoria as a Tool to Prevent Conflict and Reduce Violations of Human Rights and International Humanitarian Law. The participants, who represented thirteen West

African ECOWAS-member governments, twenty-three other countries (including prospective donors), UN agencies, the Wassenaar Arrangement, and NGOs, expressed strong support for the moratorium, welcomed the decision of the ECOWAS ministerial meeting to prepare for the declaration of the moratorium at the summit meeting in July, encouraged ECOWAS members to adopt and implement the moratorium without delay, and expressed hope that West Africa's example would encourage similar efforts in other subregions afflicted by conflicts or undergoing postconflict reconstruction and peace building.[16]

The mid-April release of the UN secretary-general's *Report on the Causes of Conflict and the Promotion of Durable Peace and Sustainable Development in Africa* also helped to catalyze and accelerate international efforts to address the roots and consequences of conflict in the region. The report underscored the problems of weapons proliferation and the responsibility of African states to take specific steps, including "implementing transparency and confidence-building measures in the military and security fields—including the signing of non-aggression pacts and security cooperation agreements, participation in joint military training exercises and patrols, and the harmonization of policies against illicit arms trafficking." The secretary-general also urged all African states to participate in the UN Register of Conventional Arms (a voluntary global annual reporting mechanism covering imports and exports of seven categories of major weapons systems, to which only eight African states contributed data in 1997) and to examine the desirability of establishing supplementary subregional arms registers. Notably, he also called on African countries to reduce their arms purchases to below 1.5 percent of gross domestic product (GDP) and to embrace a ten-year moratorium on defense budget increases. Finally, the report identified "reintegrating ex-combatants and others into productive society" and "curtailing the availability of small arms" among the critical priorities in postconflict peace-building efforts. Surprisingly, the report did not mention Mali's proposed small arms moratorium, but the timeliness, scope, and far reaching recommendations of the secretary-general's report will likely play a significant role in defining international responses to the causes and costs of African conflicts.[17]

Although ECOWAS postponed its summit planned for July 1998, work on the moratorium intensified in the context of ECOWAS's elaboration of a subregional conflict resolution framework, and international support for the moratorium continued to grow. During July 8–11, ECOWAS convened the international meeting, Conflict Management and Resolution: The Role of ECOWAS, in Ouagadougou, Burkina Faso. Attended by military and government officials of member states, journalists, scholars, and representatives of the United Nations, the OAU, and other international bodies, the forum issued the Ouagadougou Declaration, which called for adoption and implementation of the proposed West African small arms moratorium.[18] On July 13–14, the

Norwegian government organized the International Meeting on Small Arms in Oslo, the first-ever government meeting to address the full range of small arms issues. The twenty-one countries assembled there (including the United States and Mali) agreed on the text of "Elements of a Common Understanding" to combat small arms proliferation and misuse and endorsed eleven ongoing global and regional initiatives, including the proposed West African moratorium.[19] Also in July, ECOWAS met at the expert and ministerial levels in Banjul, Gambia, to develop the Mechanism on Conflict Prevention, Management and Resolution, Peace-Keeping and Security within the Sub-Region. After experts drafted the Mechanism during their July 13–22 meeting, the ECOWAS ministers of defense, internal affairs, and security met on July 23–24 to consider the draft Mechanism. They reached general consensus on all issues, endorsed the Mechanism, and adopted the draft declaration of the West African small arms moratorium, which would be implemented through PCASED. Formal declaration of the Mechanism and associated small arms moratorium was then referred for adoption at the October 30–31, 1998, ECOWAS summit in Abuja, Nigeria.[20]

U.S. Government Participation and Support

The ACDA, in cooperation with the U.S. State Department, has played a leading role in engendering U.S. support for Mali's subregional arms control initiative. The ACDA staff participated in the November 1996 Bamako Conference on Conflict Prevention, Disarmament, and Development in West Africa, where they distributed a paper on the role of arms control in conflict prevention, management, and resolution, along with model procedures for small arms disarmament/destruction and the protocol on procedures for the destruction of weapons covered by the Treaty on Conventional Armed Forces in Europe (CFE). The ACDA also facilitated the meeting of UN officials with the Friends of the Chair of the Wassenaar Arrangement in February 1997. In March 1997, the agency sent representatives to the Week of Peace program in Bamako, where they distributed papers advocating West African participation in the UN Register of Conventional Arms and providing an inventory of "micro-disarmament" proposals dealing with small arms. They also developed and presented the Light and Small Arms Registry, with technical specifications and descriptions of eight weapons categories (pistols, shotguns, rifles, machine guns, submachine guns, antitank weapons/mortars/howitzers, land mines, and others, including flamethrowers) as a contribution toward defining the range of arms that could be considered within the scope of the moratorium. This draft registry was incorporated into the moratorium concept paper.

In mid-August 1997, the ACDA hosted a visit to Washington, D.C., by UNDP's Ivor Richard Fung and the then-director of the UN Centre for Disarmament Affairs, Prvoslav Davinic, to address an interagency meeting that included representatives of the Departments of State, Defense, and Treasury (General Counsel/Enforcement, U.S. Customs Service, and Bureau of Alcohol, Tobacco and Firearms), as well as the U.S. Agency for International Development (AID), and to hold consultations with senior officials in the Departments of State and Defense and U.S. AID. These meetings were quite successful in promoting widespread awareness of Mali's initiative among many U.S. government departments and agencies, in illuminating its implications for U.S. interests and policies, and in identifying the types of international assistance required to establish and sustain the program.

The ACDA continued working with other agencies to identify possible sources of appropriate material, technical, and/or financial support for PCASED. It worked closely with the State Department's African Bureau to take advantage of the working visit of President Konare to Washington, D.C., in November 1997 and U.S. Secretary of State Madeleine Albright's trip to the region in December, and to explore ways the United States might support this initiative. Konare's visit to Washington helped to focus and crystallize U.S. views on the moratorium proposal. The United States endorsed this remarkable and unprecedented attempt to address serious regional security threats at all levels, complementing and reinforcing development aims in the region. The State Department incorporated support for the moratorium into its strategic plan and identified funds to assist its implementation. The United States is continuing its efforts to identify and provide other appropriate material, technical, and/or financial support for the establishment and effective implementation of the moratorium. The United States was also instrumental in calling for the UN secretary-general to report to the Security Council on the sources and solutions of African conflict, welcomed his report in April 1998, and is actively promoting implementation of many of its recommendations.

On the external side, ACDA officials sought to expand awareness of the proposed moratorium among other interested constituencies and governments. The ACDA also facilitated contacts between the UNDP and Canadian government agencies that are in a position to provide assistance for the moratorium, and Ottawa, too, made a substantial financial commitment. Additionally, ACDA officials participated in the two-day International Conference and Seminar on Small Arms Moratoria in Oslo in early April 1998 and led the U.S. delegation to the mid-July Oslo Meeting on Small Arms.

Conclusion

Although it is premature to draw any enduring conclusions, several important points should be highlighted about the Malian experience with conflict and its resolution. First, the Tuareg rebellion, which had deep historical and multidimensional roots, contributed to the emergence of democracy by forcing a narrowly based oppressive regime from power and generating pressure for more popular, inclusive, and elected governments. In this case, the March 1991 military coup was the first step in a political process that led to a new constitution and democratically elected government.

Second, and equally remarkable, Mali's leadership and people took the requisite and decisive steps toward conflict resolution and peace building. True, external assistance and mediation by multiple third parties, including the UN and other countries, were essential ingredients, but peace was restored without foreign military intervention or the introduction of peacekeeping forces. In this sense, Mali's experience stands in sharp contrast to many other African states, where protracted internal conflicts were aggravated, prolonged, and sometimes decided, or otherwise directly affected, by external military interventions (see chapter 2 by Kathi Austin). Surely in these respects, the Malian model of a largely indigenous, low-key, low-cost, bottom-up approach to conflict resolution should be more widely known and its lessons studied for possible application elsewhere.

Third, Mali is being widely cited as a test case of the validity and utility of the "security-first" approach to security and development, which has been endorsed by the United Nations and is gaining support within the international donor community. This new conception of the security-development nexus challenges the premises of "development" aid that preclude its use for security-related purposes and calls for well-targeted assistance to support conflict prevention, resolution, and peace building. It also suggests the need for a holistic approach to institution building with respect to the military—to establish its role as a valued and respected institution that contributes to both security and development and hence as a legitimate recipient of "development" aid for training in democracy, civil-military relations, and civic action.[21]

Fourth, and most salient for our purposes, arms control has been an integral part of the conflict resolution and peace-building process in Mali. From the outset, Mali recognized the intimate and reciprocal relationship between internal and regional security and that both domestic and external peace depended, inter alia, on establishing effective controls on the possession and trafficking of small arms. Hence, the demobilization, disarmament, and reintegration of ex-rebels were essential elements of the conflict resolution and peace-building processes (see also chapter 13 by Nat J. Colletta). The powerful symbolism of the March 1996 Flame of Peace underscored publicly and for the international community the abandonment of the culture of war in favor of a culture of peace. As Poulton and Youssouf argue, Mali's promotion of a subregional small arms moratorium should be seen as an integral part of its effort to expand "shared democratic space" within West Africa by securing peace at home and in its immediate neighborhood.

Fifth, Mali's successful promotion of a subregional moratorium should be seen in the context of the current wide-ranging international policy debates about small arms proliferation and what measures are likely to be effective in dealing with its many dimensions. The moratorium is among the few concrete proposals or efforts that has, or promises to have, far-reaching consequences, and the only initiative that is a true subregional arms control measure. Like Mali's domestic peace process, the West African moratorium is a modest but history-making arms control initiative. It is literally unprecedented: there has never been such an arms control arrangement. Moreover, considering that arms control has traditionally been the preserve of "great powers" and the product of Cold War tensions, it is remarkable that, in the post–Cold War era, such an arms control initiative should emerge from the heart of Africa. Indeed, it is fitting that Mali, a desperately poor, thinly populated, landlocked, remote country without geopolitical, strategic, or commercial value to the great powers, should assume the crucial task of resolving internal strife by creating a new political and socioeconomic order that integrated (for the first time) those who had resorted to arms as an act of desperation. It is also fitting that this extraordinary national reconciliation and subregional arms control initiative should occur largely unnoticed by the "great powers" but supported modestly by several UN agencies, neighboring states, and a small number of donors (including the United States). In this sense, Mali is an archetype of both post–Cold War conflicts and the creative and holistic approaches necessary for their resolution.

Although the ECOWAS small arms moratorium has obvious potential significance, its success is by no means assured. Mali's greatest asset is its moral authority, and it enjoys considerable international goodwill and support for its peace-building efforts. But it remains a poor, weak state, relying on low-key diplomacy to promote implementation of the moratorium.The moratorium's success will require substantial elaboration and technical specification, serious negotiations among interested states, the implementation of an unprecedented multilateral mechanism with limited resources, new forms of subregional cooperation, and long-term commitments. Whether this modest arms control initiative succeeds will depend heavily on the political will of West Africa's leaders and on international support. Now it is up to Mali, its neighbors, and well-meaning states elsewhere to "make it happen." If they succeed, the legacy and the lessons of this African arms control measure may well exceed even its promise and its pioneering spirit.

Notes

This chapter was originally presented and distributed under the title "Spiking the Barrel of the Gun: Mali's Proposed Sub-Regional Small Arms Moratorium" at the Fortieth Annual Meeting of the African Studies Association, Columbus, Ohio, November 13–16, 1997. It was updated for the Policy Workshop on Controlling the Global Trade in Light Weapons on December 11–12, 1997 and again for publication in this book.

The analysis and views presented here are those of the author and do not necessarily represent those of the U.S. government, the ACDA, or any other government agency.

1. The terms *regional* and *subregional* appear throughout this chapter. The former refers to Africa as a geographic region or political collectivity, within which West Africa is a subregion. Also, to simplify, I use the term *small arms* to include light weapons.

2. Basic data on Mali are drawn primarily from the eight-page section on Mali in Central Intelligence Agency, *World Factbook 1997* (www.odci.gov/cia/publications/factbook/ml.html). The 1995 GNP, GNP per capita, and GNP per capita ranking are from U.S. Arms Control and Disarmament Agency, *World Military Expenditures and Arms Transfers 1996* (Washington, D.C.: U.S. ACDA, July 1997), pp. 38, 43, 46.

3. Robin-Edward Poulton and Ibrahim ag Youssouf, *A Peace of Timbuktu: Democratic Governance, Development and African Peacekeeping,* UNIDIR/98/2 (New York and Geneva: UN Institute for Disarmament Research, 1998), p. 85.

4. Poulton and Youssouf, *A Peace of Timbuktu,* pp. 227–30. On the Flame of Peace, see *La Flamme de la Paix: Tombouctou—27 et 28 Mars 1996,* a fifty-eight-page commemorative booklet prepared and edited by le Commissariat au Nord, 1997.

5. On the origins and activities of the UN mission, see Ivor Richard Fung, "Control and Collection of Light Weapons in the Sahel-Sahara Subregion: A Mission's Report," Bonn International Center for Conversion (BICC), 1995 (http://bicc.uni-bonn.de/weapons/events/micro/fung.html), and "Control and Collection of Light Weapons in the Sahel-Sahara Subregion: A Mission's Report," *Disarmament,* vol. 19, no. 2 (September 1996), pp. 44–50.

6. Communiqué issued by the Conference on Conflict Prevention, Disarmament and Development in West Africa, Bamako, Mali, November 25–29, 1996.

7. See Poulton and Youssouf, *A Peace of Timbuktu,* Annex 2.6, "Note on a Regional Moratorium on Small Arms," pp. 287–91.

8. "Report to the Chairman of the Wassenaar Arrangement on the West African Small Arms/Light Weapons Moratorium Initiative," Wassenaar Arrangement, Vienna, April 8, 1997.

9. "Proposal by the Malian Government for a Moratorium on the Exportation, Importation, and Manufacture of Light Weapons: Aide Memoire." U.S. Department of State, Office of Language Services, Translation LS No. 701285.

10. "Moratoire sur l'importation, l'exportation et la fabrication des arms legeres," final document prepared by Ministerial Consultation on the proposal for a moratorium on export, import, and manufacturing of light weapons in Africa, Bamako, Mali, March 26, 1997. See Poulton and Youssouf, *A Peace of Timbuktu,* Annex 2.6, "Note on a Regional Moratorium on Small Arms," pp. 287–91, and "Rapport Final," Semaine de la Paix, Palais des Congres, Bamako, Mali, March 24–28, 1997.

11. "Programme for Coordination and Assistance for Security and Development (PCASED)," UNDP proposal, December 5, 1997. See also Tore Rose's statement, "The Programme for Coordination and Assistance for Security and Development in West Africa 'PCASED,'" International Conference on Regional Small Arms Moratoria, Oslo, April 1–2, 1998.

12. *Network: Newsletter on Arms Export Controls* (Summer 1997), p. 1.

13. United Nations General Assembly, "General and Complete Disarmament: Small Arms," A/52/298, August 27, 1997, p. 23.

14. Public statement of the Wassenaar Arrangement, Vienna, December 10, 1997.

15. African News Service, "Malian Example Points to Virtues of Preventive Diplomacy," March 18, 1998.

16. "The Oslo Platform for a Moratorium on Small Arms in West Africa," Conclusions from the Conference. For the full proceedings and papers from this conference, see Sverre Lodgaard and Carsten F. Ronnfeldt, eds., *A Moratorium on Light Weapons in West Africa* (Oslo: Norwegian Initiative on Small Arms Transfers and Norwegian Institute of International Affairs, 1998).

17. UN Secretary-General, *Report on the Causes of Conflict and the Promotion of Durable Peace and Sustainable Development in Africa* (New York: United Nations, April 1998), pp. 7, 14 (www.un.org/Docs/sc/reports/1998/s1998318.html).

18. Ouagadougou 2850, unclassified cable to the U.S. State Department, July 16, 1998.

19. "The Oslo Meeting on Small Arms, 13–14 July 1998—an International Agenda on Small Arms and Light Weapons: Elements of a Common Understanding" (see appendix B).

20. Banjul 1669, unclassified cable to the U.S. State Department, July 30, 1998; Abuja 518, unclassified cable to the U.S. State Department, September 3, 1998.

21. These points are succinctly presented in Tore Rose, "The Role of the United Nations in the International Community in Conflict Resolution and Peace-Building: The Case of the 'Tuareg Rebellion' in Mali," paper presented at the West Africa Workshop, European Conference on Conflict Prevention, Amsterdam, February 27–28, 1997. For elaboration, see Poulton and Youssouf, *A Peace of Timbuktu*. Depending on how one defines the various programs supporting the peace process in Mali, its cost has been as little as $10 million to $12 million.

8

Controlling Light Weapons in Southern Africa

Hussein Solomon

ONE OF THE MOST SIGNIFICANT threats confronting humanity as we approach the dawn of a new millennium is the proliferation of small arms and light weapons. Light weapons proliferation is a destabilizing factor in Third World polities for many socioeconomic reasons and also because it changes the balance of power between the state and substate actors, such as insurgents, warlords, and drug traffickers. This is especially evident in southern Africa, where the proliferation of small arms and light weapons has come to pose a significant threat to civil society.

Precise figures on the extent of light weapons proliferation in southern Africa are hard to come by. However, some indication of the scale of the problem is provided by Greg Mills, who, in 1994, estimated that there were 8.7 million small arms in the hands of the security forces of the southern African region.[1] To this must be added legal firearms belonging to private citizens, weapons caches that form part of the legacy of the liberation wars, weapons in the hands of mercenaries operating in the region, and arms belonging to the mushrooming private security industry.

The causes for this abundance of arms in the region are easily identified: anticolonial struggles, the warfare by liberation movements against minority regimes, Cold War proxy wars in Africa, destabilization operations conducted by the apartheid regime in South Africa, and the effects of postcolonial civil and ethnic strife. Today, the diffusion of such weapons is an integral part of the culture of violence, poor governance processes, and the crisis of the African state that characterize much of the continent.

The human and financial toll of this proliferation has been overwhelming for a region that is still coming to terms with a legacy of a quarter of a century of war. There are today in the region some 400 regional crime syndicates whose activities range from the smuggling of illegal immigrants to narcotrafficking, money laundering, and arms trafficking. Ordinary crime is also threatening human security; the movement of weapons from Mozambique into eastern Zimbabwe is a main reason that armed robberies increased by 30 percent in the last quarter of 1995 in Zimbabwe's eastern Manicaland bordering Mozambique.[2]

The ready availability of light weapons also provides the means to transform ethnic differences into open conflict, whether between the Bakalanga and Tswana in Botswana; the Ovimbundu, Kimbundu, and *mesticoes* (those of mixed Portuguese/Angolan descent) in Angola; the Ndau and Shangaan in Mozambique; or the Ndebele and Shona in Zimbabwe. The threat of ethnic secession or irredentism, in the classic style of Biafra or Katanga, requires little stretching of the imagination.[3]

The gravity of the threat posed by light weapons proliferation to regional stability is evidenced in the number of proposals by regional government and nongovernment entities aimed at eradicating this scourge. Most are based on eliminating the demand for light weapons by addressing the root causes of southern Africa's insecurity: economic, sociocultural, political, and environmental. Yet the *eradication* of light weapons proliferation will necessarily entail a long-term effort; in the short to medium term, the emphasis should be on *control.*

Curbing Light Weapons Proliferation: National Responses

Various governments in the region have embarked on a variety of measures aimed at curbing the tide of light weapons proliferation. These have included a combination of outright confiscations, amnesties, rewards, and the imposition of heavy penalties. In South Africa, such efforts have also included the progressive tightening of the Arms and Ammunition Act of 1969 along with a more restrictive approach to the granting of firearm licenses.[4] In addition, there have been joint operations between the South African National Defence Force (SANDF) and the South African Police Services (SAPS) intended to combat rising criminality and small arms proliferation. As Mills has noted, however, these efforts achieved little success in relation to the magnitude of the problem in South Africa.[5] Similar efforts by the Royal Swaziland Police's Criminal Investigation Department to curb light weapons proliferation have also proved unsuccessful.[6]

At the conclusion of the civil war in Mozambique, the government there insisted that all weapons be handed over by former combatants at designated collection points. This proved largely unsuccessful, given the fact that the human dimensions of the problem were not taken into consideration. This is clearly borne out in the following statement by a former Frelimo combatant: "Guns can mean food and a way to survive."[7] The lesson is instructive: in conditions of an apathetic government or one that is too poor and weak to provide basic necessities and security to citizens, many individuals will attempt to provide these for themselves—even if this is achieved at the expense of others. A pertinent South African example of this phenomenon is the heavily armed vigilante group People Against Gangsterism and Drugs (PAGAD). In such situations, efforts by government authorities to collect firearms will often prove unsuccessful.

These failures at the national level have resulted in a great deal of introspection on the part of the security services within the region. An understanding has gradually emerged that light weapons proliferation is a phenomenon that exists at the national, regional, and international levels and that it needs to be combated at all three strata simultaneously. The perceived importance of the regional dimension for South African security was reinforced by the fact that weapons were entering the country from Mozambique, Angola, Namibia, Swaziland, Botswana, Zimbabwe, Zambia, Lesotho, and the Democratic Republic of Congo (DRC).[8] Unilateral South African efforts at bolstering border posts simply resulted in the diversion of weapons flows to other areas.[9] The lack of success in such endeavors is evinced in the fact that the SAPS estimated that it recovers only 10 percent of all illegal weapons entering the country.[10]

Bilateral Responses

In recognition of the regional dimensions of the problem, some states in the region have responded to the problem of light weapons proliferation through bilateral initiatives of various types. Thus, in an effort to reduce cross-border flows of black-market arms, the Angolan government has embarked on a number of bilateral or joint commissions with neighboring countries, including Zambia, Namibia, Congo (Brazzaville), and the DRC.[11] South Africa, too, has embarked on the bilateral route, having signed bilateral accords with Swaziland and Mozambique. This type of bilateral cooperation has produced results. Shortly after a formal security agreement was signed between Maputo and Pretoria, joint Mozambican-South African police operations in Mozambique (Operations Rachel I and Rachel II) netted several large arms caches.[12]

Despite these successes, the bilateral route also suffers from certain weaknesses. As with unilateral endeavors, bilateral measures such as the joint Mozambican-South African police operations in southern Mozambique simply produced a change in weapons trafficking routes.[13] It soon dawned on policymakers that, in addition to national and bilateral endeavors, a regional approach to light weapons proliferation was essential.

Regional Responses

The proliferation of transnational security threats such as light weapons proliferation, combined with the perceived limitations of national or bilateral endeavors in dealing with them, has led to an increasing emphasis on regional responses.[14] Another factor in the development of regional responses arises from the post–Cold War strategic environment in Africa. While Africa was viewed as an important theater of competition during the Cold War era—a situation that provided African governments with a certain amount of leverage when dealing with the superpowers—the region no longer possesses much strategic interest for the developed countries, whether as a location for military bases or as prizes in the East-West ideological competition. The demise of communism has not, therefore, resulted in a rise in status for the developing world but rather in a demotion to peripheral status.

The reality of Africa's marginalization has, however, been precisely the stimulus that was needed to prod the leadership of the Organization of African Unity (OAU) to rejuvenate the moribund organization. This was demonstrated, most significantly, by the establishment of the OAU Division of Conflict Management in March 1992. This was followed, in June 1993, by the establishment of the Central Mechanism for Conflict Prevention, Management and Resolution. OAU Secretary-General Salim Ahmed Salim later stated,

> The establishment of the Mechanism was an act of historical significance and self-empowerment. What Africa said to the world is that yes, we may continue to need outside help in dealing with our problems, but we will be centrally involved and provide leadership in any efforts at conflict resolution. . . . We can no longer fold our hands and wait for the foreigners to come and resolve our problems.[15]

Of particular importance is the fact that the OAU Mechanism was intended to engage in close collaboration with subregional organizations, such as the Southern Africa Development Community (SADC). Thus, the development of subregional organizations was also stimulated by the OAU's revival. It is imperative that we view the formation and development of the SADC within this regional and international context.

There are no specific structures within the region tasked with curbing light weapons proliferation; however, two existing southern African institutions possess the potential to effectively deal with this scourge: the Inter-State Defense and Security Committee (ISDSC) of the SADC and the Southern African Regional Police Chiefs Cooperation Organization (SARPCCO). Each is described briefly below.

Historical Development of the SADC

The SADC was established in 1980 as the Southern African Development Coordination Conference (SADCC) with Angola, Botswana, Lesotho, Malawi, Mozambique, Swaziland, Tanzania, Zambia, and Zimbabwe as founding members; Namibia was to join soon after achieving its independence from South Africa. Its membership has expanded further in recent years: South Africa joined the organization in 1994, Mauritius in 1995, and the DRC and the Seychelles in 1997.

For the first twelve years of its existence, the SADCC operated without a legal framework or treaty. Conscious of the poor record of regional economic integration schemes in Africa and elsewhere in the developing world, the founders of the SADCC opted for a loose organization to promote cooperation and coordination rather than formal integration. Their aim was to reduce members' external economic dependence, mainly—but not exclusively—on apartheid South Africa, and to promote development. The focus of the organization, therefore, has been largely on issues of economic cooperation and development.

It was only in 1989, at the SADCC heads of state meeting in Harare, that a decision was taken to formalize the organization and to give it a permanent legal status to replace the existing Memorandum of Agreement. Four years of consultation followed before the declaration and treaty of the SADC was eventually signed by heads of state and government in Windhoek in 1992. The treaty expressed confidence that recent developments, such as the independence of Namibia and the transition in South Africa, "will take the region out of an era of conflict and confrontation, to one of cooperation in a climate of peace, security and stability. These are prerequisites for development."[16] With the change of name, the SADC's emphasis changed from "development coordination" to "development integration." In essence, the fundamental vision of the SADC became that of full economic integration within the southern African region.

A further objective of the SADC treaty is to "promote and defend peace and security." The Windhoek Declaration of 1992, which established the SADC, specifically called for "a framework of cooperation which provides for . . . strengthening regional solidarity, peace, and security, in order for the people of the region to live and work together in peace and harmony. . . . The region needs, therefore, to establish a framework and mechanisms to strengthen regional solidarity, and provide for mutual peace and security."[17] These concerns regarding regional peace and security were to culminate in June 1996 in the establishment of the SADC Organ for Politics, Defense and Security.

The SADC Organ for Politics, Defense, and Security

Right from the start, the SADC wisely decided to separate political and security considerations from the "SADC proper" (i.e., from its primary focus on economic development). Through the establishment of the Organ, the SADC moved away from an ad hoc approach in addressing common foreign and security issues. The Organ will abide by the same principles as that of the SADC, including the sovereign equality of all member states, the peaceful settlement of disputes, and the observance of human rights, democracy, and the rule of law.[18] From the perspective of arms control, the most important objective of the SADC Organ is security and defense cooperation as a first step toward the development of a collective security capacity.[19]

One of the institutions that has been absorbed into the Organ is the existing ISDSC, with its impressive system of committees on defense, police, and intelligence matters. The ISDSC is chaired by the ministers of defense of the various SADC member states on a rotational basis. It brings structure to the Organ and does so at no central expense to the SADC (since the various governments pay for their involvement in the ISDSC from their own budgets).

The ISDSC

The ISDSC is the most important substructure of the SADC Organ. In essence, it is a forum at which ministers responsible for defense, home affairs/public security, and state security meet to discuss issues relating to their individual and collective defense and common security issues. The chief of the Zambian air force has listed the objectives of the ISDSC as follows:

- Prevention of aggression from within the region and from outside the region
- Prevention of coup d'états
- Management and resolution of conflicts
- Promotion of regional stability
- Promotion of regional peace
- Promotion and enhancement of regional development[20]

In pursuit of these objectives, member states have resolved to share intelligence on such issues as motor vehicle thefts, narcotrafficking, counterfeit-currency operations, illegal immigration, forged travel documents, and the smuggling of weapons.[21] This is of immense importance in any regional effort to curb light weapons proliferation, given growing evidence that those engaged in the smuggling of weapons are also engaged in other illicit activities, such as narcotrafficking. It is also gratifying to note that member states are committed to eradicating any threat to political instability. This, too, is of grave importance. Historically, political instability has served to increase light weapons proliferation as arms smugglers respond to the demands of a potential market and as political instability reduces governments' capacity to effectively deal with arms smuggling.

The Southern African Regional Police Chiefs Cooperation Organization

Because of the increasingly transnational nature of crime and criminal syndicates, police commissioners of the various SADC nations Angola, Botswana, Lesotho, Malawi, Mozambique, Namibia, South Africa, Swaziland, Tanzania, Zambia, and Zimbabwe—have opted to pursue a more regional approach in combating crime.[22] This is evident in the establishment at Victoria Falls on August 2, 1995, of the Southern African Regional Police Chiefs Cooperation Organization by the police chiefs of the aforementioned states. SARPCCO is composed of the following bodies:

- The Council of Police Chiefs (CPC), the supreme body within SARPCCO, which is responsible for the development of policy and the efficient functioning of all SARPCCO structures. All chiefs of police of member states are members of the CPC.
- A Permanent Coordinating Committee (PCC), which consists of heads of the criminal investigation divisions (CIDs) of all member countries. The PCC is responsible for formulating strategy to combat crime in the region.
- A Secretariat, consisting of one or two officers from each member state, which, according to the SARPCCO Constitution, comprises the Sub-Regional Bureau of Interpol in Harare. As a result, the Sub-Regional Bureau of Interpol has dedicated a desk to look after all SARPCCO affairs, to follow up on all resolutions, and to coordinate the activities of all subcommittees.
- A Legal Subcommittee, which consists of officers with a legal background whose task it is to make recommendations in relation to legislation, ratification of international conventions, deportations, repatriation of exhibits, and so forth.
- A Training Subcommittee, whose objective is the improvement of training standards within the region.[23]

The importance of this structure will become apparent in the next two sections. As with the ISDSC, there is no specific structure within SARPCCO seeking to curb light weapons proliferation; however, the problem of illegal firearms trafficking is addressed in the form of the Endangered Species and Firearms Desk. Under the auspices of this Desk, a study is in progress to assess the volume of the illicit firearms trade in the region.

The ISDSC and SARPCCO: Strengths and Weaknesses

Both the ISDSC and SARPCCO must be viewed as giving practical expression to the notion that transnational sources of insecurity necessitate transnational solutions. To that extent, both of these structures are also excellent confidence-building measures, but the positive features of both structures go beyond mere confidence building. The ISDSC, for instance, is intended not only to provide a mechanism by which regional cooperation can be enhanced and coordinated but also to constitute a vehicle through which all the key players are brought together and their activities coordinated and combined in order to promote a collective approach to regional security.[24] Likewise, it is a positive feature that SARPCCO is co-located with the Sub-Regional Bureau of Interpol: light weapons proliferation is an international phenomenon, and the close relationship between SARPCCO and Interpol would be useful in mapping the interface between regional and international arms flows.

Notwithstanding these positive features, both organizations suffer from several weaknesses. In the first place, the continual expansion of the political entity known as southern Africa might have adverse consequences on the structure and organizational effectiveness of both the ISDSC and SARPCCO. In addition, it is clear that the duality of leadership within the SADC (South Africa as chair of the SADC and Zimbabwe as chair of the SADC Organ) is having a negative effect on the optimal functioning of the ISDSC, which falls under the SADC Organ. To the extent that this might also affect the workings of SARPCCO, any effort to incorporate SARPCCO into the ISDSC should be resisted (at least in the short term). Being independent also frees SARPCCO from the political machinations of the SADC. This should not lead, however, to the emergence of an antagonistic relationship between SARPCCO and the ISDSC; indeed, the strong ties currently existing between SARPCCO and the ISDSC's Public Security Subcommittee should be strengthened.

Another problem facing both institutions is the lack of capacity within the region's states. As noted by Glenn Oosthuysen, "Widespread corruption, lack of accountability on the part of officials, limited manpower, training, and operational resources are just some of the factors which mitigate against effective controls being implemented by these states."[25]

Closely related to the lack of capacity is the inability of many states in the region to exercise effective governance over the entire area of their sovereign territory. This relates to the core of the current African dilemma: the fragility of the African polity. For instance, it has been noted that Luanda's authority extends to only 20 percent of its 4,000-kilometer border.[26] A similar situation is faced by President Laurent Kabila of the DRC: Kinshasa's authority does not extend to large areas in the east of the country, where heavily armed Mai-Mai and Tutsi militia are in control. Thus, legal agreements signed within the context of the SADC and SARPCCO cannot be honored by certain state parties on account of either limited capacity or their not being in full control of large territories within their borders.

It is also clear that both of these organizations need to be considerably strengthened, in particular through enhanced capabilities in the field. In addition, the ISDSC needs to be strengthened by the creation of a permanent secretariat and the post of executive secretary, and it is imperative that specialized units be established within either or both organizations to exclusively investigate light weapons proliferation within the region.[27] These units should include officials from a variety of state structures, including defense, foreign affairs, justice, police, home affairs, customs and excise, and intelligence. This would also have an additional spin-off: highlighting the threat that light weapons proliferation poses to all aspects of states' authority in southern Africa.

As part of the SADC's proposed early warning system, a regional database needs to be established for tracking light weapons proliferation in southern Africa. Such a database could warn policymakers of an impending crisis (such as an insurrection, coup, civil war, or the emergence of organized crime syndicates), thus helping to identify areas where a strong demand for light weapons is likely to surface. With this information, authorities could take the necessary countermeasures with which to curb the diffusion of light weapons in the region.

Conclusion

All of this is, of course, a tall order. Clearly, those SADC member states that arm insurgents in other countries[28] would not welcome a regional arms database. On the other hand, governments may fear to act against arms traffickers for political reasons. In the case of Mozambique, it is a well-known fact that Renamo bases in southern Mozambique are used as depots for the arms trade;[29] the Frelimo government's failure to seize these depots could be explained as a reluctance to take steps that could lead to renewed civil war. Yet one should not be overly pessimistic about efforts to combat light weapons proliferation. Especially with help from the international community, regional policymakers could implement the following:

- Strengthening national efforts at border control.
- Building up indigenous capacities for government oversight, law en-

forcement, and customs regulation. South Africa, with its greater resources, should extend technical and logistical assistance to its neighbors. In addition, the recent initiative by the U.S. Federal Bureau of Investigation to assist South Africa in establishing its first detective academy in Pretoria should be expanded. In all cases, the transference of technical skills should be accompanied by an emphasis on human rights.
- Implementing an international ban on the transfer of arms to authoritarian governments. Given the cycle in which repressive governments stimulate the emergence of a violent opposition and an escalating demand for light weapons, the adoption of such a ban is essential to prevent the further proliferation of such weapons.[30]
- Efforts to eliminate corruption in all its forms.
- Imposing stricter controls on the private-security industry.
- Adopting a protocol similar to the recent OAS Convention on illicit arms trafficking. (See chapter 10.)

In pursuing these initiatives, it is essential not to view regional mechanisms as pertaining exclusively to intergovernment organizations such as the SADC. Complementing and reinforcing such efforts on the part of governments, dynamic partnerships are needed between international organizations, the nongovernmental organization (NGO) sector, the private sector, and regional structures. In particular, such partnerships are needed for the creation of an early warning system and for efforts aimed at the reintegration of former combatants into civil society.

Within South Africa, for instance, there are several NGOs doing excellent work on arms control, national legislation, the culture of violence, the arms trade, and illicit arms trafficking. These include, for instance, the Centre for Conflict Resolution, the Ceasefire Campaign, Gun-Free South Africa, and the South African Institute for International Affairs. Especially noteworthy is the Small Arms Programme of the Institute for Security Studies, which seeks to map and analyze the diffusion of small arms in southern Africa and ultimately propose measures for its control. In developing capacity in regional states, as discussed above, it would be unfortunate not to tap into the resources of this vibrant NGO community.

Finally, all of these regional initiatives need to be complemented by vigorous efforts at the international and national levels. At the international level, the UN Register of Conventional Arms should be expanded to include light weapons. The proposed SADC Regional Arms Register could then be fed into this revamped UN Register. At the national level, there is an urgent need to limit both the spiraling numbers of legal, licensed firearms and to crack down on the illegal arms trade. In this regard, all government armories should be subjected to greater oversight and control.

Though the obstacles to curb light weapons proliferation may appear insurmountable, governments in the region have no option but to seek the eradication of this scourge. The alternative, should they fail to do so, is as stark as it is brutal: a southern Africa wracked by civil and ethnic strife and poverty, a region on the margins of global capital flows, another region demonstrating the myth of the African renaissance.

Notes

1. Greg Mills, "Small Arms Control: Some Early Thoughts," *African Defence Review*, vol. 15 (1994), p. 45.
2. Alex Vines, "Light Weapons Transfers, Human Rights Violations and Armed Banditry in Southern Africa," paper presented to the Light Weapons Proliferation and Opportunities for Control Workshop, hosted by the British American Security Information Council Project on Light Weapons, London, June 30–July 2, 1996, p. 12.
3. Hussein Solomon and Jakkie Cilliers, "Sources of Southern African Insecurity and the Quest for Regional Integration," in H. Solomon and J. Cilliers, eds., *People, Poverty and Peace: Human Security in Southern Africa,* IDP Monograph Series, June 4, 1996, pp. 12–14.
4. Mills, "Small Arms Control," p. 47.
5. Mills, "Small Arms Control," p. 47.
6. Glenn Oosthuysen, *Small Arms Proliferation and Control in Southern Africa* (Johannesburg: South African Institute for International Affairs, 1996), p. 66.
7. Quoted in Jacklyn Cock, "Weaponry and the Culture of Violence in Southern Africa," unpublished paper (Johannesburg: Department of Sociology, University of the Witwatersrand), p. 30.
8. Cock, "Weaponry and the Culture of Violence in Southern Africa," p. 26.
9. Mills, "Small Arms Control," p. 50.
10. Glenn Oosthuysen, "Small Arms Proliferation in South Africa: The Role of Border Security," *International Update* (Johannesburg: South African Institute of International Affairs, January 1996), p. 1.
11. Oosthuysen, *Small Arms Proliferation and Control in Southern Africa,* p. 65.
12. Vines, "Light Weapons Transfers," p. 13.
13. Vines, "Light Weapons Transfers," p. 15.
14. This section is an extract from an article titled "The Southern African Development Community and Light Weapons Proliferation," written by Hussein Solomon and Jakkie Cilliers for the Towards Collaborative Peace Project, Institute for Security Studies, Halfway House, South Africa, 1997.
15. S. A. Salim, "The Front-Line States: A New Alliance for Peace and Development in Southern Africa," keynote address to the Meeting of the Ministers of Defence and Security of the Front-Line States, Arusha, Tanzania, November 10, 1994. Reprinted in *Backgrounder,* no. 17, Centre for Southern African Studies, University of the Western Cape, Cape Town, 1994, p. 8.
16. Declaration by the Heads of State or Government of Southern African States, "Towards the Southern African Development Community," in *Declaration Treaty and Protocol of the Southern African Development Community,* Windhoek, August 17, 1992, p. 2.

17. Declaration by the Heads of State or Government of Southern African States, "Towards the Southern African Development Community," in *Declaration Treaty and Protocol of the Southern African Development Community,* Windhoek, August 17, 1992, pp. 5, 10.

18. Communiqué on the establishment of the Organ for Politics, Defence and Security, Gaborone, January 1996.

19. Communiqué on the establishment of the Organ for Politics, Defence and Security, Gaborone, January 1996.

20. See R. S. Shikapwashya, "Presentation on the Aims, Roles, Functions and Organisation of the Standing Aviation Committee of the Inter-State Defence and Security Committee for the Southern African Region," paper presented at the Sir Pierre van Rhyneveld Air Power Conference, Pretoria, October 3, 1995, p. 14.

21. D. Hamman, "Paper on the Inter-State Defence and Security Committee: Defence Sub-Committee," presented at an Institute for Defence Policy roundtable seminar, South African and Global Peace Support Initiatives, Cape Town, May 17–18, 1995, p. 5.

22. Z. Lavisa (deputy commissioner, SAPS), "Police Co-operation across Borders and Ideas for Enhancement," paper presented at the Institute for Security Studies conference, pp. 1, 6.

23. F. J. Msutu, "Enhancement of the Southern African Regional Police Chiefs Co-operation Organisation," paper presented to the Institute for Security Studies Roundtable, September 22, 1997, pp. 3–4; Lavisa, "Police Co-operation across Borders and Ideas for Enhancement," p. 7.

24. Lavisa, "Police Co-operation across Borders and Ideas for Enhancement," p. 9.

25. Oosthuysen, *Small Arms Proliferation and Control in Southern Africa,* p. x.

26. Oosthuysen, *Small Arms Proliferation and Control in Southern Africa,* p. 60.

27. Oosthuysen, *Small Arms Proliferation and Control in Southern Africa,* p. 112.

28. Angola's recent arming and military support to Denis Sassou-Nguesso against President Pascal Lissouba in Congo-Brazzaville is one example.

29. Vines, "Light Weapons Transfers," p. 14.

30. Michael Klare, "Stemming the Lethal Trade in Small Arms and Light Weapons," *Issues in Science and Technology* (Fall 1995), p. 55.

Part Four

International Cooperation in Controlling Light Weapons

9

The United Nations and the Control of Light Weapons

Graciela Uribe de Lozano

CONCERN OVER THE SECURITY impact of conventional arms proliferation has been growing among members of the international community for some time. Still, constructive debate in the United Nations and other fora over potential areas for international cooperation on this issue remained elusive for many years. While many international leaders felt that establishing controls on the conventional arms trade was a matter of great urgency, there was also a feeling that improved global collaboration in this field was a long-term project.

It was not until the end of the Cold War, when the consequences of internal conflicts and other forms of civil violence became more evident, that international policymakers began to give serious attention to this issue. In particular, policymakers have come to understand that the indiscriminate accumulation, circulation, and transfer of small arms and light weapons has a direct effect on the likelihood and severity of internal conflicts. This, in turn, has had a direct impact on the work of the United Nations, in that UN peacekeeping forces have been inserted into many of these conflicts—often suffering significant casualties in the process. The global rise in criminal violence—fueled, to a considerable degree, by the illicit trade in light weapons—has also prompted UN interest in this problem. As a result, there has been a steady increase in the attention being devoted to these issues at the United Nations over the past ten years.

This interest was captured by Secretary-General Boutros Boutros-Ghali in his concept of "micro-disarmament." In the January 1995 "Supplement to an Agenda for Peace," Boutros-Ghali defined this concept as "practical disarmament in the context of the conflicts the United Nations is actually dealing with and of the weapons, most of them light weapons, that are actually killing people in the hundreds of thousands." Arguing that the worldwide accumulation of small arms and light weapons had produced a significant threat to world peace and stability, he called for new international efforts to curb the trade in such munitions: "Progress since 1992 in the area of weapons of mass destruction and major weapons systems must be followed by parallel progress in conventional arms, particularly with respect to light weapons."[1]

Similar views have been expressed by current Secretary-General Kofi Annan. "With regard to conventional weapons," he told the Conference on Disarmament in January 1998, "there is a growing awareness among Member States of the urgent need to adopt measures to reduce the transfer of small arms and light weapons. It is now incumbent on all of us to translate this shared awareness into decisive action."

This chapter traces the expansion of interest by the international community in the dilemma posed by the proliferation of small arms and light weapons, with a particular focus on developments at the United Nations.

The General Assembly's Special Sessions on Disarmament

The Final Document adopted by consensus at the conclusion of the First Special Session of the General Assembly on Disarmament, held in 1978, dealt with two major aspects of the conventional weapons issue: the reduction of armed forces and conventional weapons (especially those of the major military powers) and the limitation of the international transfers of such weapons. Elaborating on both aspects of this question, the Final Document (in paragraphs 81 and 85 of its Program of Action) states the following:

> Together with negotiations on nuclear disarmament measures, the limitation and gradual reduction of armed forces and conventional weapons should be resolutely pursued within the framework of progress towards general and complete disarmament. States with the largest military arsenals have a special responsibility in the process of conventional armaments reductions. . . .
>
> Consultations should be carried out among major arms suppliers and recipient countries on the limitation of all types of international transfers of conventional weapons . . . with a view to promoting or enhancing stability at a lower military

> level, taking into account the need of all states to protect their security as well as the inalienable right to self determination and independence of peoples under colonial or foreign domination. . . .

Following the adoption of the Final Document, a number of countries indicated that this was the first time that the United Nations had addressed these issues in a realistic and constructive way and expressed the view that these concerns had been firmly established as priority items for future deliberation by the organization.

When the Second Special Session of the General Assembly on Disarmament convened in 1982, primary attention was focused on the threat posed by nuclear weapons. This was due, in large part, to an upsurge in East-West tensions brought about by the Soviet invasion of Afghanistan and the military buildup announced by the Reagan administration. The resulting acceleration of the nuclear arms race was the principal topic of discussion during this session, and therefore little attention was given to the continuing supply of light weapons to areas of conflict in the developing world.

By the late 1980s, however, growing interest in the conventional weapons issue drew increased public attention to the economic and social consequences of the arms trade. This was evident in the studies prepared for the 1987 UN Conference on Disarmament and Development. Many of these studies, and accompanying statements at the Conference, focused on the diversion of critical resources to the military sector at the expense of economic and social development. In this context, discussion of international peace and security was broadened to include nonmilitary threats to security, such as poverty and economic insecurity.

By the time of the Third Special Session of the General Assembly on Disarmament (SSOD III) in 1988, the proliferation of conventional weapons was seen as an important dimension of the general discussion on the nature and scope of measures required to enhance international security. In an attempt to identify possible solutions to this problem, questions related to the "demand and supply" of such weapons were emphasized. On the demand side lay the history of international tensions and conflict that produced insecurity, especially among the newly independent nations; on the supply side lay the nature and character of the arms industry and the technological evolution of conventional weaponry.

In all, twenty-six nations addressed these issues in the plenary debate of SSOD III. In addition, statements by the UN secretary-general, the European Community, and the League of Arab States all made reference to the central role of conventional weapons production and transfers in international security affairs and to the need for international collaboration in devising adequate controls on these weapons. Nevertheless, some nations in the Non-Aligned Movement expressed particular sensitivity to the fact that the issue of arms transfers was being considered solely under "conventional weapons" and did not include the international transport of weapons of mass destruction or the transfer of weapons within the major military alliances.

The Forty-Third Session of the General Assembly (1988)

During the forty-third session of the United Nations General Assembly, held in 1988, many of the discussions and initiatives of SSOD III came to fruition. Citing numerous documents and studies addressing the conventional arms trade as a matter of global security, the General Assembly adopted Resolution 43/75 I. In this resolution—the first adopted by the United Nations on this issue—the General Assembly expressed its conviction that arms transfers, in all their aspects, deserved serious consideration by the international community. In particular, the resolution highlighted the following aspects of the problem:

- The potential negative effects of arms transfers in areas where tension and disorder threaten international peace and security
- Their potential negative effects on the process of peaceful social and economic development of all peoples
- The growing impact of illicit and covert arms trafficking

Resolution 43/75 I requested member states to consider, inter alia, the following measures relating to these concerns:

- Reinforcement of national systems of control and vigilance concerning the production, export, and transshipment of arms
- Examination of ways and means for eschewing the acquisition of arms in excess of those needed for legitimate national defense requirements (taking into account the specific characteristics of each region)
- Examination of ways and means of achieving greater openness and transparency with regard to international arms transfers

The resolution also reaffirmed the central role of the United Nations in this area and requested that the secretary-general take steps to "study ways and means of promoting transparency in international transfers of conventional arms."

Transparency and the Transfer of Conventional Weapons

When, in response to Resolution 43/75 I, a group of government experts began a study of transparency in 1989, the prospects for devising controls on the arms trade appeared slight. At the time, it was thought that a commitment to greater transparency in this field was the most that could be expected. However, hope was also expressed that continued attention to this problem at the United Nations might provide increased awareness of the need for a comprehensive approach to the control of conventional arms transfers.

When completed in 1991, the study on transparency reaffirmed the right of states to maintain and equip armed forces for their individual and collective defense but warned that the exercise of this right—particularly when it led to acquisitions beyond reasonable defense requirements—can have negative consequences for the security of individual states, for regional and international stability, and for the social and economic development of nations.[2] To obtain greater awareness of international arms flows and to serve as a confidence-building measure for the development of more elaborate measures, the study proposed the establishment of a voluntary Register of Conventional Arms, covering the export and import of major weapons systems. Establishment of such a register was mandated by the UN General Assembly in Resolution 46/36 of December 9, 1991.[3]

In addition to discussing the issue of transparency, the 1991 study also discussed the problem of illicit arms trafficking. In this regard, member states were urged to give high priority to the eradication of this trade and to undertake the following practical measures:

- Ensure that they have in place an adequate body of national legislation, regulations, and procedures to ensure effective control of exports and imports of arms, with a view to preventing them from getting into the hands of parties engaged in the illicit arms trade
- Ensure the effective control of borders, with a view to preventing illicit arms transfers
- Maintain an effective system of arms import/export licenses and end-user certificates (or equivalent mechanisms), as appropriate
- Provide for adequate numbers of customs officials appropriately trained to effectively enforce controls over the export and import of arms
- Cooperate with one another at the bilateral, regional, and global levels to share information on the trafficking in arms
- Intensify their efforts against bribery and corruption

In line with the recommendations of the study on transparency, the government of Colombia introduced a proposal for UN action on the illicit arms trade. The resulting measure, adopted unanimously as Resolution 46/36 H of 1991, asserts that all member states have an obligation to establish an adequate body of laws and administrative machinery for regulating and monitoring their arms transfers with a view to preventing illicit transactions. In addition, it calls on states to cooperate at the international, regional, and subregional levels to harmonize laws and regulations pertaining to arms transfers and to cooperate in aggressive law enforcement efforts against illicit traffickers.

Resolution 46/36 H also affirmed that the United Nations has a central role to play in stimulating efforts to curb the illicit arms trade. In particular, the secretary-general was encouraged to assist in holding meetings and seminars at the national, regional, and international levels to increase awareness of the destructive and destabilizing effects of the illicit traffic in arms and to explore ways and means for effecting its eradication. The secretary-general was further invited to provide advisory assistance to member states in the establishment and enforcement of laws and procedures governing the trade in arms. Finally, the resolution requested the UN Disarmament Commission to place the issue of international arms transfers on the agenda for its upcoming meetings.

The UN Disarmament Commission

The UN Disarmament Commission (UNDC) started considering matters related to conventional arms transfers during its 1994 substantive session. At its 1996 session, the Commission adopted a set of practical guidelines in response to General Assembly Resolution 46/36 H, signifying a substantial consensus on this complex and sensitive issue.

Although focused in particular on problems of the illicit arms trade, the UNDC highlighted the significance of small arms in contemporary armed conflict: "The use of small arms and light weapons in conflicts and war has a major bearing on regional and international peace and security and national stability. The alarming dissemination and illicit transfer of such weapons and the serious threat they pose require states to ensure strong and effective supervision of all aspects of the trade in such weapons." As such, the guidelines provide an important expression of the principles governing the emerging field of "micro-disarmament."

The Panel of Governmental Experts on Small Arms

Growing concern about the global spread of light weapons and the risks posed to UN peacekeepers provided the rationale for General Assembly Resolution 50/70 B, sponsored by Japan and adopted by the Fiftieth General Assembly in 1995. This resolution, on the question of how to prevent and reduce the destabilizing consequences of the excessive accumulation of small arms and light weapons, served as the point of departure for the work of the Panel of Governmental Experts, commissioned by the secretary-general, to study the issue. In preparing its report, the Panel also took into account the views submitted to the secretary-general by member states in response to the resolution and a wide range of other relevant information and materials collected by the UN Secretariat.

The task entrusted to the Panel of Governmental Experts (which began its deliberations in the spring of 1996) was to achieve further progress in clarifying the questions posed by Resolution 50/70 B. At the outset, the Panel encountered considerable difficulty in interpreting the not very clear-cut distinction between measures intended for the "reduction" of weapons accumulations and for "prevention" of further accumulations. For example, measures taken to demobilize former combatants in an area where a conflict had been terminated can be viewed as "reduction" but can also serve to "prevent" the recurrence of conflict or the outbreak of other violent activities (such as armed banditry). At the same time, it seemed obvious to the Panel that the question of reducing and preventing the excessive and destabilizing accumulation of light weapons in situations of conflict or ongoing war would prove impossible without adequately addressing the root causes of these conflicts as well as the very motives that impel countries and individuals to supply and acquire such munitions.

Trying to define to what extent the accumulation of small arms and light weapons could be considered "excessive" and needed to be "reduced" also turned out to be a difficult task, inasmuch as the accumulation of a large number of weapons in the hands of a responsible government might not appear excessive, while a small number of weapons, when placed in the wrong hands, can be both excessive and highly destabilizing. The basic problem here, of course, is in defining when a government can be considered "responsible" in matters of arms control and when such weapons are thought to be "in the wrong hands."

Ideally, there should be agreed-on international criteria regarding the potential effects of small arms and light weapons production, transfer, and accumulation and establishing the circumstances under which such accumulations become "excessive" and "destabilizing" and therefore need to be prevented or reduced. While such precision does not appear attainable, the Panel determined that weapons stockpiles that exceed the level necessary for maintaining peace and security add to instability and that the illicit trade in small arms and light weapons, which generally places these weapons in the wrong hands, is always destabilizing.

In its report, released on August 27, 1997, the Panel offered important recommendations regarding the safeguarding of small arms and light weapons against loss through theft and corruption as well as the disposal of surplus munitions and of weapons remaining after the end of conflicts[4] (for selections of this report, see appendix A).

As to recommendations on the ways and means to "prevent" and "reduce" the destabilizing effects of excessive accumulations and transfers of small arms and light weapons, specific measures were envisaged by the Panel regarding two key aspects of the issue. First is a set of measures aimed at reducing such accumulations and transfers in specific areas of the world where such accumulations and transfers have already taken place. This is followed by a set of measures to "prevent" such accumulations from occurring in the future, particularly with respect to the indiscriminate circulation of and illicit trafficking in such weapons.

The issue of civilian firearms regulations—considered by some Panel members as directly related to the "prevention" of illicit arms transfers (particularly for countries at the receiving end of such trafficking)—was left to be addressed by the UN Commission on Crime Prevention and Criminal Justice (see below). Nonetheless, the importance of curbing the illicit arms trade was emphasized in the Panel's report, and specific recommendations were made for measures to be taken by member states in this regard.

The Panel also decided to recommend that the United Nations entertain the possibility of convening an international conference on the illicit arms trade in all its aspects. It is now up to member states to take the necessary steps to convene such a conference, with the goal of reaching agreement on specific legal measures and procedures for the control of small arms and light weapons, aimed at ensuring an international framework to prevent their illicit circulation and trafficking.

In response to the report of the Panel of Governmental Experts, the General Assembly, on December 9, 1997, adopted Resolution 52/38 J, "Small Arms." The resolution "endorses" the recommendations made by the Panel and calls on member states to "implement the relevant recommendations to the extent possible" and, in doing so, to promote "international and regional cooperation among police, intelligence, customs, and border control services."

Resolution 52/38 J also authorized the secretary-general to proceed with a number of fresh initiatives in this area. For instance, the secretary-general was encouraged to "initiate a study on the problems of ammunition and explosives in all their aspects" and to carry out recommendations "for post-conflict situations, including demobilization of former combatants and disposal and destruction of weapons." Authority was also granted to begin planning for an international conference on the illicit arms trade. Finally, the secretary-general was requested to establish a new group of government experts to prepare a report on implementation of the first panel's recommendations and to propose additional measures in this area.

In the first months of 1998, Secretary-General Annan took action on several of these measures. The new Group of Governmental Experts on Small Arms was established under the chairmanship of Ambassador Mitsuro Donowaki of Japan (who chaired the original panel on small arms) to review progress in the field and to identify new problem areas.[5] (The Group is to present its report in late 1999.) Discussion also began on convening an international conference on the illicit arms trade, tentatively scheduled for the year 2001 (probably in Switzerland). In addition, in July 1998, Undersecretary-

General for Disarmament Affairs Jayantha Dhanapala released a position paper, "Coordinating Action on Small Arms," which called for such coordination within the UN system. The paper affirms that the UN Department for Disarmament Affairs (DDA) will henceforth serve as a "focal point" for all work on small arms issues being conducted by the United Nations and its associated agencies.[6]

The UN Economic and Social Council and Firearms Regulation

Parallel to the work of the various panels of government experts on small arms, the Commission on Crime Prevention and Criminal Justice (CCPCJ) of the UN Economic and Social Council (ECOSOC) has been conducting a study of international firearms regulations and developing recommendations for new controls in this area. As part of this effort, the CCPCJ collected data on the firearms regulations of member states and held a number of regional workshops on the issue in Slovenia, Tanzania, Brazil, and India in 1997–98.

Following these meetings, the Commission adopted a resolution on April 28, 1998, calling for the UN General Assembly to "work towards the elaboration of an international instrument to combat the illicit manufacturing of and trafficking in firearms, their parts and components and ammunition."[7] Such an instrument, the resolution notes, could be modeled on the Inter-American Convention Against the Illicit Manufacturing of and Trafficking in Firearms, Ammunition, Explosives, and Other Related Materials (for more on this convention, see chapter 4 by Lora Lumpe and chapter 10 by James McShane). The resolution—which has the backing of the United States—was approved by the General Assembly during its 1998 session.[8]

Conclusion

The United Nations has made great strides both in developing a body of analysis on the light weapons trade and its impact on global conflict and in devising strategies for the control of such weapons. It is obvious, however, that very little concrete progress has been made in actually curbing the trade and that much more work will be needed at the regional and international levels to actually produce results in this area.

Reversing the existing destabilizing dissemination of small arms and light weapons in society will require full cooperation and political commitment by member states. The central goal of all international endeavors in this field must be to establish binding principles and measures needed to bring small arms and light weapons—and their transnational movement—within strict government control, with the purpose of lowering and eliminating civilian casualties and human suffering caused by the indiscriminate and illicit use of such weapons.

Changes in the attitudes of governments in both exporting and importing nations, requiring concrete measures of a national, regional, and international character, are urgently needed if state members of the United Nations are to better control small arms and light weapons and thereby prevent their indiscriminate circulation and use. Moreover, if UN objectives in the field of micro-disarmament are to be achieved, a wide range of measures conducive to a climate of confidence and cooperation between states—within and beyond the military sphere—have to be promoted at the international level. Such measures should include procedures for the demobilization of ex-combatants and the collecting of military firearms to ensure that such weapons are not retained and circulated again, giving rise to new conflicts and criminal activities.

The time has come to build on the important accomplishments already made in the field of micro-disarmament and to pursue a new era of international control over small arms and light weapons, seeking to develop methods and common approaches for achieving greater stability and lasting peace. Establishing tighter controls over the production of and trade in small arms and ammunition and making those who possess them legally accountable for any damage done with these weapons is a critical international responsibility.

Notes

1. Boutros Boutros-Ghali, United Nations General Assembly, "Supplement to an Agenda for Peace: Position Paper of the Secretary-General on the Occasion of the Fiftieth Anniversary of the United Nations," UN doc. A/50/60, January 3, 1995, pp. 14–15.

2. United Nations General Assembly, "Study of Ways and Means of Promoting Transparency in International Transfers of Conventional Weapons," UN doc. A/46/301, September 9, 1991.

3. For text of the resolution and specifications of the Register, see Stockholm International Peace Research Institute (SIPRI), *SIPRI Yearbook 1992: World Armaments and Disarmament* (Oxford and New York: Oxford University Press, 1992), pp. 305–7.

4. United Nations General Assembly, "Report of the Panel of Governmental Experts on Small Arms," UN doc. A/52/298, August 27, 1997.

5. For background on this effort, see interview with Owen Greene, consultant for the Group of Governmental Experts on Small Arms, in *BASIC Reports,* no. 65, British-American Security Information Council, August 14, 1998, pp. 8–11.

6. For details of this plan, see Jim Wurst, "UN Lobbies for Coordination on Small Arms," *BASIC Reports,* no. 65, August 14, 1998, pp. 4–7.

7. United Nations Economic and Social Council, Commission on Crime Preven-

tion and Criminal Justice, "Criminal Justice Reform and Strengthening of Legal Institutions: Measures to Regulate Firearms," UN doc. E/CN.15/1998/L.6/Rev 1, April 28, 1998.

8. On the U.S. position, see Raymond Bonner, "U.S., in a Shift, Backs UN Move to Curb Illicit Trade in Guns," *New York Times,* April 25, 1998. See also "Measures to Regulate Firearms for the Purpose of Combatting Illicit Trafficking in Firearms," United Nations Economic Council, Vienna, July 28, 1998.

10

Light Weapons and International Law Enforcement

James P. McShane

TO BRING THE INTERNATIONAL TRADE in small arms and light weapons under rigorous international control will require not only the necessary laws and treaties but also effective law enforcement. Law enforcement efforts can be generalized as a function that is based on one simple premise: if something is against the law, it should be investigated and those responsible prosecuted. This, however, is a simplification of the reality of law enforcement. In most circumstances, the vigor of law enforcement is very much dictated by political will and the public environment. Laws may be "on the books," but if the political will to support law enforcement with the necessary resources and commitment is absent, or if the public environment is such that there is no support or encouragement for the investigation of particular crimes, then the laws are enforced routinely or not at all. Fortunately, in the area of firearms trafficking, this situation does not exist today.

To appreciate the current state of law enforcement cooperation in this area, it is useful to go back about six or seven years and discuss the genesis of the process that has brought us to where we are today. In 1990, the Organization of American States (OAS) began to consider the issue of international trafficking in firearms and explosives as it related to drug trafficking. This was a logical connection to make. Narcotics trafficking was, at the time, the number one concern in the region. Many countries were just beginning to admit that they had a serious drug problem, and, as rival factions began to move into these lucrative marketplaces, drug-related violence was on the increase. Many government officials suggested, moreover, that there was a nexus or a strong connection between drug smuggling and gun trafficking.

Despite the obvious appeal of this mode of reasoning, those of us in the law enforcement community avoided rushing to this conclusion. While we might agree that guns were regularly used in narcotics operations and that there probably were some swaps of guns for drugs (and vice versa), there was no documented proof beyond a few isolated cases. Our fear was that if the issue of firearms trafficking was linked to drugs, it would be swallowed up in the much larger issue of illegal narcotics. So we fought to treat the two types of trafficking as separate crimes. Our view was, and remains, that attacking illegal firearms trafficking as a crime itself is the most efficient and effective way of addressing this problem.

It took approximately two years for the OAS International Trafficking in Firearms study to get under way. For logistical reasons, the study was placed within the brief of the Inter-American Commission on Drug Control (CICAD). The first meeting of the Group of Experts was held in Washington, D.C., in October 1993. Seventeen countries sent delegations, comprising a diverse population of representatives: some countries sent their narcotics experts, others sent their military representatives, and still others sent law enforcement officers or government regulators. As at most first meetings of such a group, everyone tended to give very structured presentations. Most of these presentations covered existing national laws, not policy and problems. Nevertheless, the meeting accomplished the important goal of establishing some international relationships and setting a basis for further discussion.

The next meeting of the study group was held in Bogota, Colombia, in May 1994. While this meeting started in much the same fashion as the first, with structured discussions of national laws and regulations, some changes began to develop. The intended connection of firearms trafficking to drug trafficking was dropped. Participants began to discuss the real problems that firearms were causing in their nations. More importantly, participants began to discuss what could be done to address these problems. A consensus developed that to both comprehend and effectively combat illicit firearms trafficking, there had to be a greater understanding of how the *legal* trade occurred. There was also a growing sense that loose controls over the legal trade was the real problem when it came to illicit trafficking. Brazil proffered that there had to be a harmonized and efficient system of laws and regulations in place to control the international trade in firearms. This suggestion gained approval as a first concrete step that nations could take in confronting the illicit arms trade.

The Model Regulations

By the time that the next meeting of the Group of Experts was convened, in Caracas, Venezuela, in May 1996, sufficient momentum had developed around the need to establish a standardized and harmonized process of authorizations covering the legal movement of firearms in the Western Hemisphere. Participants were truly motivated now. From May 1996 to September 1997, there were a series of drafting meetings—culminating, in November 1997, in the acceptance of the Model Regulations for the Movement of Firearms, their Parts and Components, and Ammunition by the CICAD assembly in Lima, Peru.

The Model Regulations accomplish what the participants had envisioned in Colombia. They articulate requirements for arms transfers on the basic premise that everything must begin with an import authorization. If a government does not want certain firearms imported into its country or does not want those firearms delivered to a certain person or entity, they can halt the transaction by not issuing an import authorization. The Model Regulations further stipulate that an import authorization must contain specific information regarding the transaction and that it can remain valid only during a specific time frame.

Once issued, an import authorization becomes the basis for the issuance, by the supplying country, of an export authorization. The export authorization must contain identical information to that in the import authorization. It must contain specific information on what is being exported, right down to the serial numbers and lot numbers of the weapons involved. Moreover, the export authorization cannot remain valid beyond the expiration date of the import authorization.

The Model Regulations also instituted a new type of authorization: the in-transit authorization. The regulations require that if firearms and/or ammunition are going to pass through a third country en route between the exporting and the importing countries, that nation must issue an in-transit authorization and submit it to both the exporter and the importer. No longer would firearms simply end up in a transit country without anyone in that nation knowing about and agreeing to it. The in-transit authorization also lessens the danger of illegal diversions and transshipments to black-market dealers.

One of the important features of the Model Regulations is that the information on all types of authorizations cannot be changed; if a change is required, a new authorization must be issued, and the original document is invalidated. Furthermore, if the information on an import authorization and the application for an export authorization do not match, the export authorization application must be rejected. The regulations go further, requiring that all participating countries establish a central *point of contact* for the exchange of information and the verification of authorizations.

The OAS Treaty

In early 1997, a small group within the OAS concluded that what was needed, in addition to the Model Regulations, was a hemispheric convention against the illicit trade in firearms, ammunition, explosives, and related materials. This group, known as the Rio Group, drafted a document and presented it to the OAS for consideration and adoption. In May of that year, the draft document was accepted for consideration, and meetings on the proposal were held throughout the summer and early fall. A final document was completed at the end of October and was adopted by the full OAS on November 13, 1997.

The Inter-American Convention Against the Illicit Manufacturing of and Trafficking in Firearms, Ammunition, Explosives, and Other Related Materials is the first of its kind that addresses illegal arms trafficking. It calls for OAS member states to establish legal jurisdiction (if none exists already) over the crimes of illicit firearms manufacturing and trafficking and to strengthen their efforts to combat illicit trafficking. It also calls for a more effective system of import, export, and in-transit authorizations for firearms (in accordance with the Model Regulations) and for member states to mark firearms with specific identifiable information at the time of manufacture and importation or when placed into use by law enforcement.[1]

The OAS Convention also requires that OAS member states increase and enhance their cooperation through the establishment of central points of contact for illicit firearms issues. It encourages the greater use of enforcement tools, such as the tracing of firearms, extradition, and controlled deliveries, and calls for the confiscation or forfeiture of firearms seized in the process of illicit trafficking. More importantly, it stipulates that firearms confiscated during these illicit acts must not be allowed to reenter the marketplace through auction or sale. Member states also agreed to greater communication, cooperation, exchange of information, and exchange of training and expertise in this field.

The ECOSOC Process

While all of this was going on, the government of Japan began to be concerned about the growing number of gun-related crimes in that country. To better understand what was happening, the National Police Agency of Japan hosted a conference of law enforcement officers from other Asian countries and from the United States. Although this meeting did not produce any immediate results, it represented the beginning of discussions and understandings about problems related to illegal arms trafficking.

The discussions initiated by the National Police Agency continued on a yearly basis. More countries were brought into the conversation. However, the Japanese did not focus on action that could be taken in their own region, as occurred in the Western Hemisphere; rather, they made a decision to seek a global solution to the firearms problem through the United Nations. Specifically, they proposed that the United Nations review existing national and international firearms regulations and study the problem of firearms-related crime. A global survey was then prepared by the Commission on Crime Prevention and Criminal Justice (CCPCJ) of the UN Economic and Social Council (ECOSOC) and circulated to member nations. As part of the effort, the CCPCJ also conducted four regional workshops—in Slovenia, Tanzania, Brazil, and India—on Firearms Regulations for the Purpose of Crime Prevention and Public Safety.

This effort has also resulted in the drafting of a Declaration of Principles regarding firearms regulation. As it currently stands, the Declaration of Principles is based on the following regulatory approaches (many borrowed from the Model Regulations): firearms safety and storage; appropriate penalties for firearms misuse and/or unlawful possession; the usage of amnesty type programs to allow the surrender of illegal, unsafe, or unwanted firearms; a licensing system that would ensure that firearms cannot be distributed to individuals convicted of serious crimes or those prohibited for other reasons from possessing firearms; a record-keeping system for firearms, including a system for tracking commercial distribution; and the marking of firearms at manufacture and import.

These principles are expected to be incorporated into an international convention to be proposed to the UN General Assembly by the Commission on Crime Prevention and Criminal Justice.[2] At its meeting in April 1998, the CCPCJ adopted a resolution calling for "the elaboration of an international instrument to combat the illicit manufacturing of and trafficking in firearms, their parts and components and ammunition within the context of a United Nations convention against transnational organized crime." In particular, the resolution suggests that such an instrument include "effective methods of identifying and tracing firearms" as well as the establishment "of an import and export and in-transit licensing" regime for commercial transfers of firearms.[3]

The G-8 Initiative

Still another initiative was undertaken in 1995, when the governments of the Group of Eight (the United States, the United Kingdom, Germany, France, Italy, Canada, Japan, and Russia) decided to add firearms trafficking to the roster of transnational crime issues they sought to combat. A subgroup on this issue was formed, and law enforcement representatives from the G-8 began to review the firearms control situation and prepare a foundation on which the issue could be addressed at the intergovernment level. The foundation that was subsequently developed included the following principles: cooperation in gun-related crime investigations, exchanges of information necessary to the investigation of firearms-related crimes, the exchange of scientific and technological information useful to law enforcement, and the initiation of joint training and exchange programs.

In 1997, at the G-8 summit in Denver, these principles were presented to the heads of government, only to be rejected. From what has been reported, the principles were found to be too conservative—they did not go far enough. Hastily, these principles were redrafted, and a new blueprint was devised that drew on principles that had been established in other fora, such as the OAS process that led to the drafting of the Model Regulations. On this basis, the Denver summit adopted a new set of priorities, including the development of an international instrument to combat illicit arms trafficking, the creation of a stronger import/export regime for firearms, the establishment of a standardized system for the identification of firearms that could aid in their tracing, and the further exchange of information. These measures were then discussed at the G-8 summit in Birmingham, England, in May 1998, resulting in a commitment to support the UN initiative described above.[4]

Assessment

This has been a brief overview of a number of initiatives that have come about in a rather short period of time. As to what it all means for law enforcement, one has to look at the common threads that run through most of these efforts. The strategy of building a robust, standardized process for the legal trade in firearms appears in many of the initiatives, most notably in the Model Regulations. The concept of combating the illicit trade through an effective system of legal controls is a solid and logical one.

The biggest problem facing us for many years has been that of clearly identifying an illegal shipment. This does not, of course, arise in the more obvious scenarios, such as when five handguns are discovered in a suitcase being carried to another country. But it does arise in the case of suspicious shipments of hundreds of weapons with legal or quasi-legal documentation lending an appearance of legitimacy. To those of us in law enforcement, establishing a "paper trail" is often the only means to a successful investigatory conclusion. If the paperwork is not complete, if it is faulty, or if it is nonexistent, we lose the trail and we lose the case. For these same reasons, the inclusion of requirements for in-transit licensing greatly enhances our ability to detect and stop illegal shipments.

The requirement that appears in a number of these new proposals for the marking of firearms at manufacture and importation into a country has two beneficial effects for law enforcement. The first is the ability to trace the origins of a firearm used in the course of a crime through the manufacturer's identifiers and the serial number, and the second is that it allows law enforcement personnel to focus their attention on the most recent location/owner of a firearm. Too many times in the past, time and effort have been wasted looking in the wrong country for the last owner of a recovered firearm. Take the example of a U.S.-manufactured weapon recovered in Japan. The Japanese would concentrate their efforts on trying to trace the weapon back to the United States; however, that weapon could have been legally exported to France and legally reexported to Spain before it made its way through illicit channels to Japan. The marking requirement at time of import will allow the law enforcement officers to focus on the last legal domicile of that weapon.

Another principle contained in these initiatives—the call for greater exchanges of information and cooperation—goes beyond the usual "we'll put this in because it sounds good" provision. A number of these initiatives call for the establishment of a single point of contact in each participating country to handle requests for information and assistance as it relates to firearms issues. The intent of this principle is not to upstage or replace existing bilateral or even multilateral arrangements/organizations (like Interpol); rather, it is to ensure that there is one place where specialized law enforcement officers can call and establish communications with other law enforcement officers who are expert in the same area. The intent was also to avoid the bureaucratic "turf battles" that can exist in a country when more than one organization has jurisdiction over firearms.

The recommendation that appears in a number of these initiatives to strengthen border controls covering arms *exports* is another important accomplishment. Too often we have seen an attitude among government officials that if something unwanted is coming into our country, it is a serious problem, but that if it is leaving our country, it is someone else's problem. This is especially true for firearms. When the CCPCJ survey was being circulated, many nations answered "yes" to the question "Do you have an import problem with firearms?" while answering "no" to the question "Do you have an export problem with firearms?"[5] Yet when officials of these countries sat down together, as occurred at the regional UN workshops, they quickly saw that their import problem was caused by a neighboring country that stated that it did not have an export problem. This has been a major achievement because, once nations begin to accept the fact that they may be a contributing factor for problems occurring in another nation, half the battle is won.

The approach taken in forging the OAS Convention and the Model Regulations is the most logical stance that nations can adopt with respect to the task of combating illicit firearms trafficking. By addressing both the legal and the illegal trade, a comprehensive strategy and methodology has been formulated. A stronger, more standardized set of controls over the legal trade enables law enforcement organizations to concentrate their efforts on the illegal trade. Further, if the legal process for trafficking in arms is violated, there is considerably more evidence available to law enforcement in pursuing investigations and prosecutions.

All of this is not to say that either agreement is perfect. The United States introduced specific measures that were not accepted by the other nations involved. One of these stated that no nation shall approve the export of firearms/ammunition previously imported to that nation without the concurrence of the nation from which the firearms/ammunition had originally been imported. The purpose of this measure was to lessen the risk of diversion and transshipment to black-market dealers. This measure currently exists within U.S. regulations, and the U.S. government has taken action when it was discovered that the regulation was being violated (e.g., when it was learned that Paraguay was allowing U.S.-source firearms to be sold to Brazilian "tourists" and then transported across the border for resale within Brazil). However, other OAS member states were not prepared to endorse this measure.

Two other measures that remain to be considered are *distribution* agreements (which authorize an exporter in one country to ship firearms to another country for distribution within a recognized and approved sales territory) and *manufacturing* agreements (which authorize a manufacturer in one country to grant a license to a producer in another to manufacture copies of its products). Distribution agreements are not necessarily objectionable if they are conducted under tight control, but this does require that a comprehensive system of controls be in place in each country involved. Manufacturing agreements also require effective oversight and control in all countries involved. When a manufacturer licenses the rights to manufacture firearms in another country, adopting and enforcing controls that ensure that manufacturing ceases at the end of a specified period of time can be very difficult.

Finally, there is the question of international trade agreements. As nations enter into multilateral trade agreements and economic unions, it is essential that firearms be considered as something other than normal trade goods. Firearms and ammunition should be identified as "specified trade items" that are placed outside of the normal trade regime.

The European Union (EU) provides the best example of the problems that can occur in the effort to facilitate trade. There are those in the EU who wish to treat firearms in the same manner as tractor parts. Those people argue that, once a firearm has been imported into any of the member countries, it can be traded and transported freely throughout the Union. The identity of the firearm—an essential element to any enforcement effort—becomes lost once the original import occurs. The weapon can be shown as having been imported into the United Kingdom, but any hope of linking it to a particular illicit transaction is soon lost as it is sold and resold in other countries of the EU. This presents obvious problems to other nations and to international agreements that focus on tight control over the legal trade in firearms as a means of combating the illegal trade. It defeats initiatives such as the marking of firearms at the time of importation because, once imported to one country in the Union, the firearm has "free passage" to all member states and will not be marked again until and if it leaves the Union. The United States currently considers firearms exempt from trade agreements and will continue to articulate this position in all future negotiations.

While it is unfortunate that these additional measures did not find their way into the OAS Convention and the Model Regulations, the end products are as complete as they could be, given the political environment and the time frames available. It is hoped that it will be possible to incorporate these measures into future agreements and conventions.

Next Steps

The next step forward with the OAS Convention and the Model Regulations is their implementation. The Convention, by its very nature, will require ratification by individual governments and may take longer to implement; the Model Regulations, on the other hand, require no such ratification and can be implemented almost immediately. The interesting thing about the Model Regulations is that when one or two nations implement them, others will be forced to follow suit. Once the United States implements them, for example, other nations will be forced to do the same, or they will have to acquire their firearms elsewhere. It should be noted, moreover, that the United States intends to implement them in the very near future: regulatory changes and amendments that will be required are being passed, and there is a strong desire to put the Model Regulations into place.

After this, the priority is to use the OAS Convention and the Model Regulations as a template for similar initiatives in other areas. This could include the adoption of similar measures at a regional level—for instance in Asia—as well as the development of a global convention, as envisioned by the CCPCJ and endorsed by the G-8 in Birmingham.

Conclusion

The adoption of the Model Regulations and the OAS Convention and the steps taken by ECOSOC and the G-8 have been tremendous accomplishments. Nevertheless, much more needs to be done. As we proceed to the next steps, moreover, we need to be aware that success breeds its own problems. The complication today may be that too many initiatives have been launched. There is little opportunity to assess the results of one initiative before another is started. The OAS Convention and the Model Regulations are a perfect example of this danger, in that we were negotiating two documents from two different perspectives at the same time—and yet we had to ensure that at the conclusion they would complement and not negate each other.

We also are beginning to experience "mission creep." Some initiatives are beginning to leave their original brief and cross over into other efforts. For example, the recommendations being put forward by the UN's Panel of Governmental Experts on Small Arms are beginning to sound all too similar to the work being done by the CCPCJ. It is not only in the Panel (now the Group) of Governmental Experts on Small Arms that we are seeing such "creep"; there are other fora where the same problem is occurring. I can think of no quicker way to end an initiative—to adversely affect the political will and the public endorsement—than to bury the initiative with too much activity, too many studies, and too many meetings and assemblies.

We in law enforcement have started down a long path and have achieved considerable success because the support was there. The contacts have been established, the mechanisms have been put in place, and the context of how we are to attack the problem has been made clear. What is being accomplished has been successful because we have had the opportunity to choose the issues, construct the remedies, and form the alliances to do so. We still have a long way to go, but, unlike the situation ten years ago, law enforcement has become globally bonded to reach success, and we will have that success.

Notes

1. For the text of the Resolution, see Bonn International Center for Conversion (BICC), "Reasonable Measures: Addressing the Excessive Accumulation and Unlawful Use of Small Arms," BICC Brief no. 11 (Bonn: BICC, August 1998), pp. 45–58.

2. See Raymond Bonner, "U.S., in Shift, Backs UN Move to Curb Illicit Trade in Guns," *New York Times,* April 25, 1998.

3. UN Economic and Social Council, Commission on Crime Prevention and Criminal Justice, "Criminal Justice Reform and Strengthening of Legal Institutions: Measures to Regulate Firearms," UN doc. E/CN.15/1998/L.6/Rev.1, April 28, 1998. For text, see *BASIC Reports,* British American Security Information Council, June 4, 1998, pp. 4–5.

4. See Susannah L. Dyer, "ECOSOC, G-8 Join Forces to Combat Firearms Trafficking," *BASIC Reports,* June 4, 1998, pp. 4–5. See also Richard W. Stevenson, "Rich Leaders Turn Eye to Crime and Debt," *New York Times,* May 17, 1998.

5. See United Nations International Study on Firearms Regulation, E.98.IV.2 (New York: United Nations, 1998).

Part Five

Light Weapons, Human Rights, and Social Development

11

Light Weapons and Human Development: The Need for Transparency and Early Warning

Edward J. Laurance

OVER THE PAST SEVERAL YEARS, the international community has become increasingly aware of the deadly effects of the widespread diffusion of small arms and light weapons to areas of conflict and civil instability around the world. More and more, policymakers in national governments and international organizations, academic researchers, and the personnel of a wide range of both nongovernment relief and human rights organizations have experienced firsthand, or been accumulating data and knowledge about, the widespread death and injury caused by these weapons in dozens of conflict-ridden countries. Now, from the vantage point of 1999, the work of these different communities has produced six clusters of knowledge on which to base policy action.

The world is now dominated by intrastate or internal conflict carried out by criminals, terrorists, and irregular militia and armed bands who indiscriminately and unlawfully use small arms and light weapons. The causes, effects, and solutions related to these conflicts are international in nature, requiring a multilateral response.

There is no longer any doubt as to the increased availability of the small arms and light weapons used in these conflicts and the causes of such availability. Both supply and demand factors must be considered, alternatively calling for better governance, arms control, and security in the state experiencing the problem and/or for more controls by those states from which the arms originate.

A consensus is also emerging on the types of weapons involved in these conflicts. They are typically smaller, weigh less, and cost less and are more portable and less visible than major conventional weapons. Except for ammunition, weapons in this class do not require an extensive logistical and maintenance capability and are capable of being carried by an individual combatant or pack animal or by a light vehicle. Some of the more prevalent weapons include assault rifles, hand grenades, rocket launchers, land mines, and explosives.

The modes of acquisition of this class of weapon differ from the superpower-dominated arms supply system of the Cold War. Much of the supply and acquisition of small arms and light weapons is legal, but there has been a relative rise in illicit or illegal trade. There are at least three types of illicit acquisition that are germane to intrastate conflict: covert or secret transfer of arms to a government or nonstate actor from another government, the black market, and illicit in-country circulation.

The negative effects from the indiscriminate and unlawful use of these weapons has also become painfully clear:

- Up to 90 percent of the casualties in many of these conflicts are civilians.
- Crimes committed with these weapons are both more frequent and lethal.
- Economic, social, and political development is being disrupted by the presence and misuse of these weapons.
- Political and social conflicts are being more readily resolved by force of arms.
- There is a spiral of insecurity as citizens arm themselves against these effects.
- Societies experiencing such conflict must expend scarce resources for increased security and health services.

Human Security and Development

An important recent development has been a shift in focus from light weapons as an arms control issue to more broad-based humanitarian concerns. The successful campaign leading to the 1997 Ottawa Treaty to ban antipersonnel land mines is somewhat responsible for this. These mines were designed and manufactured for legitimate military purposes and are an integral part of most military forces in the world. Nonetheless, in December 1997 more than 120 nations decided that the continuing damage to innocent civilians caused by land mines far outweighed the military value of the weapon.

A similar approach to small arms and light weapons has begun to evolve. The international community has begun to openly discuss and indeed act on the basis of the demonstrated association between the increased availability of these weapons and their effect on human security and development. In the United Nations, the recent report of the UN Panel on Small Arms referred explicitly to this linkage as one of the commonalities among affected regions. "The crime and violence arising from the availability of small arms and light weapons have made it more difficult to conduct development projects and programmes that address the root causes of conflict. This has led to a decline in economic assistance and investment from donors."[1] This finding led directly to the recommendation that "the UN should adopt a proportional and integrated approach to security and development, including the identification of appropriate assistance for the internal security of states where conflicts come to an end and where serious problems of the proliferation of small arms and light weapons have to be dealt with urgently."[2]

Nowhere has this linkage been more explicit than in Mali. In 1992 a peace pact was signed between the Tuaregs of the north and the new government, designed to end a war that had raged for many years. This pact included disarmament and demobilization components but also contained economic, social, and political measures that would address the root causes of the conflict. Yet "the implementation proved problematic for several reasons. These included a change in government in Mali, shortage of funds for the promised development projects in the north, a rise in banditry due to insecurity and the necessity to survive, a ready supply of weapons, and the arming of law-abiding citizens to defend themselves against the increased violence."[3] In 1994 the new government requested assistance from the United Nations regarding the collection of light weapons. The response was immediate and not only has led to a very successful disarmament campaign but also has seen donor states, who did not respond to the 1992 call for assistance, return to Mali and begin funding projects once again. It is a case where the development assistance that was needed to alleviate the root causes of violence was possible only after the tools of violence were addressed. The president of Mali commented on this linkage at a recent conference on a proposed West African moratorium designed to replicate the Mali success on a regional basis. "This belief in disarmament does not proceed from idealism, or from naivete. The best strategy for prevention of armed conflict is to eliminate the means of violence."[4]

El Salvador provides another example of this linkage between the availability of weapons and the decline in human security and development. The euphoria of the peace accords of 1992 was soon replaced by the reality that over 200,000 weapons remained uncollected after the war's end. These weapons, and the unrealized hopes of civil society after the war, are proving to be a deadly combination. Thousands have taken up arms and formed criminal gangs skilled in the use of assault rifles, hand grenades, and rocket launchers.

Robberies of commercial trucks have become commonplace. At one point, 50 percent of the bus system in San Salvador was not being used, with the predictable impact on an economy struggling to recover from the war. The death rate from weapons is higher now than during the war. It was this grim picture, and a populace tired of the disruption of normal social, economic, and political life, that prompted the business community and the Catholic Church to form El Movimiento Patriotica Contra la Delincuencia (MPCD). For over a year they have been providing "goods for guns" to those citizens who voluntarily turn in military weapons.[5]

And finally, international financial institutions have begun to realize how the negative effects of the spread and unlawful use of these weapons have a direct impact on development. As noted below, the World Bank is in the process of setting up a small section on postconflict reconstruction. This office will deal with issues such as the demobilization of soldiers and their reintegration into society and the collection and destruction of weapons surplus to the security needs of the governments and societies involved. The office will bring together those parts of the World Bank that are already involved in this aspect of postconflict reconstruction.

New Policy Initiatives

As is detailed in other chapters of this book, there are numerous efforts under way—by national governments, regional and international organizations, and nongovernmental organizations (NGOs)—to specify and implement policies that can more effectively address the problem. On the supply side, it seems clear that actors at all levels could better operationalize the concept of the diffusion and spread of these weapons. The final step in this process is a readily identifiable accumulation of weapons at a specific time and place. The concepts of early warning and transparency, well developed for other issues, need to be better applied to monitoring the spread of small arms and light weapons.

Early Warning: Can It Be Applied to Weapons Flows and Buildups?

How might the early warning process be adapted to detecting arms flows and accumulations? How would it differ from the experience to date in trying to anticipate humanitarian disasters and providing emergency relief? Some of the unique characteristics of weapons and impending conflict create obstacles that do not exist in early warning associated with humanitarian affairs. First, humanitarian practitioners have learned firsthand how sensitive governments are to the revelation of human rights abuses associated with armed conflict. The topic of arms accumulations and flows is even more sensitive, especially since every state has the sovereign right to acquire arms to defend itself.

The line between defense and offense, even genocide, can be very thin, as was seen in Rwanda.

Second, even with government cooperation, tracking arms buildups is made difficult because of the small size and low price of the weapons as well as the lack of transparency associated with their transfer and accumulation. Since much of the trade is illicit and often associated with illicit trade in drugs and other commodities, attempts to gather this type of information will be very dangerous. Third, the nature of the behavior being uncovered and reported may present problems for those gathering such information. For example, there is a difference in the lethality and hence the potential for destabilization in ordinary hunting or single-shot rifles and assault rifles, let alone standoff and impersonal weapons, such as mortars and rockets. Some effort will have to be made to develop military expertise among relief and humanitarian workers working in conflict zones.

But overcoming these obstacles seems worth the effort since monitoring and reporting arms buildups has great potential to assist in predicting the human suffering endemic to these conflicts. It could theoretically allow policymakers to intervene and stop the buildup of these tools of violence. There is agreement among practitioners in conflict prevention that the emphasis should be on operational indicators of violence potential. The tools of violence would seem very ripe for such an effort, especially since it is known that perpetrators of violence always precede their efforts with an arms buildup. And in most cases these buildups take enough time to allow for an early warning process to work.

The experience of the United Nations in the worst case, the Great Lakes region of Africa, indicates that even under these conditions it is possible to detect weapons flows and give warning. Officials of both the United Nations Assistance Mission for Rwanda (UNAMIR) and the UN Commission of Inquiry reported that even their minimal presence allowed them to see arms buildups in progress. In the case of the Commission, they reported that even one inspector can disrupt the supply of weapons, even if temporarily.

Indicators of early warning

Despite the case made above regarding the necessity and feasibility of monitoring arms flows and accumulations, most of the current effort to develop early warning systems to prevent conflict do not include such monitoring. Yet such indicators can be integrated into the early warning systems being developed by NGOs and international organizations.

Beginning with the supply side, what types of information could be collected and shared that would give some advance warning of the outbreak or escalation of violence?

One of the most tragic events related to arms buildups and conflict has been the failure of the United Nations to adequately monitor the location, collection, and disposition of arms in several postconflict peace operations. It would seem relatively easy, especially politically, to improve this monitoring activity.

The post–Cold War era has been marked by the creation of an extensive surplus of small arms and light weapons.[6] States have been very reluctant to destroy this surplus, choosing instead to export it, especially to zones of conflict. A closer monitoring of this surplus and its disposition would give very advanced warning of the arrival of excessive arms into a region or country.

Most lists of early warning indicators mention external support as a key factor in the potential for escalation of conflict. External support from a country with extensive arms supply capacity and experience would be an early indication of arms supplies.

As seen in South Africa, Albania, and other countries, insecure arsenals, police stations, and other weapon storage facilities have been the source of weapons for participants in armed violence. A closer monitoring of these facilities, and especially any weapons thefts, could signal the start of an arms buildup designed to destabilize the country. In effect, that is what happened in Albania, with large quantities of weapons ultimately leaking into Macedonia and Kosovo.

By its nature, corruption is difficult to monitor. But getting a handle on corruption among officials responsible for weapons security would give some warning as to illicit arms trafficking and destabilizing buildups.

The monitoring of illicit commodities networks should also include watching for arms shipments. In general, those involved in conflict prevention and management should be receiving information on these networks.

Since so much of the trade in these weapons is illegal, monitoring black-market prices of weapons can give a good indication of the magnitude and availability of supply. For example, while an AK-47 can be purchased for a few dollars in southern Africa, it is more than a thousand dollars in Israel and the West Bank. In Albania, the price of AK-47s fluctuated from very high in the beginning, to very low ($20) when the market was saturated, and climbed once again as arms dealers began to consolidate stocks and limit availability.[7]

Very little emphasis has been placed on ammunition supplies as a potential early warning indicator.[8] Unlike most weapons found in a conflict region, which are either produced indigenously or recirculated from existing surplus stocks, ammunition for the most part must be mass produced using precision tools. It therefore is normally acquired from arms-producing states outside the region. An exception may be the presence in a conflict region of an ammunition factory previously exported under license or sold outright by an arms-producing state. Detection of excessive ammunition production and export would be a critical indicator of impending armed conflict since no military operation can succeed without adequate ammunition supplies, despite adequate numbers of weapons (as was demonstrated in the Great Lakes region).

The simple presence of a monitor in an airport could detect the supply of ammunition since, to be of use, it must be delivered in bulk.

Monitoring borders between countries of warring factions could reveal an increase in weapons flows that would warn of an impending buildup.

Violence that is increasingly promulgated by military weapons found in the armed forces of modern armies (e.g., hand grenades vs. homemade bombs) is an indicator that arms are very plentiful and becoming destabilizing. The monitoring of the weapons used by gangs would also provide a warning as to the increased availability of military-style weapons.

The increase in the legitimate acquisition of weapons by individual citizens is often a predictor of increased violence in a society since many of these weapons become the target of criminal gangs and drug dealers seeking to acquire arms through theft.

The potential for violence is often indicated by the sudden display in public of military-style weapons. The lethality of an assault rifle or a belt full of hand grenades is such that reducing its presence can significantly increase the potential for conflict prevention and control.

When government programs distribute weapons to citizens or paramilitary organizations, this is a good indicator that the potential for uncontrolled violence is increasing.

Effective monitoring of the demobilization of former combatants and redundant military personnel will provide early warning of their dissatisfaction and a return to the ways of violence of their former profession.

The Continuing Need for Transparency

The above examples indicate that early warning is possible and would enhance the likelihood of preventing conflict. As some case studies indicate, the information gatherers involved in internal conflicts have succeeded in providing some early warning. But in most cases the information was obtained with great difficulty, often too late, and in some cases at great risk to the information gatherers. What is required is increased transparency.

Transparency by itself is no guarantee that action will be taken, as was seen in Rwanda. Michael Lund's account of the 1993–94 period in Rwanda concludes that the 500 UN troops dispatched to observe were "insufficient to be able to detect the efforts being taken by the Hutu authorities not only to avoid the implementation of the [Arusha] accords but also to recruit and arm militias ready to retake the country at the first opportunity."[9] Other accounts, however, conclude that transparency was there but that the political will was not.[10]

Transparency in the production, acquisition, and proliferation of small arms and light weapons is far behind that of major conventional weapons. Among other things, given that much of the light weapons flow is illicit, simply adding this class to the UN Register of Conventional Arms is problematic. But, as hinted at in the brief discussion of early warning indicators, there are some types of information that could be made more transparent that would enhance the work of those dedicated to preventing and dampening the effects of conflict with these weapons.

First, not all of the trade in these weapons is illicit. A first approach to monitoring and transparency is to increase information on the legitimate trade flow of arms. Perhaps some types of weapon in this class could be added to the UN Register of Conventional Arms. An alternative approach is to make transparent this type of information at the regional level. In the now adopted Moratorium on the Exporting, Importing and Manufacturing of Light Arms in Africa, discussed in Bamako, Mali, in March 1997, it was suggested that "governments will be able to supplement the moratorium with various additional measures. Concerning future arms acquisitions, the governments may wish to establish a sub-regional arms register. The register would contain pertinent information regarding the acquisition of arms necessary for uniformed forces."[11]

A second possibility is to make transparent the legitimate owners of weapons, allowing the focus to be on those who would be more likely to conduct armed violence. As only one example, Brazil and Paraguay signed an agreement in October 1996 requiring that each country provide the other with a monthly list of arms acquisitions by citizens.

If arms flows themselves are too difficult to monitor, at least the manufacturers and the legitimate arms traders could be subjected to greater public scrutiny. As is contained in the 1997 Organization of American States (OAS) Convention, this would allow a more efficient monitoring of the supply of arms. A similar approach has been proposed for the European Union (EU)[12] and is proposed as an associated measure for the Mali Moratorium. The United Nations could also serve as a repository for this type of information.

A more controversial suggestion is to develop a system that registers a weapon with an international serial number on manufacture so that weapons can be traced to end users. The UN Small Arms Panel recommended that the United Nations initiate a study on "the feasibility of establishing a reliable system for marking all such weapons from the time of their manufacture,"[13] and this is also part of the EU program. In the United States, such transparency has allowed law enforcement officials to be increasingly effective in pinpointing and closing down major sources of weapons used in violent crime.

As previously noted, large numbers of light weapons have been seized, collected, and destroyed, both by national authorities and international peacekeeping forces. Keeping a record of all of these actions, making them public, and/or exchanging such information with states in the region would accomplish several things. First, it would put the focus on the fact that arms accumulations have become excessive. Second, it would provide policymakers with a better idea of the magnitude and quality of inventories. This has been proposed for the EU and the Mali Moratorium. This approach is also being increasingly used with great effect in the United States as the main sources of illicit guns are identified and eliminated.

These measures could be strengthened if arms-producing states took steps to clarify which types of weapons are strictly for military or police work as a precursor to establishing control mechanisms to restrict or prohibit ownership of such weapons by civilians. As indicated, the line between weapons ownership for individual protection versus armed violence can be thin. Developing a norm that calls for the elimination of such weapons as assault rifles, hand grenades, and other military weapons in the hands of civilians could assist work in conflict prevention. Making transparent the possession of these weapons would enhance the development of such a norm.

Finally, transparency remains critical in publicizing not only the suppliers of tools of violence but also the users. There should be no letup in the adverse publicity that increasingly accompanies the human carnage resulting from the use of these weapons; this publicity should include the widespread dissemination of photos of the weapons themselves. In the land mine campaign, effective use was made of the human and social cost of these weapons. Why is it any different that a sudden supply of hand grenades and assault rifles results in the death of thousands of civilians? In some conflicts, such as Rwanda and Burundi, much of the violence is admittedly committed with machetes, clubs, and knives. But the most lethal attacks are with military weapons such as grenades, rockets, assault rifles, and mortars. Where did these weapons come from? Are they under the control of responsible military units, or have they been distributed to militias? In the end, people kill people, but when modern military weapons are used, the lethality escalates to inhumane levels. Those who use such weapons, especially indiscriminately and purposefully against civilians, should be consistently condemned in the hope that, at least, lower levels of violence will allow negotiations on the root causes of conflict to proceed.

Conclusion

In the end, the ultimate goal of controlling light weapons is to decrease and eventually eliminate the human costs associated with the availability and unlawful use of these weapons around the world. This is truly a global problem that requires a global effort. Despite the end of the Cold War and the subsequent move toward privatization in many areas, the international system is still based on the behavior of states, especially with regard to military weapons. Governments continue to act irresponsibly when it comes to the export, procurement, use, control, and storage of small arms and light weapons. Thus, a priority of any global campaign must be to change government behavior. Further, mechanisms must be developed that provide incentives for governments to cooperate to ensure that these changes occur and are not reversed.

Another goal will be to ensure that resources are allocated by the international community to reduce the level of small arms and light weapons available for proliferation and misuse. One of the most important benefits of the land mine effort was the commitment of resources for demining that became a reality only with the signing of the Ottawa Convention. Resources must also be found to repair the damage from the spread and unlawful use of light weapons as well.

As with the antipersonnel mines, the most promising approach will be like-minded states joining with NGOs to forge new norms, develop the appropriate incentives for states to comply with these norms, and generate the resources that are so sorely needed.

Notes

The research and writing of much of this paper was supported by grants from the Carnegie Commission on Preventing Deadly Conflict and The Ploughshares Fund of San Francisco. It was published as part of the Carnegie Commission report *Light Weapons and Intrastate Conflict: Early Warning Factors and Preventive Action* (Washington, D.C.: Carnegie Commission on Preventing Deadly Conflict, 1998).

1. United Nations, "Report of the Panel of Governmental Experts on Small Arms," Report #A/52/298 from the secretary-general to the UN General Assembly, August 27, 1997, p. 20.
2. United Nations, "Report of the Panel of Governmental Experts on Small Arms," Report #A/52/298 from the secretary-general to the UN General Assembly, August 27, 1997, p. 21.
3. Bonn International Center for Conversion, *Conversion Survey: Global Disarmament and Disposal of Surplus Weapons* (Oxford: Oxford University Press, 1997), p. 156.
4. Raymond Bonner, "Nations Unite to Eradicate the Plague of Small Arms," *New York Times,* April 5, 1998.
5. Bonn International Center for Conversion, *Conversion Survey,* pp. 156., 161.
6. See "Small Arms and Light Weapons: The Epidemic Spread of Conflicts," in *Conversion Survey* (Bonn: Bonn International Center for Conversion, 1997).
7. "Albania: Hold Your Breath," *The Economist,* March 22, 1997.
8. For an exception, see Tara Kartha, "Ammunition as a Tool for Conflict Control," paper presented to the BASIC workshop on Light Weapons Proliferation and Opportunities for Control, London, June 1996.
9. Michael Lund, *Preventing Violent Conflicts* (Washington, D.C.: United States Institute of Peace Press, 1996), p. 92.
10. Alison L. Des Forges, "Making Noise Effectively: Lessons from the Rwandan Catastrophe," in Robert I. Rotberg, ed., *Vigilance and Vengeance: NGOs Preventing Ethnic Conflict in Divided Societies* (Washington, D.C.: Brookings Institution Press, 1996), pp. 213–32.

11. Proposed Moratorium on the Importing, Exporting, and Manufacturing of Light Arms, Bamako, Mali, March 1997.

12. Owen Greene, *Tackling Light Weapons Proliferation: Issues and Priorities for the EU* (London: Saferworld, April 1997).

13. United Nations, "Report of the Panel of Governmental Experts on Small Arms," Report #A/52/298 from the secretary-general to the UN General Assembly, August 27, 1997, p. 23.

12

Arms Transfers, Humanitarian Assistance, and Humanitarian Law

Peter Herby

THE INTERNATIONAL COMMITTEE of the Red Cross (ICRC) has witnessed in its work for war victims throughout the world the increasingly devastating effects for civilian populations of the proliferation of weapons, particularly small arms. The difficulties of providing humanitarian assistance in an environment where arms have become readily available to a variety of actors and many segments of society are well known to most humanitarian relief agencies today. However, until recently, the relationships between arms availability, the worsening situation of civilians during and after conflict, and the challenges of providing humanitarian assistance have not been addressed directly.

The exceedingly high levels of civilian death and injury in recent conflicts from Bosnia to El Salvador to Liberia to Afghanistan are no longer being seen simply as an inevitable by-product of these conflicts. Rather, these results are viewed, increasingly, as a result of inadequate or nonexistent control of the flow of weapons—both internationally and domestically. Although few would claim that the weapons themselves are the primary source of recent conflicts, it can be argued convincingly that the easy availability of arms and ammunition increases tensions, heightens civilian casualties, prolongs the duration of conflicts, and renders postwar reconciliation and rebuilding far more difficult.

The widespread availability of arms, particularly small arms, combined with their frequent use in violation of the most basic humanitarian norms, poses a direct challenge to the dual mandates of the ICRC: to assist the victims of conflict and to promote respect for international humanitarian law (IHL).

It is clear that the high levels of civilian casualties, which have steadily increased in the twentieth century in parallel with the development and proliferation of sophisticated military technology, are facilitated (i.e., not necessarily caused) by the availability of arms and ammunition. Weapons previously available primarily to organized armed forces are now in the hands of a wide variety of actors in conflict and postconflict situations. These include highly destructive instruments, such as automatic rifles capable of firing hundreds of rounds per minute, rocket-propelled grenades, mortars, and land mines. Whereas previously a single shot fired into a crowded market would have constituted an isolated criminal incident, the firing of several hundred bullets from the automatic weapons now readily available can unleash an orgy of ethnic killings and civil unrest.

The suffering of civilians affected by conflict grows still worse when the ICRC and other agencies are denied access to the victims owing to direct attacks, mined transport lines, or the threat of armed violence. In a large number of recent conflicts, specific regions or even entire countries have become "no go" areas for humanitarian workers on account of attacks or the credible threat of attacks on them. The ICRC field staff experienced a growing number of casualties through the mid-1990s. Although this may have been due to the changing nature of conflict, increased proximity to front lines, and the perceived politicization of humanitarian aid, the availability of small arms undoubtedly also played an important role. In addition to the impact on the safety of personnel, weapon availability increases the cost of humanitarian operations. When relief supplies have to be transported by air because land mines have been used to block roadways, the operation's cost must be multiplied up to twenty-five times.

Beyond the immediate problems described above, the widespread availability of arms threatens to undermine the fabric of IHL—one of the principal means of protecting civilians in times of armed conflict. In addition to its assistance mandate, the ICRC is charged with helping states promote knowledge of and respect for IHL. However, this body of law assumes that military-type weapons are in the hands of armed forces subject to a certain level of training, discipline, and control. When these weapons become available to broad segments of the population, including undisciplined groups, bandits, insecure individuals, and even children, the task of ensuring a basic knowledge of humanitarian law among those in possession of such arms becomes difficult if not impossible.

Compared with the distribution of arms, creating an understanding and acceptance of IHL is a much more difficult and time-consuming task. It should come as no surprise that as highly lethal arms become diffused throughout a population, the conditions for violations of humanitarian law increase. In the most generous interpretation, the direct and illegal attacks in 1996 on clearly identified Red Cross vehicles in Burundi and a hospital in Chechnya reflect a lack of understanding of basic humanitarian law norms and the role of a neutral humanitarian presence in conflict zones. Such attacks may also represent intentional attempts to destabilize an area.

Even after armed conflict has ended, the suffering of civilians continues, often for years, as the availability of arms can foster a "culture of violence," undermine the rule of law, and threaten efforts at reconciliation among former warring parties. A recent study[1] of the ICRC's medical database on weapons-related casualties (excluding land mines) showed a decrease in such casualties of only 20 to 40 percent (depending on weapon type) during the eighteen months following the end of armed conflict in a particular region. Under such "postconflict" conditions, one might have assumed a far more dramatic drop in arms-related death and injury.

Given the trends described above, the International Movement of the Red Cross and Red Crescent has become increasingly concerned with the problem of arms transfers and availability. In 1995, the Twenty-Sixth International Conference of the Red Cross and Red Crescent, including 135 states party to the Geneva Conventions of 1949, mandated the ICRC to conduct a study, on the basis of its firsthand experience, of the extent to which the availability of weapons is contributing to the proliferation and aggravation of violations of IHL in armed conflicts and the deterioration of the situation of civilians.[2] This work is currently being carried out on the basis of interviews with a wide variety of current and former ICRC field delegates, the ICRC's medical database, and its humanitarian law analysis. The preliminary findings were reviewed by a panel of experts on arms transfers in May 1998, with a final report and possible recommendations expected by the end of 1998.[3] The report will be the basis of further discussion at the Twenty-Seventh International Conference in November 1999.

In addition to the efforts of the ICRC, other components of the Red Cross and Red Crescent Movement have begun to address the issue of arms availability as a matter of humanitarian concern. The December 1997 session of the Council of Delegates, which brings together all National Red Cross and Red Crescent societies, their International Federation, and the ICRC, expressed its concern with the *easy access of combatants and civilian populations unfamiliar with the requirements of IHL to a wide variety of weapons, particularly small arms, and their frequent use against civilian populations and in violation of basic humanitarian principles.*[4] It called for the development over the next two years of a unified Movement position on arms transfers and a clarification of the role it could play in addressing the issue. This process will move forward on the basis of the upcoming ICRC study and broad consultations within the Red Cross and Red Crescent Movement.

In a preliminary assessment of the humanitarian problems caused by arms transfers, the ICRC made a number of observations and suggestions that will provide a conceptual framework for its forthcoming study on arms availability:[5]

- The unregulated transfer of weapons and ammunition can increase tensions, heighten civilian casualties, and prolong the duration of conflicts.
- The current pattern of small arms transfers, because it is largely outside of international control, is a matter of urgent concern.
- While the primary responsibility for compliance with IHL falls on users of arms, states and enterprises engaged in production and export bear some responsibility to the international community for the use made of their weapons and ammunition.
- Although states have an undisputed right under international law to retain armaments required for their security, they also have an equally solemn moral and legal responsibility, under article 1 common to the Geneva Conventions of 1949, to "respect and ensure respect" for IHL. The transfer of arms and ammunition should be examined in this light. States should, in particular, consider whether arms and ammunition can be viewed as simply another form of commercial goods.
- Given the serious threat to international humanitarian law, to international peace and security, and to the social fabric of societies that the unregulated spread and undisciplined use of weapons presents, the ICRC will encourage states to consider the elaboration of rules, based on humanitarian law and other criteria, governing the transfer of arms and ammunition.

The international community has in recent decades enacted important prohibitions and limitations on the transfer of chemical, biological and nuclear weapons, missile systems, and components of these technologies. Certain geographical regions have established controls on the transfer of major conventional weapon systems. However, until recently, little attention has been given to the transfer of small arms that have inflicted most of the death and injury in recent conflicts. Governments, regional organizations, and nongovernmental organizations (NGOs) now involved in the development of new arms transfer limitations and "codes of conduct" should consider integrating criteria based on IHL considerations into these measures. It is important to recognize that IHL is often the body of law most relevant to the stated purpose for which military arms and ammunition are transferred: to fight an armed conflict.

Although some have suggested using the worldwide campaign for a prohibition on antipersonnel land mines as a model for future work on arms availability, any attempt simply to replicate that effort is unlikely to succeed. The appalling suffering caused by antipersonnel mines could be traced to a single small weapon of questionable military utility. The proposed solution, a complete prohibition, was as simple as it was dramatic. And even regarding antipersonnel mines, decades of continued efforts to universalize the Ottawa Treaty, clear existing mines, and provide assistance to victims will be required before the process can be said to be entirely successful.

While it is clear that unregulated arms availability and the abuse of arms to commit violations of human rights and humanitarian law produce human costs that are clearly unacceptable, the prescription for addressing the issue is far from simple. The supply of small arms currently available in known and hidden stockpiles around the world is enormous. Most of the weapons concerned would not in themselves be considered illegal in humanitarian law terms. Some are held by government armed forces for legitimate purposes, others by groups seeking justice through resort to arms, and yet others by criminal elements or civilians seeking a measure of personal security in the absence of any other form of protection in situations of great violence.

Even in situations where governments wish to limit the flow of armaments into their territory, considerable resources and regional cooperation will be required. The success of the national moratorium on arms production, import, and export announced by the government of Mali in December 1997 will require significant investments in police and customs forces that are beyond the capacity of the government to provide without outside assistance. Even with such assistance, cooperation and similar moratoria of neighboring states will be required to reinforce Mali's effort.

Despite these differences, certain lessons may be drawn from recent efforts to end the "land mines epidemic." A central element in the land mines campaign was a demonstration of the link between victims and the cause of their suffering. The appalling results of unrestrained arms flows and their results before, during, and after conflicts will need to be clearly demonstrated in a manner that engages the public conscience. Credible research and its exchange through modern communications technology will be just as important as it was for the work on land mines. Specific and achievable proposals for addressing the problem will need to be advanced, this time as part of a far more multifaceted approach. As was the case with land mines, progress will demand a high level of cooperation and trust among governments, NGOs, and international humanitarian agencies—based on a sense of humanity and common purpose.

Conclusion

In the short term, the challenge will be to raise awareness of the human costs of arms availability and to put the issue squarely on the international agenda. The fatalistic acceptance of daily news reports of armed attacks on civilians for which no one is held responsible will need to be challenged. The principle needs to be established that those who supply arms to situations where violations of international law can be expected share a certain responsibility for the use of their weapons.

"Codes of conduct" for arms transfers are one promising approach to developing agreement on what constitutes responsible practice. One such draft code, drafted by a group of Nobel Peace Prize laureates led by former Costa Rican President Oscar Arias Sánchez, includes criteria based on IHL. The European Union integrated a reference on respect for IHL in the code of conduct on arms transfers it adopted in May 1998. The U.S. Congress is also discussing a code for U.S. exports that includes human rights, but not yet IHL criteria.

Success in addressing the humanitarian costs of unregulated arms proliferation will depend on creating a sense of responsibility and accountability among both those who produce and those who use arms. Weapons, as tools for implementing life-and-death decisions and for both enforcing and undermining the rule of law, cannot be considered simply another form of commercial goods to be governed by the law of supply and demand.

Notes

1. David Meddings, "Weapons Injuries During and After Periods of Conflict: Retrospective Analysis," *British Medical Journal,* no. 7120 (November 29, 1997), pp. 1417–20. See also International Committee of the Red Cross, "The SIrUS Project: Towards a Determination of Which Weapons Cause 'Superfluous Injury or Unnecessary Suffering,'" Geneva, 1997.

2. International Committee of the Red Cross, Twenty-Sixth International Conference of the Red Cross and Red Crescent, Resolution 1.8, Geneva, 1995.

3. International Committee of the Red Cross, "Arms Availability and Violations of International Humanitarian Law and the Deterioration of the Situation of Civilians in Armed Conflicts" (Oslo: Norwegian Red Cross, May 1998).

4. International Committee of the Red Cross, Council of Delegates, Resolution 8.4, Seville, November 1997.

5. International Committee of the Red Cross, "Arms Transfers, Humanitarian Assistance and International Humanitarian Law," ICRC document, February 19, 1998.

13

The World Bank, Demobilization, and Social Reconstruction

Nat J. Colletta

AFRICA WAS AMONG the first battlefronts and the final casualties of the Cold War. Many devastating conflicts have persisted there for twenty years or more. Some countries, including Chad, Liberia, Mozambique, Namibia, South Africa, and Uganda, are emerging from years of Cold War politics and internal civil strife, but pernicious internal struggles continue to plague others, such as Angola, Eritrea, Ethiopia, Sierra Leone, Somalia, the Democratic Republic of the Congo, the Central African Republic, the Republic of Congo, and Sudan.

The damage inflicted on the social and human capital as well as the economic potential of these countries has been horrific. Of the estimated 80 million to 110 million land mines spread across sixty-four countries around the world, about 20 million are believed to be strewn across the countries of Africa.[1] The impact of warfare through disinvestment, the destruction of physical infrastructure, and the deterioration of social and human capital through disability, death, and displacement is impossible to quantify. Persistent armed conflict is surely one reason why at least 250 million people in sub-Saharan Africa—nearly half the total population—are living below the poverty line in the mid-1990s.[2]

While the war-ravaged countries of Africa are among the poorest in the world, their neighbors, in which hundreds of thousands of people have sought refuge from the devastation of war, often feel the effects both environmentally and socially. Over the past decade, the African continent hosted about half of the world's displaced people, and by 1994, 21.4 million Africans had fled their homes because of conflict. Of these, 6.2 million were living abroad, representing 38 percent of the world's refugees.[3]

Despite these dire circumstances, the governments of the continent have devoted a substantial percentage of gross domestic product (GDP) to military expenditures (3.9 percent in 1992). Expenditures for defense have crowded out those for human development. Thus, in many countries of sub-Saharan Africa, defense expenditures surpass those for health and education combined.

The ideological camps that once fueled military buildups receded with the end of the Cold War, making it possible for many African governments to begin to downsize their militaries and reduce defense expenditures—thereby allowing human and material resources to be shifted to development activities. Demobilization and reintegration programs for military personnel constitute a vital part of demilitarization and the transition from war to peace.

Indeed, increased demilitarization is a precondition for reviving civil society, reducing poverty, and sustaining development in Africa.[4] The realization of this objective demands disarmament, demining, and demobilization of forces as well as the reintegration of ex-combatants into productive civilian roles. Demilitarization also requires reducing the costly and destructive flow of arms into Africa as well as the conversion of military facilities and land to civilian use.

Nevertheless, the world's arms suppliers continue to sell large quantities of military hardware to governments and substate forces in Africa's war zones, creating obstacles to a rapid transition to peace. During the Cold War, the superpowers and their allies armed local factions or entire countries; now, internal factions rely on the control and sale of precious natural resources (ranging from timber to diamonds and oil) to sustain their arms purchases. The path to peace is thus littered with mines, both literally and in the form of violent sociopolitical rivalry.

Fundamental Elements of a Demobilization and Reintegration Program

In his speech at the 1995 annual meetings of the World Bank and the International Monetary Fund, James D. Wolfensohn, president of the World Bank, declared that a priority of the Bank is to anticipate and be organized for post-conflict economic development programs.[5] The Demobilization and Reintegration Program (DRP) for ex-combatants is the key to an effective transition from war to peace. The success of this first step following the signing of a peace accord signals the end to organized conflict and potentially provides the security necessary for people affected by war to reinvest in their lives and their country.

Early on, the World Bank focused on public expenditure reallocation and the shifting of scarce financial resources away from defense to the social and economic sectors. However, as Bank experience evolved, there was a greater appreciation of the developmental linkages between demilitarization, social and economic reintegration of war-affected populations, and the overall reconstruction process.[6]

Accordingly, the basic policy/technical ingredients for success in DRP are (1) political will, (2) careful preparation based on rapid assessments of the opportunity structure and a profiling of the needs of ex-combatants and their families, and (3) transparent institutional arrangements with a simple monitoring and feedback system to ensure flexible but accountable implementation (to both donors and the community).

In turn, the essential program/operational elements of any DRP are (1) a *demobilization phase,* accenting disarmament, discharge, orientation, and relocation to a community of the ex-combatants' choice; (2) a *reinsertion phase,* marked by the provision of a transitional safety net of cash and in-kind payments spread out over a several-month period, roughly equivalent to a single growing season; and (3) *social and economic reintegration* assistance in the form of access to productive assets (particularly land and capital), training and employment, and information/counseling services.

While targeting of ex-combatants (particularly the most vulnerable) and their families is vital, area-based interventions that also provide inputs to the rehabilitation of social infrastructure in recipient communities are equally important.

Reinsertion and reintegration are not distinct phases after demobilization. Rather, they form part of a seamless web of transition from military to civilian life, without a clear beginning or end. As reinsertion and reintegration proceed, the needs of ex-combatants change and call for different support measures.

A successful DRP requires several actions: (1) classifying ex-combatants according to their characteristics, needs, and desired way of earning a livelihood (mode of subsistence); (2) offering a basic transitional assistance package (safety net); (3) finding a way to deliver assistance simply, minimizing transaction costs while maximizing benefits to ex-combatants; (4) providing counseling, information, training, employment, and social support while sensitizing communities and building on existing social capital; (5) coordinating centrally yet decentralizing implementation authority to districts; and (6) connecting to ongoing development efforts by retargeting and restructuring existing portfolios.[7]

Key Lessons from the World Bank Experience

There are several key lessons drawn from the World Bank's experiences that warrant close consideration by Bank staff, client governments, and donors in the design and implementation of DRPs. These lessons are summarized below.

Political Dimensions

When a country is moving from war to peace, demobilization and reintegration issues should be addressed at the earliest stages of the peace negotiation process. Strong political will and leadership, expressed in terms of commitment, realism, and pragmatism, are crucial factors for successful program implementation. In Uganda, for example, it was President Yoweri Museveni who requested World Bank assistance to the demobilization program.[8] In Angola, both sides reluctantly agreed to demobilization at the peace table, but Uniao Nacional para a Independência Total de Angola (UNITA) subsequently undermined implementation at every turn.

National reconciliation should be actively promoted through transparent policies and conflict resolution efforts at the community level. These can reduce suspicion and help rebuild trust. In particular, the question of land ownership and distribution needs to be treated carefully and openly. Both traditional and legal rights to the land, as well as historically rooted inequalities, have to be taken into account in this process.

Targeting

Ex-combatants constitute an especially vulnerable group in need of priority targeted assistance. Socioeconomic data should be collected to reveal their characteristics, needs, and aspirations so that appropriate program interventions can be designed.

Careful analysis of the opportunity structure for ex-combatants (in particular, the demand for labor and the availability of land, credit, information, and provision for skill development) is a prerequisite not only for program design but also for targeted counseling and adequate placement. An authentic, nontransferable, and noncorruptible identification system is of paramount importance for avoiding targeting errors.

The particular challenges confronting veterans' dependents (the family), as well as female soldiers, child soldiers, and disabled ex-combatants, warrant the development of specially targeted interventions. The Uganda program illustrates the importance of careful planning and the targeting of families as opposed to veterans per se as well as paying attention to especially vulnerable groups.

Demobilization

Ex-combatants should be released or discharged from military quarters as soon as possible so that they do not become a serious threat to security. In Mozambique, protracted stays in demobilization transit centers led to spontaneous uprisings in several instances. Prior to discharge, they should receive information about civilian life—rights and duties, opportunities and c straints. If feasible, postdischarge orientation, with a focus on social supp and economic opportunities, should be provided in the communities wh ex-combatants settle.

Especially in the transition from war to peace, neutral international mo tors can facilitate the design and implementation of effective demobilization programs.

Reinsertion

Entitlement packages, which provide a safety net during the transition from war to peace, should reflect the needs of ex-combatants and their families in different socioeconomic environments. Such packages help ex-combatants and their families bridge the difficult period between demobilization and reintegration.

Providing cash entitlements has several advantages over in-kind provision: transaction costs can be reduced, leakage can be better controlled, and beneficiaries can make more flexible use of the entitlement. By using local banks for transferring cash in installments, ex-combatants can access financial assistance throughout the reinsertion phase. These staggered payments also help to spread benefits and ex-combatants throughout the country. The capacity of the banking system or alternate payment systems, especially in rural areas, must therefore be evaluated before transfers begin. Putting financial resources into communities at the lowest level has the added impact of stimulating local economic demand for goods and services, as exhibited in Uganda and Eritrea.[9]

Reintegration

Ex-combatants should be assigned to target groups and subgroups on the basis of their choice of livelihood reflecting their differing needs and aspirations. This allows for the development of a differentiated, relevant, and cost-effective approach. Ethiopia's demobilization program was especially effective in delineating a "menu" of benefits consistent with the needs of ex-combatants as shaped by their desired mode of livelihood.

Ex-combatants should receive no more support than is necessary to help them attain the standard of living prevailing in the communities into which they are being reintegrated.

Reintegration in urban areas is more complex than in rural areas and requires a more diversified approach. All support measures should be based on a careful matching of opportunities and actual needs. Support measures should, to the extent possible, be demand driven.

Social Dimensions

It is the interplay of a community's physical and social capital and the ex-combatant's financial and human capital that ultimately determine the ease and success of reintegration. Efforts to strengthen social capital—for example, by using existing community organizations and channels of communication—enable communities to take development into their own hands and facilitate the reintegration of ex-combatants.

Informal networks of ex-combatants—discussion groups, veterans' associations, and joint economic ventures—are key elements for successful economic and social reintegration. Such associations can be extremely helpful when social capital has been depleted. AMODEG (Associacao Mocambicana dos Desmobilizados de Guerra) in Mozambique is one example of the importance of veterans' associations as a form of social capital in support of economic and social reintegration.

A community is a critical adjunct to assistance for ex-combatants. Community sensitization and political awareness are paramount in this effort. Care should be taken that ex-combatants are not stigmatized as unfit for military service or as conveyors of disease, violence, or misbehavior.

Institutional Concerns

To put scarce resources to optimal use, program components should be ranked by simplicity of implementation, with the simplest components first on the list.

Central coordination of DRPs by one civilian agency with overall responsibility—balanced by decentralization of implementation authority to districts and communities through existing organizational structures—makes for a powerful institutional arrangement. Administrative costs need to be held down. The higher the transaction (administrative) costs, the smaller the resources available to ex-combatants.

The effectiveness of program interventions in relation to ongoing development initiatives is maximized by careful coordination within government and among other project promoters. Once the major program objectives have been fulfilled, remaining activities should be integrated into the government's mainstream development efforts.

Local communities should be involved directly in decision making, especially on important local matters, so that scarce public resources are allocated in a transparent and socially accountable manner. Elected representatives of ex-combatants, as well as field-based staff, can perform crucial roles in facilitating reintegration.

Management Aspects

Staff training to improve skills and knowledge should begin before demobilization and should emphasize practical problem solving.

The most important contribution of a monitoring and evaluation system is to consistently improve ongoing operations by keeping abreast of major trends in the program and by regularly reporting to and advising management. Use of an external auditor improves management of funds. The external auditor, in addition to ensuring control of program resources and transparency, gives confidence to the donors and to the beneficiaries.

External Assistance

Timely availability of resources facilitates smooth operations. Donor budget cycles and disbursement and auditing procedures have to be closely meshed with implementation schedules for DRPs. Whereas Uganda provides a model for donor coordination, Ethiopia demonstrates the negative impact of ineffective donor coordination and a poor match with government desires and preparation.

Capacity building and close coordination among the government, nongovernmental organizations (NGOs), community-based groups, and donors are central elements of cooperation. Coordination of donor support by a lead donor has proven very effective.

Economic Impact

The peace dividend needs to be understood in social and economic terms as well as financial terms. The reinvestment of some savings from military downsizing into the development of a disciplined, high-quality defense force can itself produce a peace dividend by increasing security, building confidence, and reducing public fear.

It is useful to link a country's overall macroeconomic reform program, especially as it concerns the public expenditure mix, to the planned reintegration program.

Jump-starting the economy by rehabilitating critical infrastructure also can be linked to reintegration programs that involve training and employment schemes for both reconstructing material assets and building human and social capital.

From Demilitarization to Sustainable Peace

Continental demilitarization is a precondition for reviving civil society, reducing poverty, and sustaining development in Africa. The realization of this objective hinges on disarmament, the demobilization of forces, and the reduction of the flow of arms into the continent on the one hand and on the reintegration of ex-combatants into productive civilian roles on the other.[10]

Revitalizing civil society entails the promotion of local associations, community participation, and peer accountability—all of which reduce individual fear, enable collective condemnation of violence, and strengthen local security. These are the minimal conditions for encouraging people to reinvest in their communities both emotionally and financially.

Operational experience and field research have enlarged our conceptualization of the technical aspects of demobilization and reconstruction programs. We can now identify at least three interwoven technical phases of any DRP: demobilization, including disarmament and discharge; reinsertion, including resettlement; and reintegration. Our analysis has also brought into clearer focus the need for two more dimensions in the transition from war to peace: conflict prevention and reconciliation.

Conflict Prevention: Arms and Development

Overall, arms exports to sub-Saharan Africa have declined markedly since the late 1980s, but sales of light weapons, especially antipersonnel land mines, continue to be a lucrative business (see especially chapter 2 by Kathi Austin). The use of such weapons results in a most inhumane form of warfare that affects the civilian population more than it does the fighting army. Some 20 million land mines remain in sub-Saharan Africa, with 8 to10 million mines and unexploded ordnance deployed in Angola alone.[11]

It costs nearly $1,000 to deactivate a mine that originally cost as little as $3 to acquire. Worse yet, the mere threat of these mines has hampered market forces—the movement of people, goods, and services—and the resettlement of large tracts of arable land. As a result, agricultural development has been retarded across Africa. The donor community may be able to accelerate the pace of demining by increasing funding and promoting new mine-clearing technology, but in the long run the manufacture and sale of these weapons must be stopped—as envisioned by the 1997 Ottawa Treaty to ban land mines—if development is to be sustained.

The transition to peace also requires a reduction in the diffusion of small arms and other infantry-type weapons in the region. These weapons are the primary form of armament used by both government security forces and insurgent groups in the internal conflicts that have swept through Africa in recent years. Small arms are popular because of their low cost, widespread availability, and ease of operation—the latter characteristic making them especially suitable for use by child soldiers, who make up a large part of the combatant force in many of Africa's internal conflicts.[12] Because of their ease of operation, small arms and light weapons are also responsible for a large proportion of the civilian casualties in these wars.

The negative connection between arms proliferation and protracted insecurity on the one hand and sustainable development on the other is self-evident. In recognition of this, Nobel peace laureate Oscar Arias Sánchez has proposed a global campaign against arms trafficking. In *Human Development Report 1994,* a publication of the United Nations Development Programme, he proposed a global demilitarization fund that would finance activities from demining to demobilization. Such efforts deserve the support of the development community.

Reconciliation: From War-Torn to Civil Society

At the end of this seamless web of war-to-peace transition, reintegration in its full sense implies reentry into political and social as well as economic life. One of the legacies of protracted civil strife, in addition to the destruction of physical and human capital, has been the displacement of millions of people and the debasement of social capital. Of the estimated 70 million displaced persons in the world, about half are in sub-Saharan Africa. More than a fifth of the people in nine African countries are displaced, as is a staggering two-thirds of Liberia's population.[13]

Social capital goes beyond the basic level of human association and trust that welds a civil society together; it also encompasses organizations, networks, and unwritten mores and rules. Field data from previous DRPs in Africa point to the importance of social support—be it family, religious groups, or ex-combatants themselves—in easing the reintegration process. Such social support provides not only psychosocial sustenance to returnees but also the pathways for becoming economically productive members of society—via information and financial assistance, among other critical things.

Rebuilding social capital means a revitalization of civil society, and revitalizing civil society entails the promotion of local associations, community participation, trust and confidence building, and the establishment of peer accountability. It reduces the level of individual fear and nurtures the collective conditions that must be met if people are to reinvest in their communities emotionally and financially. The state of social capital is also a barometer for external investors.

When it comes to reintegration, donors have a role beyond promoting employment and training for ex-combatants or rebuilding service structures. This role is the promotion of civil society. In many fragile sociopolitical environments, NGOs and secular and religious groups are at work organizing reconciliation activities, open community meetings, and other activities for free and transparent public exchanges between formerly hostile groups and individuals.

In Namibia, church-led repatriation committees rebuilt trust between former adversaries in combat, now neighbors in development.[14] In Somalia, in an attempt to rebuild civil society in the wake of the breakdown of bureaucratic authority, NGOs are working to reestablish the council of elders as a time-tested means of interclan governance. In South Africa, the Truth Commission is trying to heal the wounds of years of violence under apartheid. In Mozambique, the UNESCO-sponsored Culture of Peace Program seeks to use veterans as community peace promoters.

The most desirable outcome, for a country and its people, is the prevention of conflict. Where conflict has nonetheless occurred, the work of reconciliation must be done if future bouts of conflict are to be avoided. Reconciliation means rebuilding faith and trust in civil institutions, justice, and the rule of law. In the final analysis, lasting reconciliation must be built on forgiveness.

The Sacred Trilogy

In the end, DRPs are important not only for freeing up resources but also for addressing the pressing needs of war-affected populations and restoring the confidence of nationals to invest in their own lives. Orderly demobilization, reinsertion, and reintegration of military personnel are central contributions to the restoration of civil society and the peaceful return to productive civilian life of hitherto destabilizing forces. Equally important are the establishment of a transparent legal system, a professional army and police force, an independent judiciary, and the implementation of economic reforms aimed at promoting growth and expanding employment opportunities.

The trilogy of (1) security and good governance, (2) the restoration of social capital, and (3) macroeconomic reform are critical enabling conditions for social reconstruction and sustainable development.

Development Assistance at a Crossroads

Donors are increasingly seeking to establish early warning systems and rapid response mechanisms to forestall problems with DRPs and to link relief and development efforts more closely if problems nonetheless arise. A major agenda item at the Halifax summit of the Group of Seven industrial nations in June 1995 was to address ways of preventing and responding to crises. International lending agencies and the United Nations were called on to reinvigorate coordination to facilitate a smoother transition from emergency response to reconstruction, from war to peace.

Because most conflicts, particularly in Africa, cannot be viewed as purely local problems, multilateral institutions are often cast in a prominent role. Refugees who stream across borders to avoid devastation often turn local hostilities into regional conflicts; in some cases, neighboring countries host military forces engaged in cross-border warfare. The result is the emergence of regional conflicts, involving groups of countries and subnational forces—a pattern seen, for instance, in Burundi, Rwanda, Uganda, and Zaire (now the Democratic Republic of the Congo); in Eritrea, Ethiopia, Sudan, and Uganda; and in Liberia and Sierra Leone. Regional wars will end only when regional answers are found.

Conclusion

The reform of national military and security establishments—whether in peacetime or the postconflict period—is not within the purview of the multilateral donor institutions, nor do these institutions have a comparative advantage in this area. Moreover, the World Bank cannot by itself implement projects to rebuild social capital in war-torn societies. What the World Bank and other international agencies *can* do is to promote a secure and stable environment for development by supporting the removal and nonproliferation of mines and other antipersonnel weapons, encouraging the realignment of national public expenditures from nonproductive to productive sectors, assisting in the demobilization and reintegration of ex-combatants into a productive civilian life, financing the reconstruction of physical assets, and helping rebuild social capital. By focusing on needed components for reconstruction and development in war-torn societies, the international community can play an important role in the larger transition from war to peace.

Notes

1. Carnegie Commission on Preventing Deadly Conflict, *Preventing Deadly Conflict* (Washington, D.C.: Carnegie Commission on Preventing Deadly Conflict, 1997), p. 17.

2. See Steven Holtzman, "Post-Conflict Reconstruction," Environment Department Work in Progress, The World Bank (Washington, D.C.: The World Bank, Social Policy and Resettlement Division, 1996).

3. See Nat J. Colletta, Markus Kostner, and Ingo Wiederhofer, *Directions in Development: The Transition from War to Peace in Sub-Saharan Africa* (Washington, D.C.: The World Bank, 1996).

4. Jakkie Cilliers, ed., *Dismissed: Demobilization and Reintegration of Former Combatants in Africa* (Halfway House, South Africa: Institute for Defence Policy, 1995).

5. See The World Bank, *Framework for World Bank Involvement in Post-Conflict Reconstruction* (Washington, D.C.: The World Bank, April 1997).

6. See Nat J. Colletta, "From Warriors to Workers: The World Bank's Role in Post-Conflict Reconstruction," *Leaders,* no. 204 (October 1995).

7. See especially Ramesh Srivastava, *Reintegrating Demobilized Combatants: A Report Exploring Options and Strategies for Training-Related Interventions* (Geneva: International Labour Office, 1994).

8. Nat J. Colletta and Nicole Ball, "War to Peace Transition in Uganda," *Finance and Development,* vol. 36–39 (June 1993).

9. For more on the situation in Eritrea and Ethiopia, see Bonn International Center for Conversion, "Demobilization in the Horn of Africa: Proceedings of the IRG Workshop," BICC Brief No. 4, Addis Ababa, December 4–7, 1995.

10. United Nations Research Institute for Social Development, "The Challenge of Rebuilding War-Torn Societies: Report on the Working Seminar at Cartigny, Geneva, November 29 to December 1, 1994," 1995.

11. See Saferworld, *Angola: Conflict Prevention and Peace-Building* (London: Saferworld, 1996).

12. See Mike Wessells, "Child Soldiers," *The Bulletin of the Atomic Scientists,* November/December 1997.

13. See Holtzman, "Post-Conflict Reconstruction," pp. 10–17.

14. Nat J. Colletta, Markus Kostner, and Ingo Wiederhofer, with assistance from Emilio Mondo, Taimi Sitari, and Tadesse A. Woldu, "Case Studies in War-to-Peace Transition: The Demobilization and Reintegration of Ex-Combatants in Ethiopia, Namibia, and Uganda," World Bank Discussion Paper 331 (Washington, D.C.: The World Bank, 1996).

Conclusion

14

Light Weapons and Civil Conflict: Policy Options for the International Community

Jeffrey Boutwell and Michael T. Klare

FROM THE VARIETY OF PERSPECTIVES contained in the chapters of this volume, it is clear that the unchecked flow of small arms and light weapons to areas of conflict represents a significant threat to world peace and security. While it cannot be said that such weapons are a primary *cause* of conflict, their worldwide availability, low cost, and ease of operation make it relatively easy for potential belligerents of all kinds to initiate and sustain deadly conflict. The widespread diffusion of such weapons throughout society—especially in areas still recovering from armed conflict—also contributes to the incidence and intensity of criminal violence. These factors have greatly complicated (and in some cases undermined) efforts by the international community to restore the peace in areas of conflict and to deliver emergency humanitarian assistance to the victims of war.

Accordingly, policymakers have begun to highlight the need for new international controls in this area. Much of the impetus for these efforts began in January 1995, when then UN Secretary-General Boutros Boutros-Ghali declared, "Progress since 1992 in the area of weapons of mass destruction and major weapons systems must be followed by parallel progress in conventional arms, particularly with respect to light weapons." Similar views have been expressed by his successor, Kofi Annan: "With regard to conventional weapons," he told the Conference on Disarmament in January 1998, "there is a growing awareness among Member States of the urgent need to adopt measures to reduce the transfer of small arms and light weapons. It is now incumbent on all of us to translate this shared awareness into decisive action."

Interest in the trade in small arms and light weapons has also been spurred by a growing number of national and international nongovernmental organizations (NGOs). These include many groups with a background in arms control and human rights, such as the American Academy of Arts and Sciences, Amnesty International, the British American Security Information Council (BASIC), the Federation of American Scientists, Human Rights Watch, and Saferworld, as well as prominent humanitarian aid and relief organizations such as International Alert and the International Committee of the Red Cross (ICRC). These NGOs—many of which played a key role in the international campaign to ban land mines—have conducted groundbreaking research on the trade in light weapons and have begun to lobby governments for vigorous action in this field. Along with UN officials and leaders of interested governments, these groups have also led the search for new policy prescriptions.

Before turning to a discussion of the policy initiatives that have emerged out of this effort, it is important to review the work that has already been done at the national, regional, and international levels to focus attention on the light weapons trade and to lay the groundwork for effective solutions.

International Efforts

In line with the increased attention being focused by the international community on the dangers posed by small arms and light weapons, the United Nations has been engaged in a wide variety of activities to both publicize the problem and initiate steps toward policy controls, as is described by Graciela Uribe de Lozano in chapter 9. The recommendations proposed by the Panel of Governmental Experts on Small Arms in 1997 are now being considered for action by the newly formed UN Group of Governmental Experts on Small Arms, which is expected to issue its report in August 1999. In April 1998, the UN Commission on Crime Prevention and Criminal Justice adopted a resolution on firearms regulation, which more than fifty countries have signed, calling on UN member states "to combat the illicit manufacturing of and trafficking in firearms, their parts and components and ammunition within the context of a United Nations convention against transnational organized crime."[1]

Operationally, the UN has sought to monitor the effectiveness of various international embargoes on the transfer of weaponry into areas of conflict. In 1996, the UN International Commission of Inquiry on Rwanda investigated the implementation of the UN arms embargo on Rwanda, paying particular attention to specific allegations of embargo violations. In their report, members of the Commission noted that "[we] could not fail to note the absence of an effective, proactive mechanism to monitor or implement the arms embargo the Security Council had imposed on Rwanda."[2] The United Nations has also lent its support to efforts by the government of Mali to negotiate a regional moratorium on the import and export of light weapons.

Recognizing that the spread of light weapons directly affects human rights and development as well as security and arms control, the United Nations in July 1998 began to consolidate all such efforts within the Department for Disarmament Affairs (DDA). Undersecretary-General Jayantha Dhanapala announced that the Coordinating Action on Small Arms (CASA) would involve UN departments concerned with peacekeeping, humanitarian aid, development policy, refugees, crime prevention, and children in order to "coordinate on a UN-wide basis all action on small arms."[3] Future plans for international coordination include a proposed UN conference on illicit arms to be hosted by Switzerland in the year 2001.

Other international organizations are also becoming involved in the light weapons issue, particularly as it relates to issues of economic and human development. Nat Colletta notes in chapter 13 that the World Bank is devoting resources to issues of postconflict reconstruction, particularly in regard to the demobilization of combatants and their reintegration into civil society. Also, the Organization for Economic Cooperation and Development (OECD), through its task force on Conflict, Peace, and Development Cooperation, is putting greater emphasis on the need for "timely prevention measures" (such as limiting arms flows in areas of potential conflict) in order to forestall armed violence.[4]

Regional Efforts

Particularly in Africa and the Americas, national governments and regional organizations are devising a variety of measures to better regulate the legal trade in light weapons and to combat illicit weapons trafficking. In November 1997, the Organization of American States (OAS) signed a convention on the illicit weapons trade that calls for standardization of national firearms regulations and increased law enforcement and customs cooperation to prevent illicit weapons flows within the Western Hemisphere. The OAS has also adopted a set of model regulations designed to harmonize and tighten the arms export and import procedures of member states, as described in chapter 10 by James McShane. Within the Caribbean subregion, moreover, Jamaica has proposed that similar efforts be undertaken by the fourteen-member Caribbean Community (Caricom).

In West Africa, as described in chapter 7 by Joseph Smaldone, the government of Mali has been working with the United Nations and neighboring countries (Burkina Faso, Chad, Côte d'Ivoire, Mauritania, Niger, and Senegal) to assess the regional implications of light weapons diffusion and to craft a regional moratorium on the import, export, and manufacture of light weapons. In central Africa, the UN has established a trust fund, coordinated by an eleven-member Standing Advisory Committee on Security Questions in Central Africa, with which to remove small arms and light weapons from the region. Similarly, Hussein Solomon notes in chapter 8 that the Southern Africa Development Community (SADC) has recommended the establishment of a regional database on stolen firearms and the implementation of multilateral police operations to recover such weapons.

Among the European countries, as described by Paul Eavis and William Benson in chapter 5, there are increased pressures for controlling both legal and illegal shipments of light weapons. In 1998 the European Union (EU) adopted a code of conduct that aims to impose more rigorous standards on the legal sale and shipment of small arms and light weapons to other countries, particularly those experiencing civil strife and human rights abuses. Earlier, in June 1997, the EU agreed to the Programme for Preventing and Combating Illicit Trafficking in Conventional Arms.

National Efforts

Under pressure from NGOs and citizens groups, national governments in many regions are taking steps to increase transparency in the light weapons trade and to tighten controls on gun production, sale, and ownership. In the United States, as described in chapter 4 by Lora Lumpe, the U.S. Congress has mandated the publication of detailed annual reports on all types of arms transfers (under section 655 of the Foreign Assistance Act). In response to complaints from Mexico, moreover, the United States has cracked down on illicit gun trafficking on the U.S.-Mexican border and has agreed to stronger export controls in the context of the 1997 OAS Convention. Similar efforts are under way in a number of other states, including Colombia, South Africa, and members of the EU.

In many communities, municipal authorities and NGOs have begun grassroots campaigns to remove small arms from circulation at the local level and to pressure their national governments to take the light weapons problem more seriously. In South Africa, such initiatives involve bringing various ethnic and tribal groups together to deal with the "culture of violence" plaguing that country. In countries like the United Kingdom and Australia that have experienced horrific massacres carried out by automatic weapons—notably the killings in Dunblane, Scotland, and Port Arthur, Tasmania—national groups have come together to lobby for more restrictive gun control laws, as

Natalie Goldring covers in chapter 6. Elsewhere, NGOs and grassroots organizations have put the spotlight on their own governments' responsibility for supplying weapons to areas of conflict and persistent human rights abuse.

Prompted in part by this growing activity on the part of the United Nations, international donor agencies, and NGOs, representatives of twenty-one national governments gathered in July 1998 in Oslo, Norway, and issued an appeal urging more stringent controls on the legal and illicit sale and supply of small arms and light weapons (see appendix B).[5] This was followed on October 12–13, 1998, by an international conference in Brussels, Sustainable Disarmament for Sustainable Development, involving several hundred representatives of national governments and NGOs. The conference concluded with the issuing of "The Brussels Call for Action," which outlined a wide range of measures for tackling the threat posed by light weapons to civil society and human development (see appendix C).[6]

Clearly, these are but the first steps in what must be a vigorous long-term effort to impose effective international controls on the trade in small arms and light weapons. Given the complexity of these issues and the reluctance of many states to curb their own arms exports, adopting such controls will not be easy. But much has been learned from the efforts already under way—many of which are discussed in the chapters in this volume—and it is now possible to identify the sort of measures that will be needed to ensure effective control over this trade.

The Need for New Policy Initiatives

From all that has been learned about the international trade in small arms and light weapons, it is evident that no single set of policy initiatives will suffice to deal with this problem. Unlike the relative simplicity of the land mines issue—where the international community could focus on one particular weapon (antipersonnel land mines) and recommend its total elimination—the effort to control the diffusion of light weapons will demand a host of initiatives, extending to the local, regional, national, and international levels. These initiatives must extend beyond the illicit weapons trade, moreover, to cover the legal trade that results in tens and hundreds of thousands of light weapons being sold or given away each year.

Ultimately, what is needed is the establishment of a multilayered regime covering the international transfer of small arms and light weapons, similar to the existing regimes covering nuclear, chemical, and biological weapons. Such a regime should consist of a matrix of national, regional, and international control measures—acting like a series of dams or filters—to screen out illicit sales and narrow the allowable scope for legal transfers.

Accordingly, the following initiatives represent a rough menu of the sort of steps that will be needed to subject light weapons transfers to greater international scrutiny and to reduce the flow of such munitions to areas of conflict.

Establishing International Norms

The first, and perhaps most important, step is to adopt international norms against the uncontrolled and destabilizing transfer of small arms and light weapons to areas of tension and conflict. Although deference must be made to the traditional right of sovereign states to arm themselves in the face of overwhelming threats to their survival, it must be made clear that this right has natural limits and does not extend to the acquisition of arms for the purpose of engaging in genocide or the suppression of opposition political or religious movements. It must become axiomatic, moreover, that the right to acquire arms for self-defense entails an obligation to maintain such weapons under effective government control at all times and to preclude their diversion to illicit actors or purposes.

While it may take some time to clarify and win support for such norms, the basic groundwork has been provided by the UN Panel of Governmental Experts on Small Arms. In its report, the Panel concludes, "The excessive and destabilizing accumulation and transfer of small arms and light weapons is closely related to the increased incidence of internal conflicts and high levels of crime and violence" and is, therefore, "an issue of legitimate concern for the international community." With this in mind, the report calls on member states to "exercise restraint" with respect to the transfer of small arms and light weapons and to take all necessary steps to prevent the diversion of government arms supplies into illegitimate hands.[7]

Clearly, much work is needed to strengthen these norms and to promote their acceptance by governments. As in the worldwide campaign against land mines, the media can focus public attention on the dangers posed by such weapons, especially to civilians and children. The issue is admittedly complicated by the fact that, unlike antipersonnel land mines, national governments and military and police forces can demonstrate a far greater legitimate need for light weapons for purposes of self-defense and national security. Nonetheless, the frequency with which such weapons are used in the indiscriminate killing of civilians and children points to a humanitarian aspect of small arms that is quite similar to that of land mines.

International norms could also be developed along the lines of the Geneva Conventions, where states parties would be prohibited from supplying light weapons to any government, group, or entity that does not have the resources to treat its wounded or those of the enemy or has not trained its own personnel in the laws of war.[8] There is also scope for focusing public attention on particularly lethal aspects of light weapons. In the same way that international agreements (notably the 1980 Convention on Certain Conventional

Weapons) have been developed to constrain new technologies, such as laser-blinding weapons and new types of ammunition (similar to the 1899 Hague Declaration concerning expanding bullets), public sentiment could be mobilized to support constraints on the introduction of other inhumane or indiscriminate weapons technologies.

Along the same lines, there is an urgent need for greater involvement on the part of the international medical community in helping to highlight the effects of small arms and light weapons as a public health issue. One effort currently under way at the International Committee of the Red Cross, the SIrUS Project, is investigating how traditional concepts of "superfluous injury" and "unnecessary suffering" might be applied to modern small arms and light weapons in order to impose prohibitions on their transfer and use.[9]

Finally, a number of individual countries, organizations like the EU, and a group of Nobel Peace Prize laureates led by Oscar Arias Sánchez have proposed international "codes of conduct" that would regulate the transfer of small arms and light weapons between states and prohibit their transfer to regimes that have engaged in warfare against elements of their own or neighboring populations or have been engaged in persistent violations of basic human rights.

Increased International Transparency

At present, efforts to monitor and control the diffusion of small arms and light weapons are hampered by a lack of detailed information on the production, sale, and transportation of such munitions. Whereas considerable data on the trade in major conventional weapons are available from the Stockholm International Peace Research Institute (SIPRI) and other organizations, no such data are available on the trade in light weapons. The UN Register of Conventional Arms, established in 1991, covers major weapons only. At the national level, few governments provide detailed data on imports and exports of light weapons. This means that it is very difficult to measure the flow of such weapons from centers of production to recipients around the world.

Clearly, to ensure effective international oversight of the legal trade in small arms and light weapons, it will be necessary to promote greater transparency in this area. This will require effort at the national, regional, and international levels. National governments should be required to publish detailed annual tallies of weapons imports and exports, while regional arms registers covering small arms and light weapons should also be encouraged. Finally, at the international level, the UN Register of Conventional Arms should be gradually extended to cover all types of munitions, including small arms and light weapons.

Enhanced international transparency is also necessary to curb the illicit trade in small arms and light weapons. In the absence of an effective system of international transparency, it is relatively easy for illicit dealers to conceal their operations; as information on the trade in light weapons becomes more widely available, it will become increasingly difficult to do this. Increased transparency will also facilitate joint efforts by law enforcement agencies to identify, track, and apprehend black-market dealers.

Increased Government Accountability

In the current international milieu, control over the import and export of small arms and light weapons rests with national governments; thus, efforts to better regulate the trade in such munitions will be most effective at the level of the nation-state, not with regional or international organizations. Increased government accountability is needed in two key areas: first, the establishment of effective oversight over all military-type firearms found within the national territory so as to prevent their diversion to criminal elements and black-market dealers and, second, strict controls over the import and export of such weapons so as to preclude their use for any purpose other than legitimate self-defense as sanctioned by the UN Charter.

Efforts to accomplish the first of these objectives should be guided by the work of the UN Commission on Crime Prevention and Criminal Justice. Specific measures would include a licensing system for manufacturers and gun owners, more effective identification systems to track firearms, more effective record keeping of firearms, and safe storage measures. Governments around the world should be encouraged to incorporate such measures into their national laws and regulations; those states that fail to do so should be barred from receiving arms from those states that do adopt such legislation.

Similarly, efforts to better control the import and export of small arms and light weapons should be guided by the recommendations found in the report of the UN Panel of Governmental Experts on Small Arms. These include the collection and destruction of weapons once conflict has ended, the destruction of surplus weapons no longer needed by a country's military or police forces (as opposed to selling or giving them away), and the exercise of restraint in transferring military and police weapons from one country to another. Yet another proposal would increase the transaction costs of the international trade in light weapons by either increasing taxes on weapons and ammunition sales or requiring a substantial transaction deposit (from both sellers and buyers) that would be refunded only once it had been certified that weapons shipments had reached their intended destination.[10]

States should also be encouraged to adopt a code of conduct for arms transfers (similar to but stronger than that adopted by the EU) that would bar the sale or transfer of small arms and light weapons to any state that is ruled by a military dictatorship, that fails to respect the human rights of its citizens, that violates UN arms embargoes, and that cannot ensure the security of the weapons already in its possession.

Establish Regional and International Frameworks for Control

While priority should be given to the development of effective controls at the national level, efforts should also be made to establish systems of oversight and control at the regional and international levels. Action at the regional level is particularly important because, as analyzed by Kathi Austin in chapter 2 and Tara Kartha in chapter 3, small arms and light weapons are often circulated by regional networks of illicit dealers, insurgents, and permissive government agencies. Experience suggests, moreover, that it may be easier to mobilize political support for control systems at the regional level (as shown, for example, by the OAS Convention and the arms moratorium in West Africa) than at the international level.

At the regional level, policy initiatives could include agreements for the strengthening of import and export regulations, tougher enforcement of laws against illicit trafficking, and joint operations against black-market dealers. The OAS effort is one means of fostering increased cooperation between national customs services and law enforcement agencies on a regional basis. Other such efforts could be greatly facilitated if the wealthier countries, notably the United States and Japan, provided the requisite technologies for computer databases of suspected illicit weapons traffickers. In southern Africa, national governments and intelligence agencies are sharing information and mounting joint operations to uncover and destroy large caches of weapons left over from previous conflicts.

The West African moratorium on the manufacture, sale, and import of small arms and light weapons is another initiative that can begin to reduce the easy availability of such weapons in society. As one of the more successful multilateral attempts to control the flow of small arms and light weapons both prior to and following periods of civil tension, the moratorium might provide a model for other regions beset by political and social instability. This is especially the case in central Africa, where the experience of countries such as Rwanda and Burundi demonstrated that even relatively modest numbers of light weapons ended up having horrific consequences for civilians caught in the middle of sectarian strife.[11]

Other regional approaches include the establishment of "codes of conduct" on exports of arms, such as that adopted by the European Union. Given the particularly troublesome black-market weapons activity coming out of eastern Europe and the former republics of the Soviet Union (including Russia), thought should be given to the adoption of such codes by the OECD or the Organization for Security and Cooperation in Europe (OSCE). It has also been proposed that those countries joining the North Atlantic Treaty Organization (NATO) be obliged to destroy excess weapons stocks as a condition of membership. Economic incentives could be provided for the closure of excess production capacity in eastern Europe and the former Soviet Union, or western states could buy surplus small arms and light weapons from former Warsaw Pact militaries and destroy them (as is happening with the U.S. purchase of excess Russian nuclear weapons material).

At the international level, emphasis should be placed on the adoption of measures needed to strengthen the implementation of weapons embargoes agreed to by the United Nations and associated bodies. While such embargoes may never be entirely leakproof, evidence has shown that even a modest number of international observers at airfields, seaports, and other points of entry for weapons to an area of conflict can make a difference. When supplemented by national controls on arms brokering, the transshipment of weapons, and stricter export controls, embargoes can make it far more difficult to deliver significant quantities of modern weapons to areas of conflict.

The major arms-supplying countries should also establish a mechanism (possibly as part of the Wassenaar Arrangement for conventional arms control) for consultation on arms flows to areas of current and potential conflict, along with provisions for the imposition of moratoria on weapons transfers to any state or region deemed to be at risk of ethnic slaughter, state failure, or genocide. Such moratoria should also provide for increased vigilance of black-market traffickers operating in the region in order to permit the swift apprehension of any dealers found to be in violation of international curbs on illicit arms trafficking. International inspectors should be sent to the region to ensure compliance with these measures and to suggest any other actions that might be taken to reduce the flow of arms and to promote the peaceful resolution of disputes.

Reduce Global Stockpiles of Surplus Weapons

The research collected in this volume demonstrates that much of the killing that has occurred in recent conflicts was carried out with small arms and light weapons left over from the Cold War era. Huge quantities of such weapons were manufactured and stockpiled by the two superpowers and their allies during this period in expectation of a prolonged and bitter conflict—a World War III. Some of these weapons were provided to friendly governments in the Third World, and some were smuggled to insurgent groups engaged in combat against governments linked to the opposing superpower. While a certain percentage of these weapons were lost or destroyed over time, vast numbers of them remain in working condition and are available for sale on the international market.

Addressing the problem of surplus weaponry is especially important because many states—especially those in the former Soviet bloc—are eager to sell their excess stocks for hard currency, with few or no questions asked. Because controls on the export of surplus arms are generally less strict than those on sales of newly manufactured weapons, moreover, black-market dealers generally find it easier to obtain and sell surplus arms than newly made weapons. The problem of surplus arms is especially acute in areas just recovering from armed conflict, where impoverished ex-combatants may try to sell their weapons for needed cash rather than turn them over to UN peacekeepers or other designated authorities.[12]

Clearly, reducing global stockpiles of surplus munitions should be a critical component of any international effort to constrain the flow of small arms and light weapons. Such measures can take several forms. States that can afford to do so should agree to destroy the surplus arms and ammunition in their possession and to take all necessary steps to prevent the theft of weaponry from government depots and warehouses. As one example of the former, the Dutch Ministry of Defense announced in January 1998 that it would destroy most of its surplus small arms, including 115,000 Uzis, FAL rifles, Garand rifles, Browning pistols, and M1 carbines.[13] Too often, however, such steps are the exception, not the rule.

In addition, the wealthier industrial states should create a "Nunn–Lugar" type of fund with which to buy up and destroy the surplus stocks of the former Warsaw Pact countries and to help subsidize the security of their remaining stocks of weapons. (The Nunn–Lugar program, or "cooperative threat reduction," is a U.S. effort to reduce the risk of nuclear proliferation from the ex-Soviet states by strengthening the safeguards on nuclear weapons materials in these countries and by financing the destruction of warheads being deactivated in accordance with the START treaties.) Such assistance should be given in conjunction with assurances by these states to abide by new international constraints on the trade in small arms and light weapons, as described above.

The United States and Russia should also agree to cooperate in locating and reclaiming (or buying back) weapons given by them to insurgent groups during the Cold War era. In many areas, these weapons are now being used to fuel internal power struggles and criminal violence—usually with scant regard for the political objectives once espoused by the superpowers. Taking these weapons out of circulation would close one of the most deadly chapters of the Cold War and help promote international peace and security in the current era.

Postconflict Disarmament Measures

As noted throughout this volume, a high priority should be placed on efforts to remove the large quantities of small arms and light weapons that often remain in the battle zone once a particular conflict has ended. Too often, the availability of such weapons facilitates either a renewal of the conflict (as in Angola) or the destabilization of efforts to build a peaceful civil society (as in South Africa). The limited success of disarmament programs in countries like El Salvador, which suffers from an appalling rate of criminal violence despite the collection of tens of thousands of weapons, points up the complexity and difficulty of such efforts.[14] Above all, decisions to disarm warring factions and remove small arms and light weapons from areas of conflict must be implemented uniformly and comprehensively.

Moreover, there are many societies around the world where weapons are deeply embedded in the local culture, in which case arms collection efforts may prove futile or not be politically feasible. In such cases, the primary emphasis should be on economic development and social reconstruction so that ex-combatants and civilians have viable options in the civilian economy. Nonetheless, policy options need to be explored that could combine weapons recovery and destruction programs, cross-border controls, and other measures to reduce the likelihood that small arms and light weapons will continue to be used in either armed conflict or civil violence. Recent initiatives on the part of the World Bank and a number of development and humanitarian NGOs to better integrate economic assistance programs with demobilization, the destruction of weapons, and other conflict prevention strategies are a useful step in this direction.[15]

International Capacity Building

Ultimately, any regime for the control of international trafficking in small arms and light weapons will only be as effective as the weakest links in the system. So long as black-market dealers enjoy safe havens in which they can operate with impunity, it will be difficult or impossible to enforce tougher international standards on the trade in light weapons. Accordingly, it is essential that the stronger participants in the system assist the weaker elements to establish effective and reliable mechanisms for the oversight of arms imports and exports. Such efforts can be said to fall under the heading of international "capacity building."

As part of such efforts, technology should be developed and installed on an international basis to help track the flows of small arms and light weapons, identify illicit sources of supply, and improve law enforcement and customs prosecution of illegal weapons suppliers and traders. In addition to developing computer databases and communications systems that can facilitate international cooperation on the light weapons trade, several other initiatives have been proposed for helping to increase the transparency of light weapons flows. The OAS, for instance, has proposed the marking and registration of weapons both at the point of manufacture and when such weapons are legally exported. Such marking will make it easier for law enforcement and intelligence officials to trace the supply routes of weapons that may have been acquired legally and then diverted to the black market. While some of these measures may prove difficult and expensive to implement, the international community has at least begun the process of thoroughly evaluating their potential significance.

Conclusion

In sum, increased attention to the lethal effects of small arms and light weapons, on the part of humanitarian relief agencies, national governments, international organizations, and the media, is translating into a greater public appreciation of the need to better control the production, supply, and proliferation of these weapons. Admittedly, the problem is incredibly complex, and policies to control and regulate these weapons will not come easily. Nonetheless, the scale of death and injury caused by light weapons is such that the international community must continue to search for effective means of controlling and reducing the lethal commerce of small arms and light weapons around the world.

Notes

1. United Nations, Economic and Social Council, Commission on Crime Prevention and Criminal Justice, Seventh Session, April 21–30, 1998, Vienna, Austria.
2. UN report in response to Security Council Resolution 1013, pp. 18–19.
3. Jim Wurst, "UN Lobbies for Coordination on Small Arms," *BASIC Reports,* no. 65, August 14, 1998, p. 4.
4. See Development Assistance Committee of the OECD, "Guidelines on Conflict, Peace and Development," DCD/DAC (96) 31/REV3, April 17, 1997, p. 11.
5. Raymond Bonner, "U.S. Joins 20 Nations in Urging Controls on Spread of Small Arms," *New York Times,* July 15, 1998.
6. Secretary of State for Development Cooperation, "The Brussels Call for Action," from an International Conference: Sustainable Disarmament for Sustainable Development, Brussels, October 12–13, 1998.
7. United Nations, *Report of the Panel of Governmental Experts on Small Arms,* #A/52/298, August 27, 1997.
8. See International Committee of the Red Cross, "Arms Availability and Violations of International Humanitarian Law and the Deterioration of the Situation of Civilians in Armed Conflicts," report from an Expert Group Meeting, Oslo, Norway, May 18–20, 1998.
9. See R. M. Coupland, "The Effects of Weapons: Defining Superfluous Injury and Unnecessary Suffering," *Medicine and Global Survival,* 3:A1, 1996. To cite one example, Dr. Georg Scharf has argued for a ban on mortar bombs, given their increasing use in civilian environments and to target medical facilities; see Georg Scharf, "The Effects of Mortar Bombs and Similar Weapons in Limited Conflicts," background paper for "The Medical Profession and the Effects of Weapons," International Committee of the Red Cross, 1996.
10. Peter Lock, "Illicit Small Arms Availability," research note prepared for the Third International Berlin Workshop, "Consolidating Peace through Practical Disarmament Measures and Control of Small Arms—From Civil Wars to Civil Society," Berlin, July 2–5, 1998 (Hamburg: Institute for Study of Transition, 1998).

11. Howard W. French, "Liberian Slayings Began Brutal Trend in Africa," *New York Times,* February 25, 1998.

12. See Edward J. Laurance and Herbert Wulf, eds., *Coping with Surplus Weapons,* Brief no. 3 (Bonn: Bonn International Center for Conversion, 1995).

13. Saferworld, *Arms Bulletin No. 2* (London: Saferworld, January 6, 1998).

14. In El Salvador, FMLN weapons were kept under lock and key, with FMLN commanders having one of the keys, in case the government reneged on its promise to demobilize soldiers and turn in weapons. The disarmament process carried out by the United Nations Observer Mission in El Slavador (ONUSAL) in 1992–93 resulted in the collection and destruction from the FMLN of some 10,000 small arms and light weapons, four million rounds of ammunition, and over 9,000 grenades. In terms of dismantling the FMLN as a fighting force, reducing the size of El Salvador's military, and integrating former rebels into the military, the ONUSAL mission was a success. Nonetheless, criminal and civil violence continues to plague the country. See Paulo S. Wrobel, principal author, *Managing Arms in Peace Processes: Nicaragua and El Salvador* (Geneva: UN Institute for Disarmament Research, 1997).

15. Steven Holtzman, "Post-Conflict Reconstruction," Environment Department Work in Progress, The World Bank (Washington, D.C.: The World Bank, Social Policy and Resettlement Division, 1996).

Appendix A

Recommendations of the Report of the UN Panel of Governmental Experts on Small Arms, Submitted by the Secretary-General to the General Assembly, August 27, 1997

General and Complete Disarmament: Small Arms

Note by the Secretary-General

By its resolution 50/70 B of 12 December 1995 the General Assembly requested the Secretary-General to prepare a report on small arms, with the assistance of a panel of governmental experts.

Pursuant to that resolution, the Secretary-General has the honour to submit to the Assembly the report of the Panel of Governmental Experts on Small Arms.

V. Recommendations

78. The Panel's recommendations are comprised first of measures to reduce the excessive and destabilizing accumulation and transfer of small arms and light weapons in specific regions of the world where such accumulations and transfers have already taken place. These are followed by measures to prevent such accumulations and transfers from occurring in future.

79. The Panel recommends the following reduction measures:

(a) The United Nations should adopt a proportional and integrated approach to security and development, including the identification of appropriate assistance for the internal security forces initiated with respect to Mali and other West African States, and extend it to other regions of the world where conflicts come to an end and where serious problems of the proliferation of small arms and light weapons have to be dealt with urgently. The donor community should support this new approach in regard to such regions of the world;

(b) The United Nations should support, with the assistance of the donor community, all appropriate post-conflict initiatives related to disarmament and demobilization, such as the disposal and destruction of weapons, including weapons turn-in programmes sponsored locally by governmental and non-governmental organizations;

(c) Once national conciliation is reached, the United Nations should assist in convening an inter-Afghan forum to prepare, *inter alia*, a schedule to account for, retrieve and destroy the small arms and light weapons left unaccounted for in Afghanistan;

(d) In view of the problems stemming from an excess of small arms and light weapons left over from many internal conflicts and the lessons learned from the peacekeeping operations of the United Nations, two sets of guidelines should be developed in order to:

(i) Assist negotiators of peace settlements in developing plans to disarm combatants, particularly as concerns light weapons, small arms and munitions, and to include therein plans for the collection of weapons and their disposal, preferably by destruction;

(ii) Provide assistance to peacekeeping missions in implementing their mandates, based on peace settlements;

Former peace negotiators and members of peacekeeping operations of the United Nations should be consulted in the preparation of such guidelines. In this connection, consideration should be given to the establishment of a disarmament component in peacekeeping operations undertaken by the United Nations.

(e) States and regional organizations, where applicable, should strengthen international and regional cooperation among police, intelligence, customs and border control officials in combating the illicit circulation of and trafficking in small arms and light weapons and in suppressing criminal activities related to the use of these weapons;

(f) The establishment of mechanisms and regional networks for information sharing for the above-mentioned purposes should be encouraged;

(g) All such weapons which are not under legal civilian possession, and which are not required for the purposes of national defence and internal security, should be collected and destroyed by States as expeditiously as possible.

80. The Panel recommends the following prevention measures:

(a) All States should implement the recommendations contained in the guidelines for international arms transfers in the context of General Assembly resolution 46/36 H of 6 December 1991, adopted by the Disarmament Commission in 1996;

(b) All States should determine in their national laws and regulations which arms are permitted for civilian possession and the conditions under which they can be used;

(c) All States should ensure that they have in place adequate laws, regulations and administrative procedures to exercise effective control over the legal possession of small arms and light weapons and over their transfer in order, *inter alia,* to prevent illicit trafficking;

(d) States emerging from conflict should, as soon as practicable, impose or reimpose licensing requirements on all civilian possession of small arms and light weapons on their territory;

(e) All States should exercise restraint with respect to the transfer of the surplus of small arms and light weapons manufactured solely for the possession of and use by the military and police forces. All States should also consider the possibility of destroying all such surplus weapons;

(f) All States should ensure the safeguarding of such weapons against loss through theft or corruption, in particular from storage facilities;

(g) The United Nations should urge relevant organizations, such as the International Criminal Police Organization (Interpol) and the World Customs Organization, as well as all States and their relevant national agencies, to closely cooperate in the identification of the groups and individuals engaged in illicit trafficking activities, and the modes of transfer used by them;

(h) All States and relevant regional and international organizations should intensify their cooperative efforts against all aspects of illicit trafficking mentioned in the present report that are related to the proliferation and accumulation of small arms and light weapons;

(i) The United Nations should encourage the adoption and implementation of regional or subregional moratoriums, where appropriate, on the transfer and manufacture of small arms and light weapons, as agreed upon by the States concerned;

(j) Other regional organizations should take note, and make use, as appropriate, of the work of the Organization of American States in preparing a draft inter-American convention against the illicit manufacturing of and trafficking in firearms, ammunition, explosives and other related materials;

(k) The United Nations should consider the possibility of convening an international conference on the illicit arms trade in all its aspects, based on the issues identified in the present report;

(l) To assist in preventing the illicit trafficking in and circulation of small arms and light weapons, the United Nations should initiate studies on the following:

(i) The feasibility of establishing a reliable system for marking all such weapons from the time of their manufacture;

(ii) The feasibility of restricting the manufacture and trade of such weapons to the manufacturers and dealers authorized by States, and of establishing a database of such authorized manufacturers and dealers;

(m) The United Nations should initiate a study on all aspects of the problem of ammunition and explosives.

Appendix B

An International Agenda on Small Arms and Light Weapons: Elements of a Common Understanding, Oslo, Norway, July 13–14, 1998

Concerns and Challenges

A number of states, recognizing the problems caused by the excessive availability, accumulation, and uncontrolled proliferation of small arms and light weapons, met in Oslo 13 and 14 July 1998 in order to discuss the humanitarian, developmental, and security concerns raised by this issue. In many societies, excessive accumulation and criminal use of these weapons contribute to violations of international humanitarian law, including war crimes, and abuse of human rights. They threaten security, exacerbate violence, increase human suffering and hinder socioeconomic development and political stability. They also constitute an obstacle to the implementation of peace agreements, the development of a culture of peace, and are an impediment to meaningful development cooperation. A sizable portion of all transfers of small arms and light weapons is illicit and increasingly linked to other transnational criminal activities, and there is a considerable "grey trade."

Due to its complexity the problem will have to be pursued and solutions sought in different fora and in a variety of ways. Governments bear the primary responsibility for addressing these issues. It is therefore encouraging to note the increasing number of governmental initiatives.

Governments recognize that civil society in general and NGOs in particular contribute to our work. They acknowledge the important role of NGOs in conducting and disseminating research, doing field studies, educating the public, providing advice to governments on small arms issues and in delivering humanitarian relief to war-torn societies.

Actions to Be Taken

Immediate action could focus on the *prevention* of illicit transfers and tighter control in connection with legal transfers. The great number of casualties and the extent of human suffering caused by the use of small arms in war-torn societies point to the urgent need for the *reduction* of such weapons in these situations of conflict.

Prevention Aspects

- Enhanced accountability, transparency, and improved information exchange on small arms transfers; improved control mechanisms at their manufacture, transit, and transfer, including export and import licenses and notification of shipments. Notification of country of origin after identification of unlawful small arms holdings. Regular information exchange. Strengthened adherence to UN embargoes.
- Cooperation, coordination, training, and information sharing among police, intelligence units, and customs officials within and between countries.
- Develop and strengthen laws and regulations; increase capacity to combat illicit manufacturing and trafficking; ensure strict enforcement of appropriate laws and regulations on civilian possession of small arms; improve traceability of small arms possession and transfers, e.g., through improved marking.
- Respect and ensure respect for international humanitarian law with regard to the use of small arms and light weapons; explore possibilities to strengthen international humanitarian law.
- Develop national and regional mechanisms including codes of conduct in connection with the legal manufacturing, transit, transfers, and, where appropriate, reduction of small arms and light weapons.

Reduction Aspects

- Support the demobilization and reintegration of combatants at the end of armed conflict, including income-generating activities. Collection, safe storage, and/or destruction of "surplus" military weapons and weapons not legally held. Voluntary programs for weapons collection. Integration of these issues into peace accords.
- Seek to reverse cultures of violence. Demilitarization of societies. Contribute to processes of reconciliation.

- Support efforts to establish trustworthy judicial and penal systems and to train local police. Support security sector reform in postconflict societies.

The Process Ahead

The participating states believe that in order to address these problems effectively and coherently, governments need to intensify and harmonize the efforts that have been made. This includes the need to develop further a common understanding of the issues as well as of practical ways of approaching the problems presented by small arms and light weapons.

We recognize the important role of the United Nations in global efforts. Governments need to pursue their priorities in global, regional, subregional, and national settings in a coherent manner. We encourage other governments to participate in common efforts to find practical solutions to these problems. At this point in time regional and subregional arrangements seem to be particularly promising. We also recognize the need for international cooperation, inter alia, with regard to meeting resource and technology requirements.

We welcome and commend the various endeavours currently being undertaken in different areas and at different levels. Governments are encouraged to support the existing global and regional initiatives—such as those listed in Annex I—and explore the feasibility of further initiatives, globally and in other regions and subregions.

Annex I: Global and Regional Initiatives

- The UN Secretary-General's Report on Small Arms of 1997
- The UN Group of Governmental Experts on Small Arms
- The UN Commission on Crime Prevention and Criminal Justice: Planned Transnational Organised Crime Convention, Protocol on Firearms
- Proposed International Conference on the Illicit Arms Trade in All Its Aspects
- The Inter-American Convention Against the Illicit Manufacturing of and Trafficking in Firearms, Ammunition, Explosives and Their Component Parts
- The OAS/CICAD Model Regulations for the Control of the International Movement of Firearms, Their Parts, Components and Ammunition
- The Mali Proposal on a Moratorium on the Manufacture, Export and Import of Light Weapons in West Africa
- The OSCE Principles Governing Conventional Arms Transfers
- The OECD/DAC Guidelines on Conflict, Peace and Development
- The EU Code of Conduct on Arms Exports

- The EU Programme for Preventing and Combating Illicit Trafficking in Conventional Arms

Annex II: An International Agenda on Small Arms and Light Weapons: Elements of a Common Understanding

List of Participating States

Belgium
Brazil
Burkina Faso
Canada
Colombia
France
Germany
Indonesia
Japan
Mali
Mexico
Mozambique
Netherlands
Norway
Philippines
South Africa
Sweden
Switzerland
United Kingdom
United States
Zimbabwe

Appendix C

SUSTAINABLE DISARMAMENT FOR SUSTAINABLE DEVELOPMENT: THE BRUSSELS CALL FOR ACTION, October 12–13, 1998.

The International Conference on "Sustainable Disarmament for Sustainable Development" originates from the acknowledgement by all concerned actors that their efforts to respond to post–Cold War violent conflict have been confronted with two critical developments.

On the one hand the toll of human and material destruction in war-torn and conflict-prone areas is spiralling to such an extent that development resources are more and more diverted to emergency relief and rehabilitation operations. Worse, the growing number of intra-state conflicts destroy the development potential of affected communities and impede perspectives for future sustainable development. Many actors in the field of development cooperation and humanitarian assistance have come to consider peacebuilding as a cornerstone of development cooperation strategies.

On the other hand there is an ever increasing international awareness of the need to tackle the proliferation and misuse of small arms and light weapons,* since these have become major instruments in violent conflicts. They are responsible for the bulk of the killings and woundings, serious human rights abuses, banditry and crime, and destruction of infrastructures. Their widespread availability erodes negotiated peace settlements, prolongs conflicts, and hampers conflict resolution and post-conflict reconstruction. In short, the widespread availability of light weapons and small arms perpetuates insecurity and instability, thereby undermining the basis for sustainable development.

*"Broadly speaking, 'small arms' are those weapons designed for personal use, and 'light weapons' are those designed for use by several persons serving as crew" (UN Secretary General's Report on Small Arms).

The Conference welcomes recent initiatives by international, national, and regional actors, both governmental and non-governmental from all regions of the industrialised and developing world, to reduce the flow and availability of small arms and light weapons. The Conference provides an opportunity for participants to share insights and experiences and to promote the recognition and a better understanding of the interaction between disarmament and sustainable development. It seeks to strengthen the existing momentum by adopting a "Call for Action" for the short and middle term, as a reference point for further action.

Towards an International Programme of Action on Practical Disarmament and Peacebuilding

1. The Brussels Conference calls for an International Programme of Action on Practical Disarmament and Peacbuilding to combine in a comprehensive way efforts to effectively tackle proliferation of small arms and light weapons with initiatives to promote security and to build peace as prerequisites for sustainable development.

Such a programme for practical disarmament and peacebuilding needs to integrate measures to:

- Combat illicit arms trafficking in all its aspects.
- Strengthen national legislation and controls on legal arms possession, use, and transfer.
- Ensure that weapons holdings by defence and security forces do not exceed requirements for legitimate defence and security needs, as well as measures to secure, destroy, or otherwise responsibly dispose of surplus stocks.
- Integrate post-conflict demobilisation programmes with social and economic rehabilitation policies, in close partnership with relevant local and regional actors.
- Halt the abduction and enrollment of children in armed forces and design adapted programmes for their recovery from traumas and their reintegration into society.
- Promote post-conflict reconstruction and reconciliation in a stable and secure environment as a basis for sustainable development.
- Collect and destroy illegally possessed weapons.

2. To that end the Brussels Conference endorses the conclusions and recommendations of the UN Secretary-General's Report on Small Arms. It expresses its strong interest in the "International Conference on the illicit arms

trade in all its aspects" and looks forward to the results of the work of the follow-on UN Group of Experts on Small Arms. The Conference looks forward to concrete actions to be undertaken by the General Assembly in this respect.

The Conference welcomes recent initiatives by the United Nations to operationalise and integrate the approach to disarmament, security, and development. They encourage the Secretary-General to provide assistance to member states seeking the UN's help in weapons' collection, demobilisation, and reintegration.

The Conference warmly endorses the "Elements of Common Understanding" issued by the twenty-one participating governments at an international meeting on small arms in Oslo, July 13–14, 1998, including the eleven global and regional initiatives annexed to it, and urges all governments to support them.

A Call for Immediate Action

3. While recognising that such an International Programme of Action will take time to develop, the Brussels Conference also calls upon all members of the International Community to take appropriate, timely and co-ordinated actions at national, regional, and international levels in the following areas.

A Call for Concrete Measures on Human Security and Development

4. The Brussels Conference endorses the proportional and integrated approach to security and development. It thus supports the so-called "security first" approach to donor-assistance in conflict-prone areas within an environment of good governance and respect for human rights. This approach involves the integration of appropriate security assistance with development and other cooperation programmes.

Members of the donor community are urged to review their policies and mechanisms for cooperation, and to ensure that sufficient resources are available to provide appropriate and timely assistance for such programmes. These programmes should seek to strengthen and build on indigenous capacities for conflict resolution and peacebuilding.

5. Thus, as armed conflicts come to an end, demobilisation and disarmament measures should be combined with programmes to reintegrate former combatants and their dependents into the community to guarantee security as well as to ensure that basic economic, social, and cultural needs of affected communities are met. Specific needs of special target groups in conflicts such as women and children have to be taken into account.

6. Weapons collection programmes should be an integral part of peace agreements and post-conflict reconstruction. Mechanisms should be established to identify and promote best practice and ensure adequate resources for such programmes. The conference further calls for the rapid, reliable, and transparent destruction of such collected arms.

In close partnership the donor community should support government weapons collection programmes and development programmes with communities striving to remove weapons from circulation. Furthermore, schemes need to be developed—such as provision of technical assistance and the creation of appropriate linkages with aid and debt relief (e.g., debt/arms destruction swaps)—to facilitate and increase incentives for the collection, destruction, or secure disposal of all weapons stocks that are surplus to legitimate requirements.

7. In conflict-prone areas, dynamic and representative social and political structures capable of managing change, maintaining law and order, and resolving conflict without resorting to violence or oppression need to be supported and developed to create an environment of structural stability. Such stability is a prerequisite for sustainable development and often requires, within an environment of democratic reform, prioritising:

- Reform and capacity-building of the police and security forces, of the judicial system, of customs services and border controls.
- Restructuring of armed forces under democratic control and ensuring military expenditures and roles proportionate to legitimate security needs.
- Improving transparency and cooperation at regional and international levels.

8. To promote a culture of peace, to counter the trivialisation of armed violence, to challenge the glorification of weapons, and to help resolve conflicts and disputes peacefully, public education and awareness programmes are of utmost importance, as are initiatives aimed at restoring the social fabric and creating trust between communities and legitimate police and security services.

9. The Conference calls upon states that have not already done so to adopt appropriate mechanisms for regulating the activities of non-governmental security actors.

A Call for Measures to Address the Widespread Availability, Transfer, and Use of Light Weapons and Small Arms

10. National, regional, and international regulations, policies, and practices with respect to the possession and transfer of arms should be harmonized where appropriate to strengthen international cooperation in combating the illicit arms manufacturing and trafficking.

11. Governments should take all appropriate measures to combat the illicit manufacturing of and trafficking in arms, including enhanced exchange of information and improved traceability of weapons. The Conference strongly recommends the rapid negotiation and conclusion of a protocol on firearms within the framework of the proposed UN Transnational Organized Crime Convention.

Further international measures are also needed to combat illicit trafficking in small arms and light weapons that would not be covered in such a protocol. Such measures should include agreements to strengthen and harmonise appropriate laws and enforcement mechanisms. Other measures include the effective marking and appropriate mechanisms to account for import and exports of all arms.

States should ensure strict enforcement of appropriate laws and regulations on civilian possession of weapons.

12. The international community should adopt a more systematic approach towards imposing arms embargoes or import-export moratoria in regions of violent conflict or as a conflict preventive measure in regions where tensions are building up. Where such embargoes exist measures have to be taken to ensure their strict implementation.

A Call for Care for Victims

13. An integrated approach towards restoring peace and stability requires a commitment to attend the trauma of victims of conflict and widespread violence. Special attention must be given to the plight of victimised women and children, especially where minors are abducted and forcibly integrated into armies and rebel forces.

In this respect the Conference calls upon all states and parties to armed conflicts to respect Article 38 of the UN Convention of the Rights of the Child, which demands refraining from recruiting children into armed forces. The Participants welcome any measure to raise the age limit.

A Call for Follow-up

14. In order to promote cooperation and effectiveness of measures to address these problems, the Conference agrees to:

- Work towards the development of a mutually agreeable International Programme of Action on Practical Disarmament and Peacebuilding.
- Integrate recommendations and proposals of the Brussels Call for Action in relevant agreements on conflict areas.

- Build on work in the areas of security sector reform and appropriate military expenditures (e.g., within OECD and relevant UN bodies).
- Further research into innovative concepts on peacebuilding and practical disarmament.
- Request all governments concerned that have not already done so to integrate the respect for humanitarian law and for human rights into bi- and multilateral cooperation agreements and to ensure the necessary follow-up.
- Regularly exchange information on policies, measures, and progress in the implementation and lessons learned and to hold follow-up meetings following a scheduled agenda to review such information and develop co-ordinated actions in the priority areas.

15. The Conference requests this Call for Action to be brought to the attention of the UN General Assembly and the UN Secretary-General.

Selected Bibliography

Benson, William. *Light Weapons Controls and Security Assistance: A Review of Current Practice*. London: International Alert and Saferworld, September 1998.

Bonn International Center for Conversion (BICC). *The New Field of Micro-Disarmament: Addressing the Proliferation and Buildup of Small Arms and Light Weapons*. Bonn: BICC and Monterey Institute of International Studies, June 1996.

Boutwell, Jeffrey, Michael T. Klare, and Laura Reed, eds. *Lethal Commerce: The Global Trade in Small Arms and Light Weapons*. Cambridge, Mass.: American Academy of Arts and Sciences, 1995.

Brett, Rachel, and Margaret McCallin. *Children: The Invisible Soldiers*. Stockholm: Swedish Save the Children, 1996.

British American Security Information Council (BASIC). *Deadly Rounds: Ammunition and Armed Conflict*. Project on Light Weapons Report 98.4. Washington, D.C.: BASIC, May 1998. See also other reports from BASIC's Light Weapons Project.

Carnegie Commission on Preventing Deadly Conflict. *Preventing Deadly Conflict: Final Report*. Washington, D.C.: Carnegie Commission on Preventing Deadly Conflict, December 1997.

DiChiaro, Joseph III. *Reasonable Measures: Addressing the Excessive Accumulation and Unlawful Use of Small Arms*. Brief 11. Bonn: Bonn International Center for Conversion, August 1998.

Ezell, Virginia Hart. *Report on International Small Arms Production and Proliferation*. Alexandria, Va.: Institute for Research on Small Arms in International Security, March 1995.

Gamba, Virginia, ed. *Society under Siege: Crime, Violence and Illegal Weapons*, Vols. 1 and 2. Halfway House, South Africa: Institute for Strategic Studies, 1997, 1998.

Gander, Terry J., ed. *Jane's Infantry Weapons 1997–98.* Surrey: Jane's Information Group, 1997.

Government of Canada. *Small Arms and Light Weapons: An Annotated Bibliography, Update 1996–1998.* Ottawa: Department of Foreign Affairs and International Trade, September 1998.

Government of Canada. *An International Register of Small Arms and Light Weapons: Issues and Model.* Ottawa: Department of Foreign Affairs and International Trade, October 1998.

Greene, Owen, Mike Bourne, Victoria Gardene, and Christopher Louise. *Light Weapons and Peacebuilding in Central and East Africa.* London: International Alert, July 1998.

Human Rights Watch/Arms Project. *Stoking the Fires: Military Assistance and Arms Trafficking in Burundi.* New York: Human Rights Watch, 1997. See also numerous other country and regional case studies.

Human Rights Watch/Arms Project. *Sudan: Global Trade, Local Impact.* New York: Human Rights Watch, August 1998.

International Committee of the Red Cross. "Arms Availability and Violations of International Humanitarian Law and the Deterioration of the Situation of Civilians in Armed Conflicts." Report of an Expert Group Meeting, Oslo, Norway, May 18–20, 1998. Oslo: Norwegian Red Cross, 1998.

Kartha, Tara. *Tools of Terror: Light Weapons and India's Security.* New Delhi: Knowledge World, 1999.

Klare, Michael, and David Andersen. *A Scourge of Guns: The Diffusion of Small Arms and Light Weapons in Latin America.* Washington, D.C.: Federation of American Scientists, 1996.

Laurance, Edward J. *Light Weapons and Intrastate Conflict: Early Warning Factors and Preventive Action.* Washington, D.C.: Carnegie Commission on Preventing Deadly Conflict, 1998.

Louise, Christopher. "The Social Impact of Light Weapons Availability and Proliferation." Discussion Paper 59. Geneva: United Nations Research Institute for Social Development, March 1995.

Monterey Institute of International Studies. Project Prep Com, the Web site of the Preparatory Committee for a Global Campaign on Small Arms and Light Weapons. http://www.prepcom.org.

Oosthuysen, Glenn. *Small Arms Proliferation and Control in Southern Africa.* Pretoria: South African Institute of International Affairs, October 1996.

Oxfam. "Small Arms, Wrong Hands: A Case for Government Control of the Small Arms Trade." Oxford: Oxfam, April 1998.

Renner, Michael. *Small Arms, Big Impact: The Next Challenge of Disarmament.* Washington, D.C.: Worldwatch Institute, 1997.

Saferworld. *Undermining Development: The European Arms Trade with the Horn of Africa and Central Africa.* London: Saferworld, February 1998.

Singh, Jasjit, ed. *Light Weapons and International Security.* New Delhi: Indian Pugwash Society and British American Security Information Council, 1995.

"Small Arms, Big Problems." *Bulletin of the Atomic Scientists* (special issue). Michael T. Klare, guest editor. January/February 1999.

Stohl, Rachel J. *Deadly Rounds: Ammunition and Armed Conflict.* BASIC Project on Light Weapons Research Report 98.4. Washington, D.C.: British American Security Information Council, May 1998.

United Nations. "Interim Report of the International Commission of Inquiry" (Rwanda). Report S/1998/777. New York: United Nations, August 25, 1998.

United Nations. "Measures to Regulate Firearms for the Purpose of Combatting Illicit Trafficking in Firearms." Vienna: United Nations Economic and Social Council, July 28, 1998.

United Nations Institute for Disarmament Research (UNIDIR). *Small Arms Management and Peacekeeping in Southern Africa.* Geneva: UNIDIR, 1996. See also other case studies from the UNIDIR Disarmament and Conflict Resolution Project on Somalia, Cambodia, Liberia, Mozambique, Rhodesia/Zimbabwe, and Croatia and Bosnia-Herzegovina.

United States. "Factsheet: ACDA Outlines U.S. Policy on Small Arms Issues." Washington, D.C.: U.S. Arms Control and Disarmament Agency, August 11, 1998.

Index

About the Contributors

Kathi Austin is a visiting scholar at the Center for African Studies at Stanford University and has been a consultant to the International Crisis Group, Human Rights Watch/Arms Project, and other nongovernmental organizations. She specializes in security, human rights, and Africa policy issues and has spent ten years documenting conflicts in Africa. She conducted over fifteen months of in-depth field investigations in central Africa from 1994 to 1998, focusing on the legal and illicit trade in weapons and its impact on the humanitarian crisis. She independently produced the documentary *Forsaken Cries: The Story of Rwanda* and is currently writing a book on the illicit arms trade.

William Benson works as a committee specialist for the International Development Committee in the House of Commons. A former researcher for Saferworld's Arms Trade Program, he has written a number of Saferworld reports on the arms trade and light weapons, including *Undermining Development: The European Arms Trade with the Horn and Central Africa* (1997), *Policy and Practice: UK Arms Exports* (1998), and *Light Weapons Controls and Security Assistance* (with International Alert, 1998).

Jeffrey Boutwell is associate executive officer at the American Academy of Arts and Sciences, where he directs the program on international security studies. He has written and consulted widely on issues relating to small arms and light weapons and the Israeli-Palestinian peace process. A former staff aide on the National Security Council during the Carter administration, he is currently working on a book examining the effects of increased numbers of small arms and light weapons for Palestinian and Israeli civil society and the peace process.

Nat J. Colletta earned his B.A. and M.A. from the State University of New York at Buffalo and his interdisciplinary doctorate in sociology, anthropology, and international education and development studies from Michigan State University. Since 1996 he has held the position of lead specialist for social policy in the Economic Management and Social Policy Department of the Africa Region at the World Bank and head of the War-to-Peace Transition team and knowledge manager of the Post-Conflict Reconstruction Network. He is currently manager of the World Bank's newly created Post-Conflict Unit. Dr. Colletta has written several books on war-to-peace transition, social development, and education.

Paul Eavis has been director of Saferworld since January 1996. He has co-authored and edited a number of publications, including *Proliferation and Export Controls: An Analysis of Sensitive Technologies and Countries of Concern* (1995) and *Arms and Dual Use Exports from the EU: A Common Policy for Regulation and Control* (1994). He has a first degree in physics and an M.A. in international relations.

Natalie J. Goldring is executive director of the Program on General Disarmament, based in the Department of Government and Politics at the University of Maryland. Her chapter was written largely while she was deputy director of the British American Security Information Council (BASIC) and director of its Project on Light Weapons. She has written widely on topics such as the international weapons trade, nuclear nonproliferation, conventional and strategic forces, the defense budget, and arms control. Dr. Goldring has a Ph.D. in political science from the Massachusetts Institute of Technology.

Peter Herby is with the Legal Division of the International Committee of the Red Cross (ICRC), Geneva. He has worked for many years on issues relating to chemical and blinding laser weapons and most recently was involved with the ICRC's effort on the international campaign to ban land mines.

Tara Kartha is a research fellow at the Institute of Defence Studies and Analyses, New Delhi. She has recently authored *Tools of Terror: Light Weapons and India's Security* (1999) and has been a member of the CSCAP working group on transnational crime. She is on the executive committee of the Indian Pugwash chapter and heads the institute project, Light Weapons and International Security. She has also published papers on military doctrine and is at present working on her doctoral thesis, which deals with missile issues in the developing world.

Michael T. Klare is a professor of peace and world security studies at Hampshire College in Amherst, Massachusetts, and director of the Five College Program in Peace and World Security Studies (PAWSS). He is also the academic adviser to the Arms Sales Monitoring Project of the Federation of American Scientists (FAS) and a member of the Committee on International

Security Studies of the American Academy of Arts and Sciences. He is the co-author of *A Scourge of Guns: The Diffusion of Small Arms and Light Weapons in Latin America* (1996) and co-editor of *Lethal Commerce: The Global Trade in Small Arms and Light Weapons* (1995).

Edward J. Laurance is a professor of international public policy at the Monterey Institute of International Studies, where he also directs the Program on Arms Control, Disarmament and Conversion. Since 1992 he has been a consultant for the United Nations Center for Disarmament Affairs, most recently serving with the Panel of Experts on Small Arms.

Lora Lumpe is senior researcher at the International Peace Research Institute, Oslo, Norway. Previously, she was director of the Arms Sales Monitoring Project of the Federation of American Scientists (FAS), which she founded in 1990. At FAS, she published a quarterly newsletter, *The Arms Sales Monitor,* which seeks to promote restraint in U.S. and global conventional arms production and trade. She has written and lectured widely on arms trade and light weapons issues.

James P. McShane is an adviser to the director of the Office of Defense Trade Controls in the Department of State. He was a criminal investigator for twenty-seven years with U.S. Customs—retiring in 1998—with assignments in New York, London, Rome, and Washington, D.C. Most of his career has involved investigating illegal trafficking in arms. In 1992 he was assigned as the law enforcement liaison to the Office of Defense Trade Controls, U.S. Department of State, overseeing export licenses and violations. He was a member of the U.S. negotiating team for the OAS Convention on Illicit Manufacturing and Trafficking as well as the P-8 and the UN teams involved in small arms and transnational crime issues.

Joseph P. Smaldone is director of the Office of Export Controls and Conventional Arms Nonproliferation Policy, U.S. Department of State. From 1998 to March 1999, he was chief of the Weapons and Technology Control Division of the U.S. Arms Control and Disarmament Agency, where his duties included conventional arms transfers and dual-use technology exports, the proliferation of missiles and chemical and biological weapons, and regional arms control and nonproliferation initiatives in the developing world. From 1980 to 1988 he served as chief of the Arms Licensing Division in the Office of Munitions Control at the State Department. He is also an adjunct professor at the University of Maryland, Georgetown University, and George Washington University.

Hussein Solomon is research manager at the African Center for the Constructive Resolution of Disputes (ACCORD), Durban, South Africa. Previously, he was senior researcher of the African Security Analysis Program at the Institute for Security Studies in Midrand, South Africa. His research focuses largely on sources of Southern African insecurity, foreign policy, and regional integration, and currently he is editing a book on the consolidation of democracy in Africa. He has been a senior visiting fellow at the Department of War Studies, King's College, London, and a visiting lecturer at the College of International Relations, Chubu University, Japan. He also sits on the Council of the South African Political Science Association.

Graciela Uribe de Lozano is coordinator of disarmament affairs at the Foreign Ministry of Colombia. Between 1982 and 1992 she was the Colombian delegate to the first committee of the United Nations General Assembly and all other UN and NGO forums on disarmament issues. She has written numerous articles on small arms and light weapons.